STUDIES IN IRISH HISTORY, SECOND SERIES
edited by

T. W. MOODY
Professor of Modern History
University of Dublin

J. C. BECKETT
Professor of Irish History
Queen's University, Belfast

T. D. WILLIAMS
Professor of Modern History
National University of Ireland

VOLUME III
THE POLITICS OF REPEAL

STUDIES IN IRISH HISTORY, SECOND SERIES

THE POLITICS
OF REPEAL

*A Study in the Relations between
Great Britain and Ireland, 1841–50*

by

KEVIN B. NOWLAN

Lecturer in History
University College, Dublin

LONDON: Routledge & Kegan Paul
TORONTO: University of Toronto Press
1965

First published 1965
in Great Britain by
Routledge & Kegan Paul Ltd
and in Canada by
University of Toronto Press

Printed in Great Britain
by Hazell Watson & Viney Ltd

PREFACE

~~~~~~

THE GROWTH in the volume of specialised studies, dealing with Ireland in the nineteenth century, has been one of the most welcome developments in recent years in the field of Irish history. The mid-nineteenth century has not been neglected, but much remains to be said about the structure of Irish politics in the eighteen-thirties and eighteen-forties. In this present work, an attempt has been made not merely to examine the place of the repeal agitation and of Daniel O'Connell in the shaping of modern Irish nationalism, but also to consider the influence of Irish affairs on the policies and decisions of the Peel and Russell administrations.

In my contribution to *The Great Famine* (Dublin, 1956, New York, 1957), I discussed the political problems of the famine years in Ireland. Now, in this book, I hope, I have been able to provide a somewhat fuller treatment of the period 1845 to 1850 and to put the developments of those years into the wider context of the history of the repeal movement and of the eighteen-forties as a whole.

In the preparation of this study, I have received much encouragement from my colleagues of the Department of History, University College, Dublin. My special thanks are due to Professor R. Dudley Edwards and Mrs. Maureen Wall, M.A. I should like to record also my appreciation of the advice I received from Dr G. Kitson Clark, of Trinity College, Cambridge. The task of research was greatly eased by the kind assistance of the staff of the National Library of Ireland, Dublin. To the custodians of the manuscript sources listed in the bibliography, I owe a debt of gratitude for making the material available to me.

Preface

In conclusion, I wish to acknowledge the generosity of the Senate of the National University of Ireland in providing a grant in aid of publication.

KEVIN B. NOWLAN

University College,
Dublin.

CONTENTS

ABBREVIATIONS

Add. MS   Additional manuscripts, British Museum

D.N.B.   *Dictionary of National Biography*

F.O.   Foreign Office, London

Hansard   *Hansard's Parliamentary Debates*

N. Lib. Ir.   National Library of Ireland

P.R.O.   Public Record Office of England

P.R.O.I.   Public Record Office of Ireland

R.I.A.   Royal Irish Academy

S.P.O.   State Paper Office, Dublin

INTRODUCTION

~~~~~~~~~~~~~~~~~~~~~~~~~~~~~~~~~~

THIS STUDY had its origins in an attempt to examine the influence of the great Irish famine on contemporary political developments in Britain and Ireland. But it became increasingly obvious as the work progressed that while the famine years have much in common they do not present an altogether satisfactory unity for the study of political change; too many of the factors involved stretch back into the years before 1845.

The year 1841 is in some ways a more convenient starting point. It saw the effective beginning of Daniel O'Connell's agitation for the repeal of the Act of Union and it saw, too, the beginning of the most notable phase in Sir Robert Peel's career, a phase in which Irish problems came to hold, for a time, a central position. In bringing Irish affairs into such prominence in British politics, O'Connell's repeal agitation, like the Catholic emancipation campaign at an earlier date, played a most important part. Indeed, it can be said that this concentration of attention on Irish needs was the one immediate achievement to which the repeal agitation of the eighteen-forties may lay claim. But great as may have been the influence exercised by the repeal agitation, the actual nature of the Irish problems made it increasingly difficult for British politicians to ignore them.

The project for a legislative union between Great Britain and Ireland was brought forward, at the end of the eighteenth century, primarily as a means of strengthening the British connection at a time when French revolutionary principles appeared to be making progress in Ireland. William Pitt optimistically predicted, however, that political integration and free trade between the two islands would, in practice, encourage English

Introduction

capitalists to invest in Ireland, attracted there by the supply of cheap labour. The Union, too, Pitt argued, would help to solve the Irish religious problem, since Catholic grievances could be readily met within a United Kingdom, where the Protestants in England, Scotland and Wales would ensure a permanent Protestant majority. Concessions to the Catholics need not endanger the Protestant character of the constitution.

There were, of course, those in Ireland, among the Anglo-Irish landed ascendancy, who resisted the Union and feared the consequences of the abolition of Ireland's Protestant Parliament. There were some, too, who regretted the destruction of an institution which, reformed and thrown open to Catholics of property, might have become a reasonably representative legislature. Pitt, however, had his way. The massive power of patronage and political influence was brought skilfully into play and the Irish Parliament, after an initial resistance, agreed to its own extinction. By 1801, the new United Kingdom of Great Britain and Ireland was an accomplished fact, yet forty years after the Union had been brought about Irish political movements had become in no wise fully identified with those in Great Britain.

It was a measure of the incompleteness of the Union and of the political controversy that still surrounded it that, while Chartism and free trade held significant places in English and Scottish popular politics in the years after 1838, neither movement made any serious impact on the Ireland of that time. In Ireland, the eighteen-forties were characterised, in political terms, by a body with specifically Irish aims, the Loyal National Repeal Association, which sought the repeal of the legislative Union between Great Britain and Ireland and the restoration of an Irish Parliament under the Crown.

By the year 1840 little had been done to integrate Ireland and Britain in social and political terms and the contrast remained considerable between a Britain embarking on the adventure of industrialisation and an Ireland on the edge of economic chaos. A long tradition of hostility between landlord and tenant-farmer, absenteeism, with its associated problem of inadequate investment in Irish agriculture, over-population in many areas, and widespread poverty in an essentially agricultural country, all these circumstances helped to differentiate the Irish economy

2

from that of Great Britain. But the distinctive characteristics and problems of Irish society were best revealed in the religious structure of the country.

Before the Union, and for long after it, political influence was concentrated in the hands of a numerically small Protestant landed ascendancy. That a wealthy landed class should enjoy a position of great influence was not surprising at the time. In religious beliefs and through family connections, the Irish landed class was allied with the landed interest in England. What, however, made the position in Ireland so unusual was that the great bulk of the people were neither Anglican nor non-conformist but Catholic in religious profession. This religious division had, in practice, a wide range of social and political implications.

Despite the defeat and collapse of what remained of the old Gaelic political order in the seventeenth century, very many rural areas were still Gaelic in speech in the years before the Great Famine. Though the Irish language was rapidly losing ground before the advance of English, some measure of cultural differentiation must be counted among the factors which helped, directly and indirectly, to deepen the divisions between the landed class and the Catholic masses. In economic terms, too, though some progress had been made in the eighteenth century, the Irish Catholics were still the poorest section of the community. Again, as a religious group they were accorded for long an inferior status at law, a group among whom the memory of confiscations and defeat only slowly died.

Had Pitt been able to overcome the religious scruples of King George III and had the fear of Catholicism been less powerful in early nineteenth century England, Catholics might have been freed soon after the Union from their remaining legal disabilities. But Catholic emancipation, which in constitutional terms came to mean primarily the right to sit in Parliament and secondly the right to hold high public office, did not come until 1829 and then it was only granted in the face of much and long-sustained opposition. In itself, emancipation brought little immediate change, and for many decades after 1829 the Irish Catholic was to remain in an inferior position in relation to public office and the exercise of economic power. The eighteen-thirties and forties were, indeed, to see some weakening of the

Introduction

influence and authority of the Protestant ascendancy, but for reasons we must consider in the course of this study, the process of change was slow, often slower than ministers in London would have wished.

It was only in the relatively prosperous north-eastern part of the island, where the industrial revolution was already making some impact, that integration with Britain and the acceptance of the Union made evident progress in the first half of the nineteenth century. It was in these Ulster counties, too, where Protestantism was strong, that Daniel O'Connell had least success in winning popular support for the repeal of the Union. It was Daniel O'Connell's destiny to become almost completely identified with the hopes and aspirations of a Catholic Ireland slowly emerging from that inarticulateness which had characterised it for so long. This close identity of O'Connell with Catholic claims brought with it complications. It helped to make the successive movements which he led more suspect than they might otherwise have been in Protestant circles. In the years before 1801, much of the resistance to the proposed Act of Union had come from Irish Protestant sources, yet in the eighteen-forties the great repeal movement was predominantly Catholic in membership, while the Protestant interest generally remained either hostile or aloof.

Catholic influences in the O'Connellite camp were not the only factors which helped to maintain Irish politics on a roughly denominational basis. The Act of Union had changed relatively little in early nineteenth century Ireland. Despite their initial fears, the same kind of people retained a political ascendancy after 1801 as had enjoyed it before that date. The educated, wealthy Catholic remained excluded from positions of decision. The eighteenth century, in Ireland, had been marked by a recovery in the economic power of at least a section of the Catholic community and it had also seen among the Presbyterian townsmen of Ulster a significant advance in political self-expression and in economic strength. The Union did not halt these trends and the Protestants of Ulster were to strengthen still further their existing cultural and religious links with England and Scotland. Many Irish Catholics, however, came to believe that the Union offered them no hope of an escape from that position of inferiority they had occupied before 1800.

4

As a young man, O'Connell had been one of the few Catholics who openly opposed the passing of the Act of Union. But it was the failure of the Tory administrations to meet Irish claims, in the first two decades of the new century, which gave O'Connell the opportunity to win political leadership in Ireland and bring the Catholic country people as a disciplined force into political life. Through the Catholic Association, O'Connell helped to work a major change in Irish politics which subseqent developments did not altogether destroy. O'Connell and the Catholic clergy shaped a formidable political weapon and there were many educated Catholics who recognised that this weapon could be used to aid their own advance in social and political terms. O'Connell, who understood so well the character and wants of his people, became the 'Liberator' and that he was to remain until the end. But once he turned his attention to the repeal issue, Catholic emancipation accomplished, it became evident that repeal for him could not mean a return simply to the condition of affairs which existed before the year 1800. To have accepted the pre-Union position would have been to accept what O'Connell had fought for so long to destroy, the concentration of political power in the hands of a small section of the population.

Had O'Connell chosen to devote his attention, in the eighteen-twenties, to the task of securing a repeal of the Act of Union, he might not have driven so many Protestants into the anti-repeal camp. But as a practical politician he saw, no doubt, that a demand for the repeal of a still untried Union had less emotional value than a demand that Catholics should share fully in the fruits of the Union. The Catholic emancipation campaign and the popular enthusiasm it provoked, however, made it abun- dantly clear to Irish Protestants that the Catholic masses had become a formidable political force. The fear that home rule might mean Rome rule did not first take shape in the late nineteenth century.

It would be wrong to assume that Daniel O'Connell thought simply in terms of the political claims of the Catholic majority. His attitude was more complex and less precise. He was without question the champion of Catholic claims but he was also one of the most successful liberal leaders of the early nineteenth century in Europe, It is, therefore, not surprising that throughout his career he placed a great deal of emphasis on the importance of winning both Protestant support and the support of the landed interest as a whole. He failed, however, to discover an argument which would quieten Protestant fears of the demagogue and yet suffice to hold the confidence of his Catholic followers.

Speaking in October 1840, at the beginning of the great repeal campaign, he could say: 'For my part I do not hold any distinction in point of religious creed between any men . . . but I will venture to say, that however Protestants may differ from us in other respects, they could not but admire the religious fidelity of the people of Ireland . . . The Catholic church is a national church, and if the people rally with me they will have a nation for that church'.[1] A statement of this kind, and more of a like nature could be quoted, illustrates clearly enough O'Connell's approach to the vexed problem of religious divisions in Ireland. Tolerant of other creeds, he nevertheless saw in the aspirations of his own people the driving force in Irish political life. O'Connell did not hesitate to abandon policies, when, as a shrewd man of politics, he found it prudent to do so, but this reliance on the Irish Catholics and his claim to interpret their wants remained the basis of his power.

There were Protestants who supported his campaign for Catholic emancipation, and when he launched, in 1840, his new movement in favour of repeal, a number of Protestants of nationalist sympathy joined with him. Henry Grattan, the son of the great orator, became a member of the Repeal Association. A little later, the *Nation* group included some young Protestant professional men, who, for a time at least, accepted O'Connell's leadership. Again, William Smith O'Brien, who became so prominent in the affairs of the repeal movement from 1844 onwards, was both a member of the established church and a landlord. But though the Protestants who joined the Repeal Association were often men of talent and vision, the bulk of their co-religionists did not follow them and remained profoundly suspicious of O'Connell's intentions.

O'Connell chose to use extra-parliamentary means to achieve constitutional ends. The forces of popular opinion he could bring to bear on Parliament were considerable, but in an age in

[1] *Freeman's Journal*, 9 Oct. 1840.

which property and established wealth counted for so much politically, it was obviously difficult for O'Connell to maintain a sustained and consistent campaign over a long period. He lacked the means and, perhaps, the will to do so. In practice O'Connell was prepared to abandon or to modify a policy and to do so quickly if he came to believe that some practical concessions could be won from the Government of the day. The excited political activity of the early eighteen-thirties, culminating in his motion, in the Commons, in favour of repeal in 1834, could be matched by his virtual abandonment of repealist arguments in the years between 1835 and 1840, when it appeared that the Melbourne ministry was prepared to weaken the hold of the old ascendancy in Ireland. The element of expediency, therefore, was a constant one in the political tactics employed by O'Connell. The issue of the repeal of the Union seldom took on an absolute character in O'Connell's public speeches. Even at the very beginning of his remarkable campaign for repeal, in 1840, he made his line of argument on this point reasonably clear. 'If we get the justice we require', he said at the first meeting of his new repeal movement 'then our repeal association is at an end, but I know we will not get that justice'.[2]

O'Connell's apparent willingness to make repeal a bargaining counter for concessions was to involve him in serious difficulties with those of his followers who took a more uncompromising stand, but it does help to concentrate attention on O'Connell the reformer. By inclination O'Connell gravitated to the Whigs or rather to the Radicals in British politics. Many of the constitutional changes they sought would have helped to strengthen his political position. In the eighteen-thirties, he had campaigned actively in England against the House of Lords and the constitutional powers it enjoyed. Like many of the English Radicals, O'Connell saw in franchise reform, especially household suffrage, church disestablishment and municipal reform, essential elements in any worthwhile scheme of political progress. It would, however, be wrong to assume that Daniel O'Connell and the movement he led—under so many different names—was committed to drastic social changes in Ireland. On issues which might involve a revolutionary redistribution

[2] *Freeman's Journal*, 16 Apr. 1840.

7

of wealth, such as land reform, O'Connell was always cautious in his approach. Though he often spoke of the need to remedy the Irish farmers' grievances, he advocated not peasant proprietorship and the expropriation of the landlords but a more limited measure to safeguard the tenant-farmers from arbitrary eviction. The landlord most certainly had a place in O'Connell's world and indeed in that of the great majority of his associates, including the Young Irelanders. Nor surprisingly, he regarded both militant trade unionism and the Chartist movement, especially 'physical force' Chartism, with considerable suspicion.

Whether O'Connell seriously believed he could win either a total repeal of the Union or some measure of more restricted autonomy it is now impossible to say with certainty. That he displayed, for an ageing man, both great energy and enthusiasm in organising and inspiring the repeal movement of the eighteen-forties there can be no dispute. Equally evident is the fact that the extent and vigour of the repeal movement, especially in 1843, disturbed Sir Robert Peel and his ministers greatly. O'Connell's pre-occupation with those reforms which would give Catholics a growing share in the government of Ireland was considerable, but he was prepared to play the repeal card whenever it seemed profitable. He did so possibly in the hope of gaining much less than his emphatic speeches suggested.

In practice the term 'repeal of the Union' lent itself to more than one interpretation. It is not easy to define in neat terms what O'Connell conceived repeal to be beyond saying that he wanted the creation of an Irish Parliament in which Catholic and popular influences would be considerable, especially in the House of Commons. On constitutional issues, such as the relations between Great Britain and Ireland in the fields of foreign and military policy and the degree of independence to be enjoyed by an Irish executive under the Crown, he was often vague. Isaac Butt, then the leading Conservative in the Dublin Corporation, once complained, during the course of a debate on repeal in 1843, that O'Connell 'had never told them what was the national independence at which he aimed—whether he was to be contented with the settlement of 1782 . . . or whether they were to sue for something beyond and inconsistent with that settlement'.[3] Butt pointed out that before 1800 the sovereign

[3] *Nation*, 4 Mar. 1843.

of Ireland acted on the advice of his English ministry in assenting to or rejecting Irish legislation and that the Irish executive was appointed in England. With some force, he asked were they to return to a constitutional arrangement which would give them a kingdom 'without power, without national existence, without fleets or armies, without ambassadors?'[4]

O'Connell's answer was to resort to generalisations which really did not meet Butt's objections. O'Connell's genius, however, as a political leader of a great mass movement did not lie in his ability to formulate precise definitions, but in his power to put forward emphatic, simple propositions. Repeal of the Union was as much a symbol of the claims of the Irish people to a share in government and political influence as Catholic emancipation had been before it.

Whatever qualifications may hedge about O'Connell's political nationalism, the fact remains that his Repeal Association made the claim to political independence, however limited, a serious issue in British and Irish politics in the eighteen-forties. The republicanism of the United Irishmen was dead after 1798 and the Emmett rising of 1803, but in the eighteen-forties the acceptance of full political identification with Great Britain was still being resisted by a formidable popular movement.

Though Giuseppe Mazzini, commenting on the repeal agitation, in 1847, could say that the Irish did not 'plead for any distinct principle of life or system of legislation derived from native peculiarities and contrasting radically with English wants and wishes', there were those in Ireland, in the eighteen-forties, who believed with passion in the fullness of Irish nationalism.[5] It may seem curious in the light of Mazzini's strictures that a section of the repeal movement became known as Young Ireland. O'Connell and his supporters, during the stormy controversies of 1845 in the Repeal Association, used the term 'Young Ireland' to ridicule the small opposition group in the Association and to suggest that 'Old Ireland' stood firmly with O'Connell. The name Young Ireland was, however, in

[4] Ibid.
[5] Bolton King, *Mazzini*, p. 107; Kevin B. Nowlan, 'The meaning of repeal in Irish History', in *Historical Studies IV*, pp. 1–17.

Introduction

many ways an appropriate one and it quickly came to be accepted and used by the men of the opposition too.[6]

The disputes and strains within the repeal movement increased from the end of 1843 onwards, when it became clear that the great repeal agitation would not achieve its objective quickly. In the course of this book we shall have to examine some of these disputes and controversies and in certain respects the interpretation offered must differ from the neatly rounded picture of repeal history given by the Young Irelander, Charles Gavan Duffy, in his remarkable and valuable studies of the period. The immediate problems which O'Connell had to overcome in 1845 and 1846, if he were to keep an Irish political movement in being, were greater than Gavan Duffy will allow. Again, Gavan Duffy does something less than full justice to the role of more radical men than himself, such as John Mitchel and James Fintan Lalor, in the shaping of Irish nationalism, just as he tends to place the blame for the divisions within the Repeal Association all too firmly on the shoulders of O'Connell and his friends. But though the views and programme of Young Ireland were not as well defined as Gavan Duffy suggests, in stressing the differences in approach to nationalism between O'Connell and Young Ireland, Gavan Duffy was undoubtedly correct.

Three young men, Gavan Duffy, Thomas Davis and John Blake Dillon, who were attracted to the Repeal Association in 1841–2, were responsible for the foundation of the *Nation* newspaper, with Gavan Duffy as its proprietor. The *Nation*, first published in 1842, was a journal of considerable literary quality and it soon became the rallying point of the Young Ireland group. The young men were influenced by those ideas which were changing the political climate of Europe. 'The language, which grows up with a people, is conformed to their organs . . . mingled inseparably with their history and their soil, fitted beyond any other language to express their prevalent thoughts in the most natural and efficient way.'[7] These words were written neither by Johann Gottfried Herder nor by one of his German or Slav disciples, but by the Young Irelander, Thomas Davis. The appeal to the historical, to the real or imagined lore

[6] Charles Gavan Duffy, *Young Ireland*, p. 257.
[7] D. J. O'Donoghue (ed.), *Essays Literary and Historical by Thomas Davis* p. 97.

of the people and the acceptance of nationalism and national claims as fundamental realities which could not be compromised, these were all constantly recurring themes in the *Nation* newspaper.

It is important to remember that Daniel O'Connell could make use of historic symbolism when he wished to do so. The decision to hold the 'monster meetings', in 1843, at ancient sites like Tara and Clontarf was one instance of his willingness to recall the past, but O'Connell's favourite arguments in favour of repeal were not so much historical as practical in character. In time many secondary conflicts were to add greatly to the difficulties existing between O'Connell and the Young Irelanders, but it was the differences about nationalism as an absolute value that were basic to the dispute which destroyed repeal unity. The wordy arguments, in 1846, about the use of violent means to gain political ends, at a time when nobody seriously contemplated using such means, and the Young Irelanders' objection to a new Whig alliance are only of importance when seen in the context of the fundamental disagreement. Much the same can be said of the controversies, in 1844, about federalism and the possibility of accepting, as a final solution, a measure of political autonomy more limited in scope than a repeal of the union. Nevertheless, the significance of these secondary disputes should not be underestimated. They help us to learn much about the qualities and limitations of the contestants both in their conflicts with each other and in the wider struggle for some measure of national independence. The men of the *Nation* group came to criticise many aspects of the Repeal Association and of O'Connell's leadership. Lax financial management, the potential place-hunters, the demagogic methods employed to rouse popular feeling, and the clerical influences at work in the Association were seen as defects in the repeal movement by Davis, Gavan Duffy and their supporters.

The causes of the Young Irelanders' uneasiness are readily enough understood. O'Connell's rough, boisterous organisation had won the support of the ordinary people, especially of the countryside, in the eighteen-twenties and again in the eighteen-forties. The movement's strength lay in the Catholic masses, but the difficulty with such a popular force was that its very character and its dependence on one man, O'Connell, made it by no means attractive to many of the middle-class urban electors. O'Connell wanted such people in his movement, as we have seen, but he did not consider well enough the kind of concessions which would have to be made in order to induce them to join him. In contrast, the Young Irelanders, attached to the ideal of a comprehensive nationalism, saw in the task of winning the support of the landlords and of the middle-class Protestants a major challenge for the repeal movement.

Effective committee rule, a lessening of O'Connell's personal authority and of the political influence of his family, an avoidance of clerical themes at Association meetings, these were among the changes the Young Irelanders sought. They were demands which O'Connell, an elderly man, was unwilling to concede, conscious as he was of his great and enduring influence on the Catholic population and of the numerical weakness of the Young Ireland group in the country as a whole.

Controversy on issues of such a kind was sharpened by the fact that some of the leading Young Irelanders were drawn from the Protestant middle-class. They were, therefore, conscious both of the importance of winning over Protestant opinion to repeal and of preventing the Association from assuming too Catholic a character. For Thomas Davis and, to a lesser extent, William Smith O'Brien, this fear of clerical domination was, as we shall see, a major preoccupation. In the task, however, of uniting 'Orange and Green', landlord and tenant-farmer, the Young Irelanders were to be no more successful than O'Connell, despite their more subtle methods. Cut off from any really direct approach to the people of the countryside by the strength of O'Connell's influence, they made but few converts to repeal and nationalism among their contemporaries of the upper and middle classes. In Ulster, the Protestant population, as a whole, remained unmoved, though nonconformist Ulster was to give to Young Ireland and Irish nationalism a man of remarkable political stature and personal courage, John Mitchel, whose name will often appear in this study.

Like O'Connell, the Young Irelanders believed that the ending of the Union and the restoration of an Irish Parliament would provide the means of curing Ireland's woes. The *Nation* could, for example, urge that '. . . Repeal would abolish absenteeism and foreign taxation, and would give Irish offices and rewards to Irishmen . . . would secure the peasant from oppression, the mechanic from premature competition, and, with justice, would bring order, industry and riches'.[8] The claim of Ireland was for 'unbounded nationality', but no more successfully than Daniel O'Connell did they define the character of the connection that would exist between Great Britain and Ireland once the Act of Union was repealed. One thing alone was evident, there could be no return to that position of constitutional subordination to the British Parliament and executive which was occupied by the old Irish Parliament and executive before 1800.

The control of the colonies, the status of Ireland when Britain went to war, and the question of diplomatic representation under a common crown were problems which were only to be resolved with reasonable precision when dominion status became a reality in the present century. It was customary in all repeal factions to disclaim any serious interest in the management of the British colonies. On the subject of Ireland's relations with the Crown, one Young Irelander, Michael Joseph Barry, in an essay published in 1845, came close to proposing something like a commonwealth solution. 'Now, an Irish minister responsible to the Parliament of Ireland only would not advise the sovereign to declare war', he wrote, '*on the part of Ireland*, except when sure of the approbation of the Irish Parliament; and, on the other hand, would advise such a step, when he was certain of its approval, notwithstanding, the British minister might oppose such a declaration, *on the part of England*.'[9] Interesting as an exercise in political speculation, such an advanced theory was most unlikely to appeal to any section of Tory or Whig opinion in mid-nineteenth century England.

The famine and the events in France, in 1848, helped to concentrate the attention of some Young Irelanders, such as John Mitchel and Devin Reilly, on republicanism and on the methods of rural agitation, but, even in 1848, it seems fair to conclude that very many Young Irelanders continued to think in terms of the repeal of the Union and the maintenance of some constitutional links with England under a common crown. The

[8] *Nation*, 30 Sept. 1843.
[9] *Essays on the Repeal of the Union*, pp. 78–9.

main contribution of Young Ireland to the shaping of Irish nationalism was its doctrine of a comprehensive Irish nationality, which could not be compromised, superior to religious differences and group prejudices, This belief, expressed with eloquence in the pages of the *Nation* newspaper, was to become in due time part of the common inheritance of Irish nationalism.

Warm hearted, often impetuous and frequently ruthless in his words and judgements, Daniel O'Connell was in many ways a remarkable contrast to the man he came to regard as his major opponent in political life, Sir Robert Peel. The process of change in Peel's approach to Ireland was characteristic of his ways in politics. As a young man, he had come to Ireland to occupy the post of Chief Secretary and he held that post for six years until his resignation in 1818. During that period he became identified with the party of ascendancy and of resistance to Catholic claims. And it was during those years, too, that the deep hostility and mutual lack of understanding between Peel and O'Connell took shape. In 1815, the two men would have fought a duel had it not been for the intervention of O'Connell's wife. Peel left Ireland condemned by O'Connell as 'Orange Peel', while O'Connell was to remain for Peel always a violent demagogue who could not be trusted. Peel was a cautious, sensitive and conscientious man, and his career, taken as a whole, was to show him as being a great administrator rather than a major reformer. He was prepared for innovations when the necessities of efficient government demanded them, and once he had accepted a new course he followed it with firmness and much courage. The changes he was to make in Ireland, between 1841 and 1846, however, tended to be piecemeal, inadequate and often rather short-term in their implications.[10]

The fact nevertheless remains that Peel, the leader of the Conservatives, had come to accept, by the early eighteen-forties, the need for some change in the pattern of government and even of social policy in Ireland as well as in Britain. His move towards free trade was not the only indication of development in Peel's political views. The man who had for so long resisted O'Connell's demand for Catholic emancipation could write, in 1843: 'What is the advantage to the Roman Catholics

[10] Norman Gash, *Mr. Secretary Peel: the Life of Sir Robert Peel to 1830*, pp. 225–36; G. Kitson Clark, *The Making of Victorian England*, pp. 40–6.

of having removed their legal disabilities, if somehow or other they are constantly met by a preferable claim on the part of Protestants, and if they do not practically reap the advantage of their nominal equality as to civil privilege ?'[11]

Sir Robert Peel had formed no very high opinion of the qualities of the Irish Tory connection as a political factor. His own experiences as Chief Secretary had left in him a deeprooted suspicion of 'those who are constantly trying for their own purposes . . . to foment discord between the chief authorities in Ireland'.[12] He often warned his colleagues in Ireland to beware of this 'old Irish game . . . played with consummate dexterity' even by those who claimed to be the friends of the administration.[13] As Prime Minister, therefore, he showed a willingness to take some Catholics into the public service, much as his Whig predecessors had done, but in practice he was never able to free himself from dependence on that Irish Tory connection he viewed with so much reserve. The continued opposition of O'Connell to his Irish policy and the loyalty of the Catholic population to the Liberator, made the task of building up a Catholic Tory connection in Ireland even more difficult than the creation of a vigorous Whig party independent of O'Connell.

When the Irish potato crop partially failed, in 1845, Peel and his Home Secretary, Sir James Graham, had already certain reforms to their credit, and these reforms had in some cases encountered much opposition among their own supporters. Peel could claim, too, that he had halted O'Connell's agitation and made the first serious attempt to win Catholic goodwill for a Tory Government, even at the risk of irritating some members of the old Tory connection in Ireland. But, in 1845, the Irish small farmers and cottiers were not better able to meet the disaster of a potato failure than they had been five years previously. The reforms which Peel and his colleagues were responsible for were of a secondary kind, and no more comprehensive than those brought forward by the Whigs before 1841 or,

[11] Peel to Earl De Grey, 22 Aug. 1843, Peel papers, Add. MS 40478, ff. 160–7.
[12] Peel to Lord Eliot, 23 Dec. 1843, Peel papers, Add. MS 40448, ff. 124–9.
[13] Ibid.

indeed, after 1846. Yet these changes helped to show that there were men of all parties in Great Britain who were thinking, though only in very tentative terms, about reform and change in Ireland.

Between five hundred thousand and a million people may have died as a consequence of the Great Famine and the diseases which followed in its wake.[14] The famine showed in a terrible way how necessary was a reform of the social system, if any practical advances were to be made towards political or economic stability. In the period we have to consider, that necessity for reform was becoming clearer to men in public life, but many were slow to advocate any changes that might endanger the property rights of the landed class. The solution of the Irish social problem involved much more than limiting the power of the landlords to evict their tenants, yet no really successful attempt was even made to meet the tenant-farmers' immediate grievance, insecurity of possession, since no ministry, in the mid-nineteenth century, proved willing to make it a primary objective of its policy.

O'Connell believed that the Whigs, under the leadership of Lord John Russell, would prove more ready to make generous and constructive concession than the Tories. Events between 1846 and the fall of the first Russell ministry in 1852, were to demonstrate that, if O'Connell under-estimated Peel's good intentions, he seriously over-estimated both the will and the ability of Russell and his colleagues to put through Parliament reforming measures of any lasting importance. The Whig leaders had undoubtedly one advantage Peel did not enjoy, they knew that the majority of their parliamentary following favoured liberal concessions in Ireland. The difficulty lay, however, in the nature of the concessions the Whig ministry was prepared to offer and in the inability of its members to reach agreement on any bold measures fitted to meet the evils of Irish society.

The Russell administration took office under difficult circumstances in 1846. The support it enjoyed in Parliament was uncertain and the famine was to bring about in the course of a

[14] Sir William P. MacArthur, 'Medical History of the Famine', in R. D. Edwards and T. D. Williams (eds.), *The Great Famine; Studies in Irish History 1845–52*, pp. 308–12.

few months a major social disaster. Again, in matters such as municipal reform, the tithes and education, the Whig ministries of the eighteen-thirties had already put through a number of reforming measures. Any new reforms of a similar kind would have involved bitterly controversial subjects, such as disestablishment, a thorough reform of the Irish franchise and the payment by the state of the Catholic clergy. These, too, were issues on which there was no agreement even within the ministry itself. The tragedy of the years between 1846 and 1852 lay, however, in the fact that neither the ministry nor Parliament succeeded in really freeing themselves from the bonds of accepted economic doctrines and from the powerful, persistent influence of the landed interest.

The hesitant, doubting steps taken to meet the Irish famine in 1846–7, involved an important decision to abandon for a time the cherished principle of non-intervention by the state in economic affairs. But the decision seems to have exhausted whatever collective enthusiasm the Russell ministry may have had for the task of solving the problems of poverty and unrest in Ireland. It would be wrong to conclude that individual members of the Government were not concerned about reform and change in Ireland. Russell, as we shall see, came to the point of recognising that something like tenant-right, a virtual co-ownership between landlord and tenant, was necessary to resolve the agrarian problem. Again, Russell's ambitious scheme for capital investment in land development, which he outlined to Parliament in 1847, was another sign of his willingness to consider the Irish question. But Russell never came to enjoy a personal authority in the cabinet such as Peel had known. He might speculate on bold reforms but in the face of the massive opposition of Lords Palmerston and Lansdowne, both Irish landlords, his plans for agrarian reform seldom progressed far beyond the memorandum and private letter.

The Prime Minister was tempted to experiment, but he was fearful of abandoning accepted economic and political conventions and incapable or unwilling to silence the conservative opposition to change within his own cabinet. As a result Russell remained at best a somewhat confused and, at times, petulant chairman, rather than a decisive force in the shaping of a cabinet policy on Irish problems.

Introduction

In any objective assessment of the difficult years of the great
repeal agitation and of the famine, an old mistake must be
avoided, the tendency to discover a constant, uniform element,
'the British Government', with a set policy of antipathy towards
Ireland, and possessing a hateful desire somehow to exterminate
the Irish people. The surviving material rather shows how wide
and varied could be the differences of opinion on Irish affairs
even within the same ministry and how great could be the
differences in outlook between the Government in London and
the administration in Dublin on many issues. But if no sustained, deliberate policy of antipathy can be identified, it must
nevertheless be said that throughout the first half of the nineteenth
century a tragic failure to understand the needs and aspirations
of the people characterised the approach of many British
politicians and administrators to Irish issues. Often the easy, un-
just assumption that the Irish alone were to blame for their
woes hid a depressing lack of knowledge of Irish affairs among
those who sought to govern Ireland from London.

In Ireland, it was only rather slowly, under the pressure of
famine, that economic issues came to hold a really central place
in the deliberations of the organised political movements.
Repeal of the Union was the primary aim and other issues
tended to be subordinated to it; and though they often denounced the evils of the land system, Irish nationalists, in the
eighteen-forties, for a time hesitated before accepting a policy
which laid a clear emphasis on the necessity for prompt,
extensive agrarian reforms. Gradually, however, the demand
for 'tenant right', for some reasonable measure of security of
possession for the tenant farmer, acquired an importance almost
equal to that enjoyed by the demand for the restoration of an
Irish Parliament. By 1847–8, men of all shades of repeal
opinion had acknowledged the immediate urgency of the
tenant-right issue in a land burdened by hunger and evictions.
Some of a more radical temper, like John Mitchel and James
Fintan Lalor, saw, at this time, in a vigorous, militant agrarian
agitation the most effective means of rousing an apathetic and
famine-tried people to action. In the eyes of Mitchel and his
followers, the governing classes were, by 1848, guilty of mortal
crimes against the poor. For Mitchel and those who thought
like him, the Irish landlords had come close to losing all serious

18

claim to the protection of society, because of their failure to meet the tenants' grievances and to take their proper place in the ranks of the repeal movement.

The massive agrarian agitation of a militant kind did not take shape in 1848 or 1849, but it is nevertheless true to say that, for a time at least, economic demands became the dominant ones in Irish political life. It was one of the signs of the final disintegration of Daniel O'Connell's old repeal movement that, in the twilight years between 1848 and 1851, many turned away from political nationalism to concentrate their attention on the vexed problem of the relations between landlord and tenant farmer.

The agitation for the simple repeal of the Union had ended, but later generations of Irish nationalists were to seek many of their arguments and much of their inspiration in the events of those stormy and tragic years, when O'Connell created anew a great popular political movement and the Young Irelanders elaborated their doctrines of nationality. In terms of British politics the eighteen-forties brought a growing awareness of the need for special remedial action in Ireland, but none of the major political parties was prepared to take that bold action which might have saved the Union. Only marginal groups, like the Chartists, spoke in radical terms on Irish issues, and their influence on contemporary politics was much too limited to be effective. A later generation would come to accept the need for land reform in Ireland and even for some modification of the Act of Union. But by that time Fenianism, the land war, and the Home Rule movement would have created new aspirations and new grievances to complicate the relations between the peoples of the two neighbouring islands.

I

PEEL AND IRELAND, 1841–2

~~~~~~~~~~~~~~~~~~~~~~~~~~~~~~~~

WHEN THE WHIG ADMINISTRATION finally abandoned office, after the elections of the summer of 1841, an important and at times not unpromising experiment came to an end. O'Connell, weak in parliamentary following though strong in popular support, had achieved a working arrangement with the Government of the United Kingdom between 1835 and 1841. From 1840 onwards, it is true that the prospects for the alliance were not encouraging, and that from 1838 onwards O'Connell was somewhat ill at ease, but the remarkable thing about the experiment was not so much its shortcomings as the fact that it worked at all. The results of the Whig-O'Connell alliance were modest, but not without value. Though they lacked a dramatic quality, they nevertheless contributed to the administrative and social development of the country. The national schools left some Catholics and many Protestants dissatisfied, but the national system was nevertheless superior to the school systems which had preceded it. The tithe commutation legislation did not go as far as O'Connell and his supporters wanted, yet it was one of the first practical steps taken towards a new ecclesiastical settlement in Ireland, while the personal influence of the Marquess of Normanby, as Lord Lieutenant, and Thomas Drummond, as Under-Secretary, helped to lessen the suspicion with which Irishmen viewed government from Dublin Castle. Catholics were appointed to public offices, and the Boards of Poor Law Guardians, set up under the 1838 Poor Law, brought

20

a measure of popular representation into local government. Before the Whigs left office something had been done to give Ireland better municipal government and to bring Catholics a little closer to the administration; and one of the last gestures of the Melbourne ministry, in 1841, was to try, though without success, to give Ireland a wider parliamentary franchise based on a more liberal system for registering voters.

Though the Government showed a willingness to attempt reform, the opponents of change were strong in the Tory ranks. Warning signs were not lacking. Lord Stanley's registration bills, of 1840 and 1841, for example, contrasted sharply with the Government's proposals, since their effect would have been to limit still further the franchise in Ireland rather than to widen it.[1] Nor surprisingly, the differences between the two British parties were very clearly defined for O'Connell. Almost on the eve of the fall of the Whig administration, O'Connell could say that while the Whigs had done justice to Ireland when they could, Peel, as Chief Secretary for Ireland, 'was not two years in office till he came down to the House and asked for three coercion bills'. He warned Peel that, while the Irish people had a prospect of some relief under the Whigs, their patience was now clearly exhausted, especially as they 'had no hope if the gentlemen opposite came into power'.[2]

O'Connell had not forgotten his bitter struggles in the past. With the Whigs it was, he felt, possible to bargain and negotiate, with the Tories there was only one weapon to hand, the one they themselves had used, coercion.[3]

The Tory successes, in the 1841 general election, and the replacement of the enfeebled Whig ministry by a strong administration led by Peel, seemed to open the way to a period of greater stability in British political life. But for O'Connell the situation was by no means an encouraging one. The Whig peace had been marked by a slackening in the intensity of political activity and interest in Ireland, and though O'Connell established yet another new political organisation, in April

[1] *Hansard*, lvi. 220–37, lvii. 1074–91, 1274–89; *Annual Register*, 1841, pp. 62–3.

[2] *Hansard*, lviii. 1056–65.

[3] D. O'Connell to P. V. Fitzpatrick, 28 Jan. 1841, Fitzpatrick, *Correspondence of Daniel O'Connell*, ii. 257–8.

1840, he was careful not to make the breach with the Whigs appear too sudden or too complete. The new association was first given the cumbersome but cautious title of the 'National Association of Ireland for full and prompt justice or repeal'. At its initial meeting, on April 15, O'Connell emphasised that the new movement fully disclaimed the use of violent means to achieve political ends and that he was prepared to abandon his campaign for a repeal of the Act of Union if full justice were done and Ireland put on a basis of equality with Great Britain.[4] Three months later he took another step forward. Having declared that it was 'idle now to expect anything from the imperial Parliament', he asked the members to call 'this association what it really is, "a Repeal Association" . . .'.[5] The organisation was, therefore, renamed the Loyal National Repeal Association, a title it retained throughout its troubled history.

Though O'Connell worked hard to arouse popular enthusiasm, he made only hesitant progress in 1840–1. The Catholic clergy in general, he complained, showed little interest in the repeal cause, though the formidable and outspoken Archbishop of Tuam, John MacHale, did join the Association as early as August 1840.[6] O'Connell was also anxious to secure the support of liberally minded Protestants, assuring them that 'there will be no religious differences amongst us . . . we have one common good to share and one common country'.[7] The response, however, was not encouraging. The small but influential group of Ulster reformers, whose most important member was probably William Sharman Crawford, not only kept aloof from the Repeal Association but founded their own Ulster Constitutional Association, in August 1840, on the model of the radical associations in Great Britain.[8] Sharman Crawford, in calling upon the Liberals in Ulster to form the Constitutional Association, specifically repudiated O'Connell's repeal agitation as tending 'to divide the friends of liberty in Ireland and to separate us from our British countrymen'.[9] With even less

[4] *Freeman's Journal*, 16 Apr. 1840.

[5] Ibid., 14 July 1840.

[6] D. O'Connell to P. V. Fitzpatrick, 19 Feb. 1841, Fitzpatrick, *Correspondence of Daniel O'Connell*, ii. 260–1; *Freeman's Journal*, 18 Aug. 1840.

[7] Ibid., 29 Oct. 1840.   [8] Ibid., 17 Aug. 1840.

[9] Ibid., 24 July 1840. William Sharman Crawford (1781–1861), a wealthy co. Down landlord, was a resolute champion of such varied causes as

prospect of success could O'Connell have hoped to make progress among the Irish conservatives, who remained resolute in their suspicion of his intentions.

At the beginning of 1841 the financial position of the Repeal Association was unsatisfactory and the receipts from the O'Connell tribute—one of O'Connell's principal sources of funds—was disappointing.[10] 'It comes across my mind', he wrote, 'that my career will terminate just at the moment that Ireland ceases to have friends.'[11] Nor were the results of the general election a source of much encouragement to him. The limited Irish £10 franchise was an obstacle, for it gave the advantage to his opponents who could normally rely on a wealthier following than O'Connell could.[12] Out of a population of some 8,000,000 in 1841, the franchise could be exercised by at most 100,000.[13] This meant that the popular movements he organised could exercise, at best, only an indirect influence on parliamentary life, and it remained one of O'Connell's most difficult tasks to balance the violent power of the unrepresented masses against that parliamentary policy he sought to pursue with limited means.

O'Connell, putting himself forward as a professed repealer, fought the election campaign of 1841 with some vigour.[14] But he had to contend with many difficulties. The Conservatives, especially in Dublin, were well organised, and, as the Limerick city contest showed, it was sometimes difficult to find a suitable repeal candidate, even when the Repeal Association was asked to provide one.[15]

It is difficult to give an exact figure for O'Connell's parlia-

[10] Repeal Assoc. meeting, 2 Jan., *Freeman's Journal*, 4 Jan., 1841.

[11] D. O'Connell to P. V. Fitzpatrick, 19 Feb. 1841, Fitzpatrick, *Correspondence of Daniel O'Connell*, ii. 260–1.

[12] N. Gash, *Politics in the Age of Peel*, pp. 50–64.

[13] *An Abstract and Summary for the whole of Ireland, of the Returns relative to the Registration of Electors in Ireland . . .*, H.C. 1843 (293), l. 287–8.

[14] Repeal Assoc. meeting, 14 June, *Freeman's Journal*, 15 June 1841.

[15] Irish Metropolitan Conservative Society meeting, 14 June, *Freeman's Journal*, 16 June 1841; *Saunder's News Letter*, 5, 9 July 1841.

Catholic emancipation, tenant-right, parliamentary reform and 'federalism' as a possible answer to the demand for repeal of the union. He represented the borough of Dundalk in parliament from 1834 until 1837, but refusing to profess himself a repealer, he was not re-elected. He was M.P. for Rochdale from 1841 to 1852.

mentary following after the 1841 election, since the Repeal Association at no time in its history succeeded in exercising an effective control over the selection of parliamentary candidates. Potential candidates with the necessary wealth and local influence were relatively few among the Catholics and nationalists, and this scarcity of candidates made the enforcement of any rigid repeal test quite impracticable. Of the 62 Liberals returned for Irish constituencies in 1841, some 15 were described as repealers in one estimate, while a more optimistic analysis put O'Connell's following at 22.[16] But of this latter total a number proved themselves to be rather conventional Whigs, as for example, the O'Conor Don, the member for County Roscommon, Richard Lalor Sheil, the member for Dungarvan, and John Patrick Somers, the member for Sligo. Again the difficulty of making any clear distinctions in 1841 is illustrated by the description given of John O'Brien, the member for Limerick. He appears in the *Freeman's Journal* list of members as a radical reformer 'and all but a repealer'.[17] In contrast to the repeal movement, the Tories, in 1841, secured some 42 or 43 seats and defeated O'Connell in the Dublin city contest, a defeat which was hardly made good by his election to Parliament for County Cork and to the office of Lord Mayor of Dublin.[18]

To make matters still more difficult, the leaders of the Whigs in opposition resolved to maintain only the most distant contacts with O'Connell. This was the consequence of O'Connell's public declaration that for the future he would support only a ministry which would leave repeal of the Union an open question.[19] This irritated Lord John Russell, a convinced supporter of the Union, while O'Connell's demand for an extension of the Irish reform act alienated still further the aristocratic Whigs.[20]

[16] C. R. Dodd, *The Parliamentary Companion for 1843*, passim; *Freeman's Journal*, 24 July 1841.

[17] Ibid.

[18] *Morning Herald*, 24 July 1841; C. R. Dodd, *The Parliamentary Companion for 1843*, passim.

[19] Repeal Assoc. meeting, 31 Oct., *Nation*, 5 Nov. 1842.

[20] Russell to Duncannon, 8 Sept. 1841, Palmerston to Russell, 12 Oct. 1841, Russell papers, P.R.O. 30/22/4; Russell to Lansdowne, 12 Nov. 1841, G. P. Gooch, *The Later Correspondence of Lord John Russell*, i. 49–50; Howick to Russell, 20 Nov. 1841, Russell papers, P.R.O. 30/22/4.

From the beginning of the new session, O'Connell found himself largely isolated from his former associates. In office was the man he regarded as one of the major foes of progress in Ireland, while his own supporters were still disorganised and the future of the repeal movement remained uncertain. It is a tribute to his energy and resourcefulness that within two years, though no longer a young man, he turned the Repeal Association into a formidable political force, and made the Irish question a central and an urgent one for both Government and Parliament.

When Peel took office the political scene in Ireland, if not encouraging, was at least quiet. The Repeal Association was active through 1841, but for the moment it did not constitute a threat to the existing order in the United Kingdom.[21] It was rather in Britain that Peel and his colleagues found their most pressing problems and it was in relation to British affairs that Peel first showed that cautious change and the new Conservative ministry were not incompatible. The question of the modification of the Corn Laws occupied much of the attention of Parliament in the first six months of 1842. This and the rest of the Government's fiscal and tariff policy left little time for Irish questions. In the debates between February and April, the Irish members played an insignificant part, and it is perhaps characteristic of the attitude of the Government of the time that no mention whatever was made of Ireland in the Queen's speech at the opening of the session. The Corn Laws, the revenue and the distress in the manufacturing areas were the principal themes, and the principal concern of the Government.[22]

Yet it would be wrong to assume that, in its first year in office, the Government entirely ignored Irish affairs. The neglect of Ireland was more evident on the legislative than on the administrative level. Though the decisions taken on Irish issues were largely on matters of secondary importance, a study of the way in which they were handled is of value if only because the developments in Irish administration, in 1841-2, reveal much of the future character of Peel's Irish policy in both its weakness and its strength.

[21] Peel to Graham, 21 Oct. 1841, Peel papers, Add. MS 40446, ff. 76-7.
[22] *Hansard*, lx. 1-5, 620-4.

However much they may have disagreed on other issues, neither Peel nor O'Connell had many illusions about the difficulties Peel would encounter in Irish affairs. O'Connell warned Peel of the difficulty of trying to satisfy Tory opinion and of meeting the demand for impartial government in Ireland.[23] Peel knew well the power of the Irish Orange connection, but it was evident from the outset that there was to be no blind reaction from what the Whigs had been doing in Ireland.[24] Peel's approach was in many ways different from that of the Whigs. He had less patience with Irish nationalists and the burden of the Irish Tory party weighed heavily on his Irish administration, but the readiness to make cautious reforms survived the change of government.

The composition of Peel's Irish executive was not, as it proved, a happy one. It represented an attempt to meet the fear of the Irish Conservatives while providing some expectation that high Toryism would not be the key-note of the new administration. The Lord Lieutenant, Earl De Grey, was a staunch Conservative, firmly attached to the existing order and connected by his marriage to a daughter of the first Earl of Enniskillen, with one of the great Irish Tory families.[25] From the correspondence, he emerges as a man of very set ideas, anxious to keep as much authority in his own hands as possible. This tendency provoked complaints from the Chief Secretary, Lord Eliot, who appears to have been an enlightened and liberal man, though he was not an administrator of the highest quality.[26] The third important figure in the Irish executive was Edward Lucas, the Under-Secretary, and in practice the political head of the civil service. Lucas, an Irish Protestant landlord, was an invaluable link between the Government and its Irish supporters. He knew his worth and, throughout the

[23] Ibid., lix. 390–400.
[24] Peel to De Grey, 27 Nov. 1841, Peel papers, Add. MS 40447, ff. 90–3.
[25] *D.N.B.*, xxiii. 208.
[26] Graham to Peel, 17 Oct. 1842, Peel papers, Add. MS 40447, ff. 245–50. Edward Granville Eliot, third Earl of St Germans (1798–1877), entered Parliament, 1824, for Liskeard. A Lord of the Treasury, 1827. In Spain, 1834, an as envoy extraordinary. He helped to humanise the Carlist war by the Eliot convention which halted reprisals. Succeeded to the Earldom in 1845. Lord Lieutenant of Ireland under the Aberdeen administration, Dec. 1852.

years 1841–4, his repeated threats to resign caused embarrassment and irritation in London. Almost until the end of 1842,
the story of Peel's handling of Irish affairs is largely concerned
with his efforts to reconcile the growing differences within the
Irish administration.

From the beginning, Peel advised restraint and caution in
Ireland.[27] The Government's policy, both he and Graham felt,
should be based on a steady discountenancing of the repeal
party and a clear preference for those 'who advocate British
connection in union with an impartial and liberal policy, and
equal justice administered to Roman Catholics'.[28] This policy
of consideration for Catholic opinion but no firm promises to
any party soon provoked difficulties in Dublin. Both the Lord
Lieutenant and the Under-Secretary tended to favour the traditional Conservative interests, while Eliot, at times with greater
enthusiasm than his superiors in London, sought closer connections with the Liberal and Catholic elements. Minor disputes over the appointment or dismissal of subordinate officials
increased the strain between Eliot, De Grey and Lucas, but the
first major issue of policy that divided them was the future of
national education in Ireland.[29]

The dispute over the national schools, like the Maynooth
question, is of importance to the study of Peel's policy on the
vexed issue of the place of the Catholic majority in the official
life of the country. After Catholic emancipation, the establishment of the national schools by the Whigs, in 1831, probably
represented the most substantial measure of reform in Ireland
in the first half of the nineteenth century. The question of
elementary education had long been a difficult one, especially
as the Catholic hierarchy had come to view with considerable
suspicion the activities of the private educational societies which
were essentially Protestant in character. Both Catholic and
Protestant churchmen would have preferred elementary school
systems under the control of their respective churches, but the
funds were not there to make such a clear division possible and

[27] Peel to De Grey, 18 Sept. 1841, Peel papers, Add. MS 40447, ff.
16–17.
[28] Graham to Peel, 21 Oct. 1841, Peel papers, Add. MS 40446, ff. 74–5.
[29] Peel to Graham, 29 Dec. 1841, Graham to Peel, [Dec. 1841], Peel
papers, Add. MS 40446, ff. 262–3, 266–7.

the state proved unwilling to endow strictly denominational schools in Ireland in the eighteen-thirties.[30]

Because of Catholic criticisms, the Government in 1831 withdrew its financial aid from the Kildare Place Society, which had been established in 1811 to provide education for the poor, and instead brought forward a new scheme of its own. Introduced by Lord Stanley, the Chief Secretary for Ireland, the new arrangement enabled the state, through grants and public inspection, to assume some direct responsibility in the field of elementary education. A board of seven commissioners, including Dr Daniel Murray, the Catholic Archbishop of Dublin, was set up to administer the scheme. In the recognised state-aided schools, teaching was to be conducted on the basis of combined secular education for all and separate religious education for the children of the different persuasions.[31]

After ten years of trial, the system had the merit that it worked reasonably well despite opposition from some of the Catholic bishops and from a majority of the Church of Ireland episcopate.[32] But it was equally evident that as a system of mixed, that is to say—combined Catholic and Protestant education, it had in a large measure failed. The original idea of combined secular education and separate religious instruction, supplemented by the optional use of approved scriptural texts, had to a very great extent given way to a system of separate education for Catholics, members of the established church, and Presbyterians.[33]

Apart from the Archbishop of Dublin, Richard Whately, and the Bishop of Meath, Charles Dickinson, both of whom were members of the board, the leading episcopalian ecclesiastics were profoundly opposed to the national schools. De Grey, in a letter to Peel, put clearly the point of view of the Primate, the

[30] T. Ó Raifeartaigh, 'Mixed education and the Synod of Ulster', in *Irish Historical Studies*, ix. 281-99.

[31] *Ninth Report of the Commissioners of National Education in Ireland, for the Year* 1842, H.C. 1843 (471), xxviii. 93-352.

[32] Stanley to Peel, 30 Nov. 1841, Parker, *Sir Robert Peel*, iii. 35-6; *Seventh Report of the Commissioners of National Education in Ireland, for the Year* 1840, H.C. 1842 (353), xxiii. 217-21.

[33] *Ninth Report of the Commissioners of National Education in Ireland, for the Year* 1842, H.C. 1843 (471), xxviii. 93-352; Graham to Peel, 24 Nov. 1841, Peel Papers, Add. MS 40446, ff. 142-4.

Archbishop of Armagh, as well as his own when he stated: 'A joint education of the two sects I firmly believe to be *now* impracticable, the public grant of money therefore nominally appropriated to the education of all will virtually be used for the benefit of the Catholics only.'[34] The Primate, Lord John George Beresford, possibly the best advocate of the episcopalian case, argued that an education not founded on the reading of the scriptures was unacceptable to churchmen.[35] The Lord Lieutenant favoured the Primate's point of view and urged the need for a commission to examine the Irish educational system.[36] In contrast, Lord Eliot stressed that any change in the existing system would be interpreted in the worst possible way by the Archbishop of Dublin and would possibly lead to his resignation, leaving the board almost exclusively Roman Catholic.[37]

This open disagreement over the schools put Peel's ministry in a difficult position.[38] At the beginning he was prepared to admit that there might be no alternative to abandoning mixed education.[39] His opinion in favour of the national schools, however, rapidly hardened, and in November 1842 Graham was instructed to advise the Lord Lieutenant that the Government was opposed to any enquiry into Irish education. Protestant opinion was known, and an enquiry would only lead Catholics to believe that the national system was to be ended. Likewise it was held to be inconsistent with sound principles to make special grants to Protestant schools, since 'the great object is to extend the principle of united education'.[40]

A number of factors prompted the cabinet to take this stand on education, which so obviously ran counter to the wishes of a majority of those on whom the Tory party in Ireland traditionally depended, namely the country gentry and the clergy of

[34] De Grey to Peel, 6 June 1842, Peel papers, Add. MS 40477, ff. 207–12.
[35] *Hansard*, lxv. 173; Peel to De Grey, 2 June 1842, Peel papers, Add. MS 40477, ff. 201–6.
[36] De Grey to Peel, 6 June 1842, Peel papers, Add. MS 40477, ff. 207–12.
[37] Eliot to Peel, 4 June 1842, Peel papers, Add. MS 40480, ff. 76–8.
[38] *Hansard*, lxv. 171–2, 173, 207, 211–16; De Grey to Peel, 11 Oct. 1842, Peel papers, Add. MS 40477, ff. 287–90.
[39] Peel to De Grey, 27 Nov. 1841, Peel papers, Add. MS 40477, ff. 90–3.
[40] Graham to De Grey, 9 Nov. 1842, Graham papers; Peel to Eliot, 13 Nov. 1842, Peel papers, Add. MS 40480, ff. 145–8.

the established church.[41] Graham, for example, favoured the existing national school system, because he felt that if changes were made it might 'degenerate into a system of pure Roman Catholic education'.[42] On similar grounds, Lord Stanley believed that the national schools would have to be maintained, though he felt that full consideration should be given to the possibility of granting some special aid to Protestant schools.[43] But for Peel what weighed most in favour of the existing system was that any change could only result in 'three systems of national education—each a religious system' providing separate education for members of the established church, Catholics and Presbyterians. He feared, too, that the resulting controversy would only disturb the existing tendency towards religious peace in Ireland.[44]

Education was an instrument in the policy of tranquillising Ireland, and any change which would endanger that end or provoke religious discord was to be avoided. Even more clearly than in the case of primary education was this to be seen in the handling of the question of Maynooth, the state aided seminary for the education of the Catholic clergy. Maynooth and the problem of higher education for the Catholic laity were later to become issues of major importance. But, even in the early years of the Peel administration, Maynooth was a vexed question and played its part in provoking further discord between De Grey and Eliot.

Maynooth college had been founded in 1795 under an act of the Irish Parliament which not merely permitted the college to be established but authorised a grant towards the cost of the foundation out of public funds. The decision to allow the Catholics to have such a seminary in Ireland was taken at a time when the Catholic church was coming to be recognised as a potential ally in the struggle against French revolutionary influences in Ireland. Indeed, the immediate reason for the foundation of the college was the difficulty experienced by the ecclesiastical authorities in having the Irish clergy educated

[41] *Hansard*, lxv. 173; Eliot to Graham, 15 July 1842, Peel papers, Add. MS 40480, ff. 182–4.
[42] Graham to Peel, 24 Nov. 1841, Peel papers, Add. MS 40446, ff. 142–4.
[43] Stanley to Peel, 30 Nov. 1841, Parker, *Sir Robert Peel*, iii. 35–6; *Hansard*, lxv. 216–18.
[44] Peel to De Grey, [1841], Peel papers, Add. MS 40477, ff. 308–9.

abroad because of the hostile attitude of the anti-clerical revolutionaries to seminaries and religious houses.[45] Originally intended for the education of lay as well as clerical students, Maynooth soon became an exclusively clerical college. Maynooth had been in receipt of annual parliamentary grants of less than £9,000, but the funds available were quite inadequate for the proper management of the seminary.[46] Shortly after Peel took office, in 1841, a memorial from the Catholic hierarchy was transmitted to London seeking an increase in the grant.[47] Peel's immediate reaction was to avoid any step which might commit the Government to an early decision in favour of Maynooth. Graham, therefore, advised the Lord Lieutenant to tell the Irish Catholic bishops simply that no increase or decrease would be made in the parliamentary grant.[48] Caution was again prompted by the fear that religious passions might be aroused, which, as Peel put it, 'if their slumber be not disturbed *may* peaceably die away'.[49]

On the schools issue, the Government had sympathised with Eliot's views, but on Maynooth Peel, and in particular Graham, found themselves, in 1841–2, unable to go as far as the Chief Secretary wanted them. They were conscious of Protestant susceptibilities and were alarmed lest Eliot would compromise himself and the Government in his discussions with the Catholic representatives.[50] Eliot favoured a commission to enquire into the working of Maynooth as a preliminary to an increased grant, but Peel rejected this as likely to provoke controversy.[51] The upshot of the protracted discussion was that when the Catholic bishops renewed their application in November 1842, it was again turned down. It is a measure of Peel's tactful handling of the question that Eliot could, in November, bring himself to admit that 'it would not be expedient at the present moment to propose an increased grant to Maynooth'.[52]

[45] W. E. H. Lecky, *A History of Ireland in the Eighteenth Century*, iii. 348 seq.
[46] *Hansard*, lxv. 379.
[47] Graham to De Grey, 16 Nov. 1841, Graham papers.
[48] Graham to De Grey, 27 Nov. 1841, Graham papers.
[49] Peel to Eliot, 13 Nov. 1842, Peel papers, Add. MS 40480, ff. 145–8.
[50] Graham to Peel, 17 Oct. 1842, Peel papers, Add. MS 40477, ff. 245–50.
[51] Peel to Eliot, 27 Sept. 1842, Peel papers, Add. MS 40480, ff. 120–3.
[52] Eliot to Peel 18 Nov. 1842, Peel papers, Add. MS 40480, ff. 149–52.

That tempers were ruffled, there could, however, be no doubt. Eliot felt himself overlooked and his views neglected by the Lord Lieutenant, while De Grey accused Eliot of allowing himself to be unduly influenced by the Catholics.[53] The disagreements were even carried into the House of Commons, when the Irish Solicitor-General, Joseph Jackson, a bitter opponent of the national schools, clashed with Eliot over Irish education.[54] Even the intervention of Lord Stanley to explain the Government's attitude could not disguise the fact that the Irish administration was divided.[55]

All these differences had the inevitable effect of slowing up the business of government, much to Peel's annoyance. In a sharp complaint to Graham, in October 1842, he wrote, 'we are invited, not merely to govern Ireland in detail, but to solve the difficulties arising from discrepancies of opinion of those upon the spot'.[56] The intervention by Graham and Peel brought promises of better behaviour from both De Grey and Eliot, but the improvement was of short duration.[57]

In December, the strains and stresses in Dublin threatened to develop into a serious crisis, and at a most inconvenient time. The Lord Lieutenant complained that Eliot failed to consult him frequently enough about the draft measures he was preparing for submission to Parliament, while Eliot wrote to Peel that an efficient Lord Lieutenant, like De Grey, left little for a Chief Secretary to do in Ireland.[58] The new quarrel filled Peel with alarm, for he feared lest a breakdown in the government of Ireland, on the eve of the re-assembly of Parliament, might have a serious effect on Irish politics. 'If it takes place', he wrote, 'we shall have a decisive proof that the government of Ireland can-

[53] De Grey to Graham, 29 May 1842, Graham papers; De Grey to Eliot (copy), 17 July 1842, Peel papers, Add. MS 40477, ff. 246–9; De Grey to Peel, 18 July 1842, Peel papers, Add. MS 40477, ff. 242–5; Graham to Peel, 16 Sept. 1842, Graham papers.

[54] Graham to Peel, 17 July 1842, Peel papers, Add. MS 40477, ff. 45–8.

[55] *Hansard*, lxv. 208–18.

[56] Peel to Graham, 20 Oct. 1842, Parker, *Sir Robert Peel*, iii. 39.

[57] Graham to De Grey, 22 Oct. 1842; De Grey to Graham, 25 Oct. 1842, Graham papers; Eliot to Peel, 18 Nov. 1842, Peel papers, Add. MS 40480, ff. 149–52.

[58] De Grey to Graham, 13 Dec. 1842, Graham papers; Eliot to Peel, 12 Dec. 1842, Peel papers, Add. MS 40480, ff. 200–5.

not be satisfactorily administered under the present constitution of it.'[59] Peel knew from personal experience, that the task of defining the exact duties of Lord Lieutenant and Chief Secretary was no easy one. He made the suggestion to Graham that the lesser of the two evils might be the abolition of the office of Lord Lieutenant.[60] This major question was, however, not to be decided either by Peel or his successor in office. Through Peel's tactful handling of Eliot and Graham's of the Lord Lieutenant, the dispute was again patched up, though, as Graham ruefully observed, more than six months truce could not be expected.[61]

The first year of the Peel administration in Ireland was an unsatisfactory one. The deep cleavage in outlook between a liberal-minded Chief Secretary and an old-fashioned Lord Lieutenant made every act of government a painful process. Had Peel shown the same active interest in Irish affairs as he was to do in 1844–5, things might have been better. But as it was, his intervention was spasmodic and his inclination was to postpone decisions on Irish questions whenever possible.[62]

Graham once observed in writing to De Grey, that Maynooth and Roman Catholic education 'form the most difficult problem of practical government' in Ireland.[63] These were, undoubtedly, highly important issues, but the most difficult of all Irish problems, the question of the relations between the landlord and the tenant-farmer, had no place among the practical problems of government in 1841–2. Eliot alone realised the political use which O'Connell could make of the issue of fixity of tenure, and was anxious that the Government should do something to anticipate him. For his pains, however, Eliot earned the rebuke from Graham that 'It is impossible to interfere by legislation with the terms on which land is held in Ireland without shaking to their foundations the rights of property.'[64] In grasping the political significance of the Irish land question Eliot undoubtedly

[59] Peel to Graham, 15 Dec. 1842, Peel papers, Add. MS 40448, ff. 73–6.
[60] Ibid.
[61] Peel to Eliot, 23 Dec. 1842, Peel papers, Add. MS 40448, ff. 124–9; Graham to De Grey, 18 Dec. 1842, Graham papers; Graham to Peel, 22 Dec. 1842, Peel papers, Add. MS 40448, ff. 110–11.
[62] *Hansard*, lxiv. 197.
[63] Graham to De Grey, 27 Nov. 1841, Graham papers.
[64] Graham to Peel, 14 Nov. 1842, Peel papers, Add. MS 40447, ff. 325–8; Graham to Eliot, 15 Nov. 1842, Graham papers.

showed a keener appreciation of the immediate needs of Ireland than his more senior colleagues.

Yet the policy of Peel's Government in Ireland had something positive about it too. On educational questions, Peel saw the necessity of maintaining and improving the existing system, while in the matter of appointments there was a modest break with the old Tory tradition. The main appointments in Ireland still went to Protestant Conservatives, many of them hostile to the Government's own educational policy, but Peel was anxious to encourage men of more moderate views, if and when they could be found. This change of emphasis was particularly evident in the case of Catholics. There was an awareness of the importance of winning a measure of Catholic goodwill, and this feeling was to gain in strength.[65] The names of Catholic lawyers began to appear on the lists of persons suitable for promotion to office, and Peel found it necessary to express to De Grey the cabinet's concern at the continued practice of excluding Roman Catholics from juries.[66] But while the Government's policy alienated Irish Tory opinion sufficiently to make it expedient for the new Solicitor-General, Thomas Barry Cusack Smith, to withdraw from the by-election for Dublin University, in September 1842, to avoid defeat, the measures taken by Peel to liberalise government were not sufficient to silence opposition criticism.[67] The exclusively Protestant character of the appointments was denounced. 'As far as the executive is concerned', said Richard Lalor Sheil, 'they act as if Catholic emancipation had never been carried.' A judgement which, if its implications were not altogether fair, was hard to answer in the summer of 1842.[68]

The legislative programme of the new Government was even more subdued than its administrative actions. Eliot introduced a bill to remedy an Ulster grievance. It was a retrospective measure designed to legalise marriages between members of the

[65] Graham to Peel, [Sept.–Oct. 1841], Peel papers, Add. MS 40446, ff. 58–9; Graham to Peel, 16 Sept. 1841, Peel papers, Add. MS 40446, ff. 74–5.
[66] Graham to Peel, 16 Sept. 1842, Peel papers, Add. MS 40447, ff. 158–61.
[67] Smith, who subsequently became Attorney-General for Ireland, in October 1842, was returned to Parliament for Ripon, in 1843. *D.N.B.*, xviii. 564–5.
[68] *Hansard*, lxv. 243–64; *Morning Chronicle*, 9 Sept. 1842.

Presbyterian and established churches which had been solem-
nised by a Presbyterian minister. The measure found favour in
the Commons, but its reception in the Lords was lukewarm and
it was not to reach the Statute Book that session.[69] The only
other Irish measure of any importance was a land drainage
bill, which, though it encountered some criticism from the
Irish peers, was ultimately passed.[70] Apart from these measures
and the decision to raise the duty on spirits distilled in Ireland
instead of extending the income tax to that country, Irish affairs
were left alone by a Parliament which was occupied with other
issues.[71] Even the question of devising a more satisfactory system
for the registration of voters in Ireland, which had appeared so
urgent to Whig and Tory alike in 1840–1, was not taken up.
Peel announced that nothing would be done regarding Irish
registration until the principle on which English registration
should be based had been determined, which meant that there
would be no Irish bill that session.[72]

A variety of factors, then, contributed to the Government's
inactivity in Ireland, but it was a dangerous inactivity. 1842 was
a year of social stress in Britain. In Ireland it was one of acute
hardship and uncertainty for the ordinary people. In the summer, the traditionally hungry months, there was widespread
hunger and distress especially in the west of Ireland. The Government admitted the existence of hardship and privation and
praised the 'exemplary patience' of the people, but nothing was
done to remedy the conditions which created that distress and
give a practical answer to the question put by the Archbishop of
Tuam to Peel, when he wrote: 'Is it just to expect that any
people would be content who must part with the produce
raised by the labour of their own hands, and often, as just now,
experience at the close of the season all the horrors of starvation?'[73]

While the Government took its time, the repeal movement in
Ireland was growing in strength. It was to confront a startled

[69] *Hansard*, lxi. 501–2.

[70] Ibid., lxv. 317–22.

[71] G. Goulburn to W. E. Gladstone, 17 Feb. 1842, Gladstone papers,
Add. MS 44162 ff. 14–15; *Hansard*, lxi. 422–76.

[72] Ibid., lxiv. 94.

[73] Ibid., lxiii. 1493, lxiv. 700–1, 1171–9; John MacHale to Peel, 24 June
1842, O'Reilly, *John MacHale Archbishop of Tuam*, i. 597–601.

and largely unprepared administration with a challenge which made the Irish question once more an urgent theme in British politics. In November 1842, a Tory newspaper could say: 'Never during the last twenty years have Irish affairs attracted less notice in England . . . than during the last six months'.[74] In another six months that statement could not have been made.

[74] *Morning Herald*, 4 Nov. 1842.

II

THE CHALLENGE OF REPEAL
1842–3

REBUILDING THE REPEAL ORGANISATION was a slow task. Throughout 1841–2 O'Connell addressed meetings of the Repeal Association, and to his often repeated arguments in favour of the repeal of the Act of Union, was added an urgent appeal to the people to organise.[1] As late as the summer of 1842, O'Connell was full of despair, yet that year was to see the beginning of a dramatic growth of the organisation with its repeal wardens in every Catholic parish.[2] In Ireland, 1842 was a year of hardship, of bad crops, and much distress. In Parliament, O'Connell and his supporters had drawn attention to the state of the country; outside Parliament, with energy and great determination, he preached repeal.[3] Skilfully woven into the arguments in favour of this political aim were others more likely to appeal to a popular audience. Repeal was 'the only remedy for all the woes of Ireland', he argued. Only a native Irish Parliament would abolish the tithe rent charges, give the tenant-farmer security of possession and protect home industries. An Irish Parliament, too, would sweep away the unpopular Poor Law and introduce in its place medical charities more

---

[1] C. Gavan Duffy, *Young Ireland*, pp. 4–9.

[2] D. O'Connell to P. V. Fitzpatrick, 11 July 1842, Fitzpatrick, *Correspondence of Daniel O'Connell*, ii. 289.

[3] Repeal Assoc. meeting, 5 Jan., *Nation*, 7 Jan. 1843.

suitable to the needs of the people.[4] By turning repeal into a great charter of practical reforms, O'Connell succeeded in taking it out of the sphere of mere political speculation and debate. He spoke, too, with assurance of success, 'I want three million of repealers . . . Let me have repeal wardens in every parish, and my plan is complete and success is certain . . .'.[5]

At the weekly meeting of the Repeal Association, in Dublin, O'Connell played on these themes in many combinations, but the basic lesson remained the same; the removal of the Act of Union was the only sure way to social and economic progress and reform.[6] In his speeches and public letters he tended to place greatest stress on those subjects which he knew to be the source of most dissatisfaction. The Irish Poor Law with its rigid workhouse test was unpopular.[7] O'Connell denounced the system as an impost which bore heavily on the small tenant-farmers without giving adequate aid to the needy. Writing to the Poor Law guardians of County Cork, he forecast that, unless the existing law was abolished or drastically modified, it might lead to 'a sanguinary and general insurrection'.[8] If there had to be a Poor Law, he thought it should be financed by a tax on incomes over £500. His own preference was for a partly voluntary, partly state-aided scheme which would distribute aid to the sick poor.

The second subject which he tended to stress was the need for some effective measure of land reform. O'Connell denounced uncertainty of tenure for the small farmer as the 'great evil of Ireland'.[9] But in 1842–3 he did not devote much attention to the detail of measures to reform the land system. Though he spoke of fixity of tenure, he appears to have favoured an arrangement which would have given to an evicted tenant merely compensation for the full value of all improvements he had made on his farm. Again, O'Connell considered that no landlord should have a legal right to recover rent unless he granted the tenant a twenty-one year lease. However, to give to

[4] Ibid.   [5] Ibid.
[6] Repeal Assoc. meeting, 21 Nov., *Nation*, 26 Nov. 1842.
[7] Graham to De Grey, 2 Jan. 1843, Graham papers; *Hansard*, lxvii. 1347–69; *The Times*, 30 Jan. 1843.
[8] *Nation*, 31 Dec. 1842.
[9] Repeal Assoc. meeting, 6 Feb., *Nation*, 11 Feb. 1843.

the tenant a permanent right to hold land, so long as he paid his rent, would, O'Connell argued, set up one monopolist, the tenant, in the place of another, the landlord.[10] Even as late as May 1843, he could declare that on the land question the public 'might be sure that until the Irish Parliament was about to sit, no plan could be adopted', and contented himself with the hopeful formula that the landlords should join with the repealers 'in preserving to the tenant the value of his improvements and leaving to the landlord dominion over the land'.[11]

O'Connell sketched his policy in bold strokes. He avoided the details of land reform just as he avoided the constitutional niceties that a repeal of the Union could involve. But his methods suited well the kind of campaign he was to undertake in the spring and summer of 1843. Already in the closing months of 1842, large popular meetings in favour of repeal were being held in the provinces, attended by the small farmers, but these were soon to be overshadowed in size and enthusiasm when O'Connell began his great tour of the country.[12] In January and February, repeal meetings were held in counties as far apart as Cork, Clare and Queen's County, and, before the end of February, O'Connell was able to boast that the movement was making rapid progress in the south of the country, and that Connacht 'for the first time had become perfectly enlivened'.[13] But what seems to have helped to establish the reputation of the repeal movement with the better educated section of the community was O'Connell's remarkable contribution to the debate in the Dublin Corporation on repeal, which began on February 28.

The discussion took place on a motion tabled by O'Connell to petition Parliament for a repeal of the Act of Union. He laid emphasis on the importance of the British connection to Ireland, just as he warned his listeners that this link might be broken unless the Act of Union was repealed. If this were done, Protestants would have nothing to fear from the Catholic majority. He put his case with restraint and skill and though Isaac Butt, then an alderman and leader of the moderate

[10] Repeal Assoc. meeting, 11 Apr., *Nation*, 15 Apr. 1843.
[11] Repeal Assoc. meeting, 10 May, *Nation*, 13 May 1843.
[12] *Nation*, 26 Nov. 1842.
[13] Repeal Assoc. meeting, 20 Feb., *Nation*, 25 Feb. 1842.

Conservatives in Dublin, replied at length, he did not seriously weaken the effect of O'Connell's speech. The debate, which lasted three days, aroused widespread interest in Ireland and Britain.[14] O'Connell's words showed that he remained essentially the practical reformer, the man who was prepared to accept less rather than to lose all. 'Let them give us even a dependent Parliament. I never said it before, but I am always for taking an instalment when I cannot get the whole, and I will take that.'[15] O'Connell's motion was carried by 41 votes to 15. But his victory outside the Corporation was greater.

The Catholic Bishop of Killaloe, Dr P. Kennedy, joined the Association, because O'Connell had shown himself ready, if necessary, to accept less than a full repeal of the Union.[16] Then there followed the announcement that after Easter the great tour of Ireland would begin, as a demonstration of the people's peaceful disposition and their desire for a repeal of the Union.[17] With the beginning of the 'monster meetings' came the first signs of that alarm in Britain which was to mount rapidly over the summer months. In Ireland, the decision to hold the meetings was a signal for still greater activity in support of the repeal cause.[18] The influential and outspoken Archbishop John MacHale, of Tuam, wrote praising repeal and repudiating the suggestion that Catholics sought an ascendancy, and the Catholic Bishop of Ardagh, with more enthusiasm than accuracy, declared, at a monster meeting, that all the Catholic bishops of Ireland were repealers.[19] Though Archbishop Murray, of Dublin, was careful to repudiate the statement so far as he was concerned, there could be no doubt of the growing popularity of the Repeal Association among the Catholic clergy and laity.[20] By May 29, the weekly repeal rent, for example, had jumped to £2,205: 16: 3 compared with £683: 9: 2½ at the beginning of the same month.[21]

[14] *Freeman's Journal*, 3 Mar. 1843; *The Times*, 2, 8 Mar. 1843; *Nation*, 4 Mar. 1843.
[15] *Nation*, 4 Mar. 1843.   [16] *Nation*, 18 Mar. 1843.
[17] Repeal Assoc. meeting, 6 Apr., *Nation*, 8 Apr. 1843.
[18] *The Times*, 10 Apr. 1843; *Morning Chronicle*, 15 Apr. 1843.
[19] *Nation*, 6, 14 May 1843.
[20] Archbishop Murray to the clergy of Dublin, 22 May 1843, *Nation*, 27 May 1843; De Grey to Peel, 6 May 1843, Peel papers, Add. MS 40478, ff. 39–44.   [21] *Nation*, 6 May, 3 June 1843.

The monster meetings were the source of this new enthusiasm. Though the services of many speakers were enlisted, the heavy burden of the campaign fell on O'Connell. The pattern of the meetings, both in organisation and in the subject matter of O'Connell's speeches, was surprisingly uniform. A public meeting in the open was followed in the evening by a banquet which was usually attended by the local Catholic clergy and the leading repealers of the district. O'Connell's speeches had a remarkable sense of urgency about them. No law was to be violated, because the Association was pledged to employ only peaceful methods, but provided the people did what he asked of them the repeal of the Union was inevitable. Their first aim was to enrol three million members. In April he announced that this figure should be achieved in three months.[22] Then with three million members enrolled, each district in Ireland would express its 'confidence' in individuals who were to meet 'spontaneously' in Dublin as a Council of Three Hundred to plan a bill for the repeal of the Union. In this way O'Connell hoped to constitute a virtual parliament without, however, breaking the law.[23]

O'Connell's exciting cry 'repeal was coming', was heard in the months of April and May by remarkably large crowds, even when every allowance is made for exaggeration.[24] The Lord Lieutenant had to admit that the growth of the movement had been astonishing and had taken the administration in Dublin by surprise.[25] The scale of the meetings, the fact that so many of the clergy and middle classes were joining the Association, and its good organisation alarmed the Government just as much as its sudden emergence. But the difficulty was to decide what could legally be done to check the agitation.[26]

The orderly thousands of small farmers and labourers who flocked to the repeal meetings formed the firm foundation of O'Connell's power. But what impressed the Lord Lieutenant was the numbers drawn from other classes who were finding their way into the Repeal Association. Some may have been

[22] Repeal Assoc. meeting, 27 Apr., *Nation*, 29 Apr. 1843.
[23] Repeal meeting, Sligo, 4 May, *Nation*, 6 May 1843.
[24] De Grey to Peel, 6 May 1843, Peel papers, Add. MS 40478, ff. 39–44.
[25] De Grey to Graham, 30 Apr. 1843, Graham papers.
[26] Graham to De Grey, 8 May 1843, Graham papers.

opportunists, as De Grey thought, but not all.[27] It was, for example, in the early summer of 1843 that many of those who were to be most closely linked with Young Ireland, like Thomas MacNevin and Michael Joseph Barry, joined the Repeal Association.[28] The Repeal Association was in many ways a continuation of O'Connell's political organisations of the eighteen-twenties and thirties under another name. It was predominantly Catholic in composition, with just a few Protestant followers to prevent it becoming completely so. With a minimum of theory and much stress on practical matters, the Repeal Association reflected O'Connell's approach to politics. But it was in one respect new: it attracted to its ranks a number of men, mostly young, who approached nationalism in a different way to O'Connell. Drawn from predominantly middle-class backgrounds, one of the most outstanding things about them was that they set up as their ideal a nationalism which could rise above distinctions of creed and origins. Those who came first to the movement, before the great agitation of 1843, remained, generally speaking, the most significant. They included Thomas Davis, a young Protestant barrister, educated at Trinity College, Dublin; Charles Gavan Duffy, an Ulster Catholic journalist; and John Blake Dillon, another young lawyer and a Catholic graduate of Trinity College. It was these three who founded the *Nation*, as a weekly newspaper, in October 1842. Much more than O'Connell they were influenced by the new trends in thought which inspired nationalists in other lands. The *Nation* became a focal point for all who were attracted by the ideas of Thomas Davis and his two companions, and with the influx of new members into the

[27] De Grey to Peel, 6 May 1843, Peel papers, Add. MS 40478, ff. 39–44.
[28] *Nation*, 3 June 1843. Thomas MacNevin (1814–48), a barrister, was actively associated with the *Nation* newspaper and was an enthusiastic supporter of Thomas Davis. MacNevin was a talented writer and speaker, but mental disease brought his public career to a sudden end. He died in an asylum in Bristol in Feb. 1848. Michael Joseph Barry (1817–89), was a barrister and journalist. The author of an important prize essay on repeal, published by the Association, in 1845, he was arrested near Cork, in August 1848, following the suspension of the Habeas Corpus Act. Regarding the failure of the rising of 1848 as a final defeat, he abandoned the repeal cause on his release from imprisonment. He held the position of a police magistrate in Dublin for a short time, in 1871–2.

repeal movement, the *Nation* group grew both in numbers and talent.[29]

In the tense excited atmosphere of 1843, there was little room for differences to appear between the *Nation* group and the rest of the repeal movement. The *Nation* liked the firm tone adopted by O'Connell in his speeches and described his contribution to the Dublin Corporation debate as 'a wonderful one, even for him'.[30] Again, Thomas Davis did not hesitate to approve of the admission into the Association of those who did not go so far as he did in demanding the full repeal of the Union.[31] There were, it is true, some minor points of friction. The *Nation* group were not as opposed to the existing Poor Law as O'Connell and his son John were, while O'Connell disliked some of the literary contributions the *Nation* printed on the ground that the authors of the articles wrote in favourable terms about known opponents of repeal.[32] But these were slight differences and they were only to assume an importance in the light of what was to happen later. In the summer of 1843, O'Connell was still the leader of a disciplined repeal movement which grew daily in strength.

At the beginning of 1843, there was in the Government's Irish programme no indication that the approaching session would see any remarkable legislation on Irish questions. The main

[29] Gavan Duffy, *Young Ireland*, pp. 58–72; T. W. Moody, *Thomas Davis, 1814–45*, passim; R. Dudley Edwards, 'The contribution of Young Ireland to the development of the Irish national idea', in *Féilscribhin Tórna*, pp. 115–33. Thomas Osborne Davis (1814–45) was born at Mallow, Co. Cork. His father was an Englishman, an army surgeon. His mother was Irish. Attracted by the study of politics and history, he contributed articles of a nationalist kind to the press in 1840–1. Joining the Repeal Association with his friend John Blake Dillon in 1841, he quickly won for himself considerable influence in repeal circles both as an advocate of a comprehensive nationalism and as the author of ballad poetry with a wide popular appeal. Davis's qualities of character were highly respected by his contemporaries. Under strain, however, he was, at times, intolerant of opinions and policies differing from his own. Though his influence on men like Gavan Duffy, and the *Nation* group generally was of an enduring kind, Davis's teachings were to win still greater significance when they were adopted by a later generation of Irish nationalists at the end of the nineteenth century. Following a short illness, Davis died, in Dublin, on 16 Sept. 1845. For Gavan Duffy, and Dillon, see p. 75, n. 79 and p. 113, n. 21.

[30] *Nation*, 4 Mar. 1843.

[31] Repeal Assoc. meeting, 5 June, *Nation*, 10 June 1843.

[32] Gavan Duffy, *Young Ireland*, p. 64; *Nation*, 31 Dec. 1842.

interest was concentrated on the Poor Law and the possible reorganisation of the fever hospitals and public dispensaries, which were largely controlled by private subscribers though in receipt of public monies.[33] But it was in an unhurried way that the question of amending the Irish Poor Law was discussed.[34] Between the opening of the session on February 2 and the end of April, the only Irish question that received any prolonged consideration was poor relief. There was still no Irish registration bill, and the Poor Relief (Ireland) Bill when it was introduced won little praise from the Irish members. The bill made only minor changes in the existing law; the most important being that, for the future, rates on property valued at less than £4 in the country and £8 in the larger towns would have to be paid by the landlord instead of the tenant.[35] In essentials the system remained as before. The bill was eventually passed into law, but the debate on it was soon overshadowed by more serious developments in Ireland.

As late as April the resistance to the payment of rates in some country districts was almost regarded in official circles as a more critical matter than the repeal agitation.[36] By the beginning of May, however, De Gray was endeavouring to explain why the repeal campaign had come as such a surprise to him by telling Peel that until a few weeks previously the repeal agitation 'was utterly undeserving of notice'.[37] Once the scale of the problem was realised, however, Peel and his colleagues did endeavour to resolve it. The great difficulty, from the outset, was to discover some legal means of stopping the monster meetings. O'Connell was careful. He claimed that the meetings were held merely to petition Parliament for the repeal of the Act of Union. This, he argued, was quite legal.[38] In Parliament, Graham, when

[33] *Report of the Poor Law Commissioners on Medical Charities, Ireland, pursuant to the 24th Section of the Act of 1 and 2 Vict. c. 56*, H.C. 1841 (324), xi. 1–96.

[34] Graham to De Grey, 26 Jan. 1843, Graham papers; Graham to Peel, 30 Jan. 1843, Peel papers, Add. MS 40448, ff. 222–3.

[35] Graham to De Grey, 10 Feb. 1843, Graham papers; *Hansard*, lxvi. 307, lxviii. 1318–47; *The Times*, 8 May 1843.

[36] Peel to Graham, 14 Apr. [1843], Peel papers, Add. MS 40448, ff. 273–4; Graham to De Grey, 15 Apr. 1843, Graham papers.

[37] De Grey to Peel, 6 May 1843 ,Peel papers, Add. MS 40478, ff. 39–44.

[38] D. O'Connell to Sir Edward Sugden (Lord Chancellor of Ireland), 27 May 1843, Parker, *Sir Robert Peel*, iii. 49–51.

questioned, had to acknowledge the orderly character of the meetings.[39]

A distinct reluctance on the part of Peel to take drastic action and an obvious unwillingness on O'Connell's part to wander too far from the forms of law prevented the crisis of 1843 from ending in civil war. The phrase 'civil war' was on many lips and in many speeches, but O'Connell, when he wrote to Lord Campbell in September suggesting that Russell should offer Ireland a wide programme of reforms, showed that the practical politician and not the maker of revolutions was still at the head of the campaign.[40] Yet the tension was often great and the demands on the Government for strong action persistent. Some false steps were taken by Peel, but they were few. Only the decision, to prosecute O'Connell, seriously lessened the political advantages Peel had won in his struggle with the new democracy in Ireland.

The main demand for strong action came from Ireland. There the law officers and the officials of the Irish administration joined with De Grey in seeking special legislation. But Eliot stood out against coercive legislation, and Peel and Graham felt unwilling to act until some breach of the peace had been committed.[41] Caution, Graham pointed out, was particularly necessary because the Anti-Corn Law League was organised on the same lines as the Repeal Association: 'if one be suppressed and the other left untouched, an impression of unequal justice would be given—if we attack both, we shall embark on a sea of trouble . . . '.[42] However, silence would, the Government felt, be construed as weakness, and a middle course was therefore determined upon. An announcement was to be made in both Houses of the Government's resolve to maintain the Union inviolate by every means available.[43] Peel's statement in the Commons, on May 9, was a strong one. On the part of the Queen, he was authorised to say that she would do all in her power to uphold the Union, and that the Government would, if necessary,

[39] *Hansard*, lxix. 983.

[40] D. O'Connell to Lord Campbell, 9 Sept. 1843, Fitzpatrick, *Correspondence of Daniel O'Connell*, ii. 290–1.

[41] De Grey to Graham, 4 May 1843, Graham papers; Graham to Peel, 6 May 1843, Peel papers, Add. MS 40448, ff. 289–92.

[42] Graham to Peel, 7 May 1843, Peel papers, Add. MS 40448, ff. 297–300.

[43] Peel to De Grey, 9 May 1843, Peel papers, Add. MS 40478, ff. 49–50.

prefer civil war to the dismemberment of the Empire. The ordinary law, he added, would be employed, though if necessary they were prepared to go further.[44]

This defiant, but careful statement, naturally provoked a sharp reaction in Ireland. O'Connell was quick to see the weakness in what Peel had said; for Peel had made no specific charge that the activities of the Association had been illegal. So O'Connell could answer defiance with defiance. 'I will observe', he said, 'the spirit of the law—the letter of the law. I will, to be sure, shear it to its closest limits, but I will obey; and I set their blustering at defiance.'[45] Matters might have stayed like this had not the Government decided to take another step by removing, in a rather abrupt and high-handed manner, a number of repealers from office as magistrates. This decision had the unexpected effect of strengthening the repeal position since it brought a number of influential Irish Liberals into the Repeal Association.

From the beginning of the repeal agitation some action against the magistrates had been contemplated. No decision was, however, taken until the Government's statement on repeal had been made.[46] Then the Irish Chancellor, Sugden, removed a number of repealers from the bench and he did so without issuing any formal warning against taking part in repeal activities. This action had the Government's approval, but Peel and his colleagues soon regretted the speed and lack of graciousness with which the Irish administration went about the task.[47] The dismissals provoked much criticism in Ireland, especially as it was argued that it was quite legal for any subject to seek the repeal of the Act of Union in an orderly way.[48] Sir Colman O'Loghlen, an eminent lawyer of moderate liberal views, and a number of his colleagues joined the Repeal Association as a gesture of protest, while William Smith O'Brien, the Whig member for County Limerick, resigned his magistracy. The events of the succeeding months were to convince Smith

[44] *Hansard*, lxix. 23–5.

[45] Repeal Assoc. meeting, 18 May, *Nation*, 20 May 1843.

[46] Graham to De Grey, 28 Apr. 1843, Graham papers.

[47] De Grey to Graham, 31 May 1843; Sugden to Graham, 31 May 1843, Graham papers; Peel to Sugden, 1 June 1843, Parker, *Sir Robert Peel*, iii. 51–2.

[48] *Hansard*, lxix. 1064–94, lxx. 1099–1184.

O'Brien that he, too, should take the more decisive step and join the Repeal Association.[49]

If the repeal movement continued to grow, so did the difficulties confronting the Government. Having reproved Sugden, the Irish Chancellor, for dismissing the magistrates in the way he did, Peel had to give his attention to yet another cause of friction in Ireland.[50] At this critical moment, Lucas, the Under-Secretary, decided to offer his resignation, partly because he considered that the Government was not active enough in putting down the agitation and partly because of disagreements over the staffing of his office.[51] The Government in London was prepared to let him go, but De Grey pleaded that he could not do without him at such a time, since Lucas enjoyed the confidence of the Irish Conservative landed interests. The Lord Lieutenant had his way and Lucas was induced to stay, placated by the removal of a subordinate official he regarded as being too liberal in his views.[52]

More serious than the stresses within the Irish administration were the problems the Government had to face in Parliament. The first clear attack on its policy came with the debate on the

[49] *Nation*, 3 June 1843; *Morning Chronicle*, 1 June 1843. William Smith O'Brien (1803–64), an Irish Protestant landowner descended from the ancient line of the O'Briens of Thomond. He was first elected M.P. in 1828 (for Ennis, Co. Clare). He supported Catholic emancipation and, in the eighteen-thirties, advocated educational, ecclesiastical and parliamentary reform. A man of firm purpose but slow to come to final decisions on political issues, he did not openly support the repeal cause until the end of 1843. His subsequent associations were mainly with the Young Irelanders. He was prominent in the activities of the Irish Confederation, in 1847–8, and led an Irish delegation to Paris in March 1848. He took part in the abortive rising of 1848. Sentenced to death for high treason, in October 1848, the sentence was subsequently commuted to transportation for life and he was sent to Tasmania. Smith O'Brien received a conditional pardon in 1854, and in 1856, under the provisions of an unconditional pardon, he was allowed to return to Ireland. Though he took no further active part in Irish politics after his return, his influence, of a moderating kind, remained considerable in nationalist circles.

[50] Sugden to Graham, 5 June 1843, Graham papers.

[51] De Grey to Peel, 8 June 1843, Peel papers, Add. MS 40478, ff. 67–9; Graham to De Grey, 16 June 1843, Graham papers; Graham to Peel, 17 June 1843, Peel papers, Add. MS 40448, ff. 321–2.

[52] Peel to De Grey, 10 June 1843, Peel papers, Add. MS 40478, ff. 71–4; De Grey to Graham, 21 June 1843, Graham papers.

Arms (Ireland) Bill. This was a police measure primarily intended to prolong legislation for the licensing of arms and the punishment of persons illegally in possession of them. The bill was the signal for a sharp attack by the Whigs, who saw in the increased punishments proposed for illegal possession arms a confession of the Government's inability to govern Ireland.[53]

The sharpness of this assault in Parliament and the pressure from Ireland for more vigorous measures put Peel's ministry under a severe strain. Though they resisted De Grey's arguments that legislation should be introduced suspending the right to petition in Ireland, and thereby make it easier to suppress the 'monster meetings', they could not avoid the consequences of the rumours which followed De Grey's request.[54] Before the cabinet had even considered the matter, Daniel O'Connell issued his fiery defiance at Mallow, County Cork: 'The time is come when we must be doing . . . you may soon have the alternative to live as slaves or die as freemen . . .'.[55] The atmosphere was hardly improved by Sir James Graham's outburst, in the course of the Arms Bill debate, a few days later, when he said that 'unless the House is prepared to adopt the principle of fixity of tenure or agree . . . that the Protestant establishment must be overthrown . . . I do not see what measures of further conciliation can be proposed'.[56]

Both O'Connell's defiance and Graham's statement were put in words which over-dramatised the situation. Graham was quick to regret the damage his words might do, and O'Connell was equally prompt in reasserting that the struggle would be a bloodless one, once it became known that the right to petition was not to be suspended in Ireland.[57] On July 7, Sir James Graham explained to the House of Commons that what he had said in the debate on the Arms Bill was meant merely to imply that concessions in the hope of conciliation had been carried to an unexampled length 'considering the space of time over which it had ranged'.[58] Some further advances, he cautiously

[53] *Hansard*, lxix. 996–1063.
[54] Peel to De Grey, 12 June 1843, Peel papers, Add. MS 40478, ff. 79–84.
[55] Repeal meeting, Mallow, 11 June, *Nation*, 17 June 1843.
[56] *Hansard*, lxx. 44–53.
[57] Graham to Peel, 18 June 1843, Peel papers, Add. MS 40448, ff. 328–31; Repeal meeting, Galway, 28 June, *Nation*, 1 July 1843.
[58] *Hansard*, lxx. 809–23.

hinted, were not impossible but Graham's explanation made it evident that nothing of a fundamental kind, so far as land and the churches were concerned, could be expected. Wedged between the reformers inside and outside Parliament on the one side and their own English and Irish ultra-Tory supporters on the other, the ministry was given little space in which to manoeuvre in the summer and autumn of 1843.

The Government's position, too, was complicated by the excited state of public opinion in Britain. The summer of 1843 saw the anti-Corn Law agitation gain a great deal in strength and the Rebecca troubles in Wales were a disturbing symptom of working-class discontent. Though Irish affairs, at this time, did not occupy a very prominent place in the speeches of the anti-Corn Law agitators, there was always the danger that British and Irish radicals might come together.[59] John Bright, for example, on the occasion of his return to Parliament in the Durham city by-election, denounced the Government for not helping the people, 'with insurrection threatening them more or less near, in Ireland, in Wales, in the north of England'.[60]

Meetings in favour of repeal were held in the industrial areas of England and in expressing sympathy with the Irish cause the advocates of complete suffrage appear to have been particularly vocal.[61] The Liberal and Chartist press, too, put forward views either favourable to repeal or critical of the Government's policy in Ireland.[62] *The Northern Star* proclaimed that no Chartist would 'lift his finger against Ireland', while the moderate Whig *Morning Chronicle* asserted that England would not pour forth her armies and money to maintain 'the cruel injustice' of the established church in Ireland.[63]

While the repeal agitation in Ireland gained momentum, in Britain the Irish Liberal members of Parliament made efforts to win still greater support for a policy of speedy reform in Ireland. On July 18, on the requisition of 19 Irish members, a meeting was held, in the Reform Club, to decide whether or

[59] Peel to De Grey, 12 June 1843, Peel papers, Add. MS 40478, ff. 79–84.
[60] *Morning Chronicle*, 31 July 1843.
[61] *Nonconformist*, 14 June, 2 Aug., 27 Sept. 1843.
[62] Ibid., 31 May 1843.
[63] *Nation*, 20 May 1843; *Morning Chronicle*, 13 June 1843.

not it would be advantageous to sponsor public meetings in England to draw attention to the needs of Ireland. The opinion of the meeting, which was attended by Lord John Russell, was however against the Irish proposal for such extra-parliamentary activity.[64] Again, at the end of the session, 29 Irish Liberal members of Parliament issued an address to the people of Great Britain so as to put on record their solemn protest against the government's failure to redress Irish grievances.[65]

It is an interesting document because it sums up clearly the kind of problems which were providing O'Connell with the material for his campaign and the Whigs in the House of Commons with the material for their criticisms of the Government. Without putting forward any positive proposals the Irish Members drew attention to the need for some adjustment in the relations between landlord and tenant and to the irritation caused by the maintenance of the established church on its existing basis. They went on to urge the need for a wider franchise and a reform in local government. Finally they asked than an end should be put to the practice of virtually excluding Catholics from office.[66]

In Parliament, Irish and English members of the Opposition united in criticising the Government's Irish policy. As in the Irish Liberals' protest, there was the same avoidance of positive proposals and the Whig leaders appear to have been in agreement that they should abstain from putting forward specific measures.[67] This in effect meant that the discussion tended to concentrate on the defects in the Government's policy rather than on the detailed steps which should be taken to repair them. Russell had to admit, for example, that it was difficult to advise how improvements could be made in the matter of landlord and tenant relationships, though he felt that much more attention should have been given to the question by the Government.[68]

[64] Russell to Lansdowne, 19 July 1843, Gooch, *The Later Correspondence of Lord John Russell*, i. 64–5.

[65] *Morning Chronicle*, 24 Aug. 1843.

[66] Among those subscribing to this remonstrance were Thomas N. Redington, M. J. O'Connell, Thomas Wyse, Henry Grattan and William Smith O'Brien, *Morning Chronicle*, 24 Aug. 1843.

[67] Palmerston to Russell, 22 June 1843, Russell papers, P.R.O. 30/22/4; *Hansard*, lxx. 711–19.

[68] Ibid., lxx. 53–64.

Palmerston went even further and said that for Parliament to interfere between landlord and tenant 'would be to establish a principle of confiscation'.[69] Even so constant a champion of reform as William Smith O'Brien, while believing that something ought to be done to protect the tenant's interest, had to admit in the course of a great five-day debate on the state of Ireland, which began on July 4, that it might prove impossible to meet the existing evils 'by direct interference between landlord and tenant'.[70]

Like the Irish Liberals, the Opposition leaders felt on firmer ground in urging that the Tories should appoint Catholics to public offices and in demanding some alteration in the religious settlement in Ireland in favour of the Catholic church. Yet on this ecclesiastical issue there was no effective agreement among the Whigs beyond the point that something should be done. Viscount Howick would have the Catholic church established alongside the Protestant and at the latter's expense. At the other extreme, Palmerston believed that the primacy of the Protestant establishment should be maintained.[71] Small wonder that Lord John Russell did not make public, as O'Connell suggested in September 1843, 'a magniloquent epistle' which among other things would have declared his determination to abate 'the church nuisance in Ireland'.[72]

If the Whig criticism was essentially of a negative kind, it lost nothing from the fact that Russell and the other speakers were able to strengthen their case by pointing to the state of Ireland and to the inactivity of the Government in Irish matters from 1841 onwards. Even the long-awaited registration bill had not been brought forward, and patronage still favoured the Protestant interest in Ireland, as indeed Peel and Graham were only too well aware.[73]

The Government had, however, to face difficulties as well within the ranks of its own supporters. Already disapproving of

---

[69] Ibid., lxx. 279–91.   [70] Ibid., lxx. 630–77.

[71] Ibid., lxx. 877–93; Palmerston to Russell, 22 June 1843, Russell papers, P.R.O. 30/22/4; *Hansard*, lxx. 279–91.

[72] D. O'Connell to Lord Campbell, 9 Sept. 1843, Fitzpatrick, *Correspondence of Daniel O'Connell*, ii. 308–9.

[73] 'We must take a new departure in the management of our affairs and the stream of patronage must be turned into some new channels' (Graham to Peel, 15 July 1843, Peel papers, Add. MS 40448, ff. 352–5).

Peel's policy on education, the more conservative among the Irish Tories found his apparent inactivity in the face of the repeal campaign alarming.[74] Led by great landowners like Lords Donoghmore, Roden, Glengall and Clancarty, they formed a vocal body in both Houses, and, perhaps even more important, they had considerable influence over the Duke of Wellington who was still to a large extent responsible for the management of Government business in the Lords.[75] To meet the immediate situation they wanted more decisive measure, and Wellington, from his discussions with Donoghmore and Glengall, came quickly to the conclusion, in June, that, 'Ireland is in truth no longer in a social state. There is neither property nor safety for life remaining except for those in the ranks of the repealers of the Union'.[76] To avert the civil war he believed to be imminent, Wellington proposed that the northern Protestants should be armed and trained as a yeomanry or volunteer force under officers holding commissions from the Crown, a proposition which Graham felt could only lead to a religious war in Ireland.[77]

In pressing for a more vigorous approach to the repeal question, the Irish Conservatives and Wellington could count on the goodwill of both De Grey and Lucas. In contrast to the Lord Lieutenant and the Under-Secretary, Eliot persisted in the view that a civil war was by no means inevitable, a difference of opinion which did not make for any better relations within the Irish administration.[78] In the circumstances, therefore, it needed some careful negotiations by Peel and Graham to keep Wellington from adopting openly too extreme a stand on the Irish question. They were successful in their efforts, and Wellington, though he had hitherto been satisfied that civil war would come, could write, on September 6, that his firm belief was 'that the legal and constitutional powers of the Crown in Ireland, if energetically and invariably exercised . . .

[74] *Hansard*, lxx. 1121–30.
[75] Wellington to Graham, 10 June 1843, Graham papers; Graham to Peel, 16 Sept. 1843, Peel papers, Add. MS 40449, ff. 29–30.
[76] Wellington to Graham, 10 June 1843, Graham papers.
[77] Graham to Peel, 18 June 1843, Peel papers, Add. MS 40448, ff. 325–7.
[78] Eliot to Graham, 20 June 1843, Graham papers; Graham to Peel, 9 July 1843, Peel papers, Add. MS 40448, ff. 344–5; Peel to De Grey, 11 July 1843, Peel papers, Add. MS 40478, ff. 103–4.

is too strong even for that giant of mischief the Roman Catholic religion as there prevailing'.[79]

It was under this cross-fire from left and right that Peel's ministry had to formulate its Irish policy in the closing months of 1843, and it did so under two broad headings. The first was concerned with the immediate task of halting the progress of O'Connell's agitation. The second related to the more complex task of making practical reforms in Ireland. Though the measures taken against the repeal agitation were to bring with them some dramatic developments, the same could not be said of the reforms, which remained essentially long term and limited in scope, though by no means free of controversial elements.

The repeal movement, by the autumn of 1843, was a formidable opponent for any Government. The repeal rent was high, the monster meetings were enthusiastically supported, and a steady stream of new members, clerical and lay, were joining the Association.[80] Outside the ranks of the Repeal Association the demand for the repeal of the Act of Union had its influence on liberal opinion, for not merely were the Irish Whigs pressing vigorously in Parliament for generous reforms, but the case for a compromise solution, short of repealing the Union, began to win support. Federalism never became a popular cause, but it appealed to a small, educated and not uninfluential group of reformers, including Sharman Crawford, the advocate of land reform, and to some of the more conservative among the Catholic clergy.[81] Before the proclamation of the Clontarf meeting, in October, the federalists were seen as possible and welcome allies, but after the collapse of the repeal campaign, the federalist scheme was to take on a new and more disputed role in Irish nationalist politics.[82]

O'Connell, in August and September, was at the height of his power, yet there were signs that he was not altogether satisfied with the way affairs were developing. These mis-

[79] Wellington to Graham, 6 Sept. 1843, Graham papers; Graham to Peel, 16 Sept. 1843, Peel papers, Add. MS 40449, ff. 29–30.

[80] *Nation*, 19 Aug. 1843; *The Times*, 1 Aug. 1843.

[81] *Hansard*, lxx. 943–4, 1359–60; Repeal Assoc. meeting, 26 July, *Nation*, 29 July 1843; B. A. Kennedy, 'Sharman Crawford's federal scheme for Ireland', in H. A. Cronne, T. W. Moody and D. B. Quinn (eds.), *Essays in British and Irish History in Honour of James Eadie Todd*, pp. 235–54.

[82] *Nation*, 5 Aug. 1843.

givings were not lost on the Government, nor it would appear on the Whig leaders in Britain.[83] He spoke of the elections for the Council of Three Hundred and promised that it would meet before Christmas provided they went about their task in an orderly way, yet no effective steps were taken to organise the elections.[84] By the middle of September he was, however, warning his audiences that he might have to proceed slowly before summoning the Council, but that he was prepared for the jibes this statement would provoke.[85] However forceful his speeches, he was careful to keep within the law and at a time when anti-British feelings were strong in both the United States and France, he was firm in his resolution to avoid any dangerous alliances.[86] To the question of what was to happen when the monster meetings ended in October or if the Council of Three Hundred could not be convened he gave no clear answer.

The members of the Government were quick to realise that once O'Connell had aroused public feelings to the extent he had, then he must either go forward and take the kind of risks he was anxious to avoid or else try to disengage himself from the struggle with the minimum loss in prestige and popular support. As early as June 20, Lord Eliot had written that the repeal leaders were not prepared to face a civil war.[87] At the beginning of September, he was able to report that O'Connell was anxious to restrain the impatience of his followers: 'He talks now of time and deliberation and of the necessity of caution and of strict obedience to the law'.[88] Graham regarded

[83] Eliot to Graham, 20 June 1843, Graham papers; Graham to Peel, 22 Sept. 1843, Peel papers, Add. MS 40449, ff. 47–50; Palmerston to Russell, 22 Oct. 1843, Russell papers, P.R.O. 30/22/4, and Gooch, *The Later Correspondence of Lord John Russell*, i. 65–7.

[84] Repeal meeting, Baltinglass, *Nation*, 12 Aug. 1843.

[85] Repeal meeting, Clifden, *Nation*, 23 Sept. 1843.

[86] Discussing a proposed visit of the French radical, Ledru Rollin, to Ireland, O'Connell declared, 'They sought no foreign alliance, they were determined not to seek it . . . if the British government were to use force against them . . . they would be glad in such an event to get allies and supporters anywhere. But that was an event he did not foresee . . . and he was convinced now that it could not possibly occur' (Repeal Assoc. meeting, 4 Aug. 1843, *Nation*, 5 Aug. 1843).

[87] Eliot to Graham, 20 June 1843, Graham papers.

[88] Eliot to Graham, 1 Sept. 1843, Graham papers.

these developments as a proof of the wisdom of their policy in avoiding exceptional or coercive legislation, especially as the police reports were confirming, before the end of September, the opinion 'that the heat of the repeal fever has somewhat abated'.[89]

If the opinion was gaining ground that O'Connell was finding himself in a difficult predicament, the scale of the repeal agitation remained a constant challenge. Though Peel and Graham could not subscribe to all Wellington's fears and plans, they were nevertheless deeply perturbed by the course of events in Ireland. Graham, in a characteristically gloomy moment, wrote to Lord Stanley, 'It is a religious struggle directed by the R. Catholic hierarchy and priesthood, on which we are about to enter, and I very much doubt whether any political considerations enter into the causes or objects of this strife, which will lead to bloodshed and convulse the empire'.[90] Troops were sent to increase the Irish garrisons, and Graham considered that force should be employed if O'Connell attempted to assemble his Council of Three Hundred. Again, the authorities in Dublin and London were watchful for seditious libels in the repeal press, though Graham for one felt that the Irish law officers were lacking in courage in not promptly instituting proceedings against the newspaper editors.[91]

Peel appears to have taken a somewhat calmer view of the situation than the Home Secretary, though again he was prepared, as late as September, to discuss their plans on the assumption that outbreaks might yet take place in Ireland.[92] As long as the repeal agitation continued it represented a threat which could lead to complications. Any course of action which could put a stop to it, without involving new legislation and embittered debates in Parliament, was bound to attract the government.[93] There was, however, another consideration which cannot be ignored. By the autmn of 1843, the ministry was in agreement on the necessity of adopting new

[89] Graham to Peel, 23 Sept. 1843, Peel papers, Add. MS 40449, ff. 51–2.
[90] Graham to Stanley, 16 July 1843, Graham papers.
[91] 'I begin to despair of the Irish executive; it does not only sleep, but it is dead' (Graham to Peel, 5 Sept. 1843, Peel papers, Add. MS 40449, ff. 23–6).
[92] Peel to Graham, 18 Sept. 1843, Graham papers.
[93] Graham to Peel, 28 Sept. 1843, Peel papers, Add. MS 40449, ff. 67–8.

and more effective measures to tranquillise Ireland and to weaken the Irish opposition to the Government by winning some Catholic support.[94] The repeal agitation and O'Connell's power stood in the way.

The opportunity to strike came with O'Connell's criticism of the Queen's speech proroguing Parliament on August 24, which had reaffirmed the indissoluble nature of the Union, and with the injudicious public notice announcing the final 'monster meeting' of the year.[95] The Irish law officers considered O'Connell's words sufficient to sustain a sedition charge.[96] Any doubts on the question were, however, dispelled by the mention of 'repeal cavalry' and the use of other military terms in the notice issued in connection with the meeting which was to take place at Clontarf, Dublin, on October 8.[97] O'Connell was quick to sense danger. As soon as the offending notice was brought to his attention he disavowed it.[98] But it was too late. De Grey, the Lord Lieutenant, who had been in England, hurried back to Dublin and though there were some delays, caused by last-minute legal doubts on the part of Eliot and the law officers, a proclamation forbidding the meeting was eventually issued on the day before that fixed for the meeting.[99] The proclamation was obeyed by O'Connell and his supporters. Encouraged by the easy triumph at Clontarf, the Government took the bold step of having the leaders of the Repeal Association arrested.[100]

The immediate effect of the Government's actions was to

[94] Peel to De Grey, 22 Aug. 1843, Peel papers, Add. MS 40478, ff. 160–7; Graham to Peel, 23 Sept. 1843, Peel papers, Add. MS 40449, ff. 51–2.

[95] *Hansard*, lxxi. 1005–10; Repeal Assoc. meeting, 4 Sept., *Nation*, 9 Sept. 1843.

[96] Graham to Peel, 26 Sept. 1843, Peel papers, Add. MS 40449, ff. 59–64

[97] Graham to Stanley, 7 Oct. 1843, Graham papers; Eliot to Graham, 7 Oct. 1843, Graham papers.

[98] Repeal Assoc. meeting, 2 Oct., *Nation*, 7 Oct. 1843.

[99] De Grey to Graham, 7 Oct. 1843, Graham papers; Graham to Lord Lyndhurst, 15 Oct. 1843, Graham papers. 'It is very fortunate that there was no collision at Clontarf. The shortness of the notice would have imposed a heavy responsibility' (Peel to Graham, 10 Oct. 1843, Graham papers). *Morning Chronicle*, 9 Oct. 1843.

[100] Eliot to Graham, 7 Oct. 1843, Graham papers; Graham to Lyndhurst, 15 Oct. 1843, Graham papers.

create a confused situation in the repeal movement. On the one hand, the arrest of O'Connell and his companions on charges of seditious conspiracy and of exciting disaffection among the troops brought a sudden influx of sympathisers into the movement, including Smith O'Brien and Caleb Powell, the members of Parliament for County Limerick.[101] On the other hand, the attempt to devise at short notice some plan of action to replace the one Peel had challenged led to the first significant conflict on policy within the Association.

In a statement made immediately after the proclaiming of the Clontarf meeting, O'Connell demanded that his followers should show 'the most perfect obedience to everything having the shape of legal authority . . . as long as it kept itself legal, even by name'.[102] The same quality of anti-climax attached to his proposals to substitute parish meetings for the monster meetings and to establish the much discussed arbitration courts throughout the country as substitutes for the magistrates' courts. Neither plan was in fact destined to achieve any practical significance, but the temporary enthusiasm which O'Connell displayed for federalism provoked a feeling of uneasiness among the *Nation* group which foreshadowed the more serious dispute on the same issue a year later.[103]

In his definition of what he conceived repeal to be and in his public correspondence at this time with Joseph Sturge, the English Radical and friend of self-government for Ireland, he went far towards accepting the federalist case without, however, winning the confidence of Sharman Crawford and the other leading Irish federalists. O'Connell was prepared to accept a settlement whereby 'the Irish Parliament should have control within Ireland and that for all other administrative functions the British Parliament would have the control . . .'.[104] Palmerston likened such a proposed parliament to 'a large quarter session meeting in College Green for merely local and domestic

[101] Repeal Assoc. meeting, 23 and 24 Oct., *Nation*, 28 Oct. 1843. The Association's new headquarters, Conciliation Hall, was opened on 23 Oct. 1843 (*Nation*, 28 Oct. 1843.)

[102] Repeal Assoc. meeting, 9 Oct., *Nation*, 14 Oct. 1843.

[103] *The Times*, 12 Oct. 1843; Repeal Assoc. meeting, 9 Oct., *Nation*, 14 Oct. 1843; Charles Gavan Duffy, *Young Ireland*, pp. 212–23; *Nation*, 9 Dec. 1843; Eliot to Graham, 18 Oct. 1843, Graham papers.

[104] Repeal Assoc. meeting, 30 Oct., *Nation*, 4 Nov. 1843.

purposes', while the *Nation*, which clearly felt uneasy about this definition of repeal, explained O'Connell's words as meaning that Ireland should have 'all the power she possessed in 1783'.[105] But Sharman Crawford pointed out that without Irish representation in an imperial Parliament, O'Connell's plan would leave foreign affairs completely in British hands, a solution he could not accept.[106]

O'Connell quickly and understandably dropped the federalist question on the ground that his plan 'was almost suspected by the repealers and was not joined by the federalists'.[107] But the whole incident emphasised his anxiety to gain allies at this time. The monster meetings had isolated him still further from the English Whig leaders. Melbourne looked with no favour on any connection between the Whigs and O'Connell, while Palmerston felt that though 'a certain number of our Irish friends . . . have of course been compelled by fear of constituents to become repealers *pro forma*', the Whigs ought to persevere in their resistance to O'Connell's views on repeal.[108] In this opinion, Palmerston and Russell were in full agreement.[109]

Though O'Connell was to go on employing the language of repeal, he was soon to find, in the controversies which surrounded the Government's reform measures, a field in which he could use his talents well. It was not the way to repeal but rather to a new, if never very cordial, understanding with the Whigs and to discord within the Repeal Association.

[105] Palmerston to Russell, 22 Oct. 1843, Russell papers, P.R.O. 30/22/4, and Gooch, *The Later Correspondence of Lord John Russell*, i. 65–7; *Nation*, 9 Dec. 1843.
[106] Sharman Crawford to Rev. T. O'Malley, 7 Dec., *Nation*, 9 Dec. 1843.
[107] Repeal Assoc. meeting, 27 Nov., *Nation*, 2 Dec. 1843.
[108] Palmerston to Russell, 22 Dec. 1843, Russell papers, P.R.O. 30/22/4.
[109] Russell to Lansdowne, 11 Nov. 1843, Gooch, *The Later Correspondence of Lord John Russell*, i. 68–9.

III

CONSERVATIVE REFORM IN
IRELAND, 1843-4

WHEN O'CONNELL, in November 1843, claimed that the
Devon Commission (appointed in the same month to examine
the Irish land question) had been conceded by the Government
because of the repeal agitation, he was hardly guilty of exaggeration.[1] From the autumn of 1843 onwards it is evident that
the members of the Government were prepared to think more
clearly and consistently about Irish affairs and the importance
of reform. By August, Peel, Graham, Eliot and Stanley had
reached the conclusion that more would have to be done to
bring Irish Catholics into the public service though De Grey
continued to argue that there was no practical way of finding
suitably qualified Catholics for such employment. Peel, however, was quick to tell him that the necessary thing was to
influence the 'many Roman Catholics of intelligence, tired of
excitement and agitation, on whom a favour of the Crown
bestowed on their body would have a beneficial effect . . .'.[2]

It was realised that more would have to be done than simply
to find places for Catholics in the Government service. Positive

[1] Repeal Assoc. meeting, 13 Nov., *Nation*, 18 Nov. 1843.
[2] Graham to Peel, 15 July 1843, Peel papers, Add. MS 40448, ff. 350-1;
Peel to De Grey, 22 Aug. 1843, Peel papers, Add. MS 40478, ff. 160-7;
De Grey to Peel, 18 Aug. 1843, Peel papers, Add. MS 40478, ff. 150-1;
Eliot to Graham, 1 Sept. 1843, Graham papers.

reform measures were accepted as being necessary, along with the suppression of the repeal movement, if good order were to be restored in Ireland. Shortly after the arrests of O'Connell and his companions, Peel wrote to Graham: 'It is clear that mere force, however necessary the application of it, will do nothing as a permanent remedy for the social evils'.[3] The setting up of the Devon Commission and the first tentative efforts to improve the relations between the Catholic church and the state marked the beginning of an experiment in reform which was to survive many vicissitudes into 1845–6.

If the repeal agitation pointed to the necessity for change in Ireland, the sudden ending of the great agitation had equally the effect of concentrating O'Connell's attention on reforms. Indeed even the attempt to turn from repeal to federalism, in 1844, may, perhaps, be seen as part of an effort to confine political aspirations within a more limited, practical framework. Having refused to answer force with force in October 1843, O'Connell wasted little time in formulating what he conceived to be the reforms which, if adopted by a British government, 'would deprive me of many of my present adherents'.[4]

In a letter to Charles Buller, which appears to have been widely circulated among the Whig leaders at the beginning of 1844, O'Connell gave these reforms as seven in number.[5] He recommended complete religious equality, preferably to be achieved by having no established church in Ireland, the restoration of the law of landlord and tenant to the form it took at the time of the Union, a generous extension of the parliamentary franchise, a further measure of municipal reform with greater popular representation, and a heavy absentee tax, and finally he suggested that the problem of fixity of tenure should be given careful consideration.[6]

[3] Peel to Graham, 19 Oct. 1843, Peel papers, Add. MS 40449, ff. 105–6.
[4] D. O'Connell to Charles Buller, 9 Jan. 1844, Russell papers, P.R.O. 30/22/4.
[5] Charles Buller (1806–48), whig M.P. for Liskeard, 1832–48. Another copy of the letter in the Monteagle papers, National Library of Ireland, Dublin.
[6] In suggesting that the law of landlord and tenant should be restored to the form it took at the time of the Union, O'Connell apparently had in mind the repeal of the statutes 56 Geo. III, c. 88 and 58 Geo. III, c. 39 which enabled landlords to recover possession of property in certain

Though O'Connell ended this letter on the note that he expected nothing from the Whigs, the Earl of Clarendon thought O'Connell's proposals on the whole moderate even if expressed 'in a disagreeable manner'. They led him to believe that, if Russell were in power again, it would be possible to come to terms with O'Connell and end the cry for repeal.[7] But the practical changes suggested by O'Connell also bore in certain ways a resemblance to the legislative and administrative programme which Peel and his colleagues were devising. There was the same recognition of the need for a change of some kind in the ecclesiastical settlement, for a reform of the Irish franchise and possibly for some amendment in the law of landlord and tenant. Except on the issue of repeal, the kind of reforms Peel and O'Connell regarded as desirable or necessary for Ireland differed not so much in kind as in the extent to which they should be realised in practice. Whig, Tory and repealer tended to cover much the same ground in their plans for reform, and it was, on the whole, a limited area, whatever implications those reforms might have for the future. Yet old enmities and traditional loyalties were to keep repealers and Tories firmly apart. O'Connell could not bring himself, and indeed neither could Russell, to admit that Peel as Prime Minister would carry reforms of any value, while, for Peel, O'Connell remained the dangerous and irresponsible demagogue.[8]

That the hostility between the ministry and the repealers should have remained a rather steady factor throughout the closing years of the Peel administration is not surprising. No matter how distant the aristocratic Whigs, like Palmerston or Lansdowne, might be from O'Connell, he had his direct personal links with the Whig leaders through people such as Lord Bessborough and Richard Lalor Sheil, and he could count on

[7] Clarendon to Russell, 25 Jan. 1844, Russell papers, P.R.O. 30/22/4, and Gooch, *The Later Correspondence of Lord John Russell*, i. 69–70.

[8] Russell to Lord Monteagle, 22 Aug. 1843, Monteagle papers; *Hansard*, lxxii. 683–726, lxxiii. 185–206; Peel to Graham, 12 Dec. 1843, Peel papers, Add. MS 40449, ff. 257–8.

instances by civil bill proceedings in the assistant barrister's court. The statutes effected a saving in costs in ejectment proceedings. J. P. Kennedy, *Digest of Evidence taken before Her Majesty's Commissioners of Inquiry into the State of the Law and Practice in respect to the Occupation of Land in Ireland*, pt. ii, 835, 853–5.

much goodwill among the English Radicals.[9] With the Tories there were no such links.

Other considerations, too, made any narrowing of the gap difficult. Despite an abiding desire to reach an understanding with the Irish Catholics, there remained in Government circles a feeling of distrust towards the Catholic church, particularly as they found it in Ireland.[10] In this the members of the Government were but Englishmen of their age. The storm over Maynooth was to show the strength of that suspicion and it was by no means absent among the leading Whigs.[11] What, however, tended to emphasise this distrust among the Tories was the party's own recent history and the fact that the ultra-Tory faction, which was strong in the Lords and vocal in both Houses, was an influence the Government could not ignore completely even if it wanted to.[12] Again, from its beginning in November 1843 to O'Connell's successful appeal to the House of Lords, in September 1844, the ill-managed state trial in Dublin remained a disturbing background which made more difficult the Government's task of building a bridgehead of confidence in Ireland.[13]

Though the course of reform was to some extent hindered by considerations which had little bearing on the value of the reforms as such, it is possible to see in the measures adopted a certain pattern and continuity. By the beginning of 1844, the broad outline of the Government's reform policy was fairly well

[9] Bessborough to Russell, 20 Sept. 1844, Russell papers, P.R.O. 30/22/4; D. O'Connell to Richard Lalor Sheil, 19 June 1844, Fitzpatrick, *Correspondence of Daniel O'Connell*, ii. 322–4.

[10] Writing to Peel on the necessity of improving the status of Maynooth, Graham could say: 'the experience of each succeeding year has demonstrated more plainly the dangerous consequences of an establishment . . . sending forth an annual swarm of rebellious priests, unconnected with the government, to exercise a fatal influence over the most bigoted people in the world' (Graham to Peel, 12 April 1844, Peel papers, Add. MS 40450, ff. 14–5).

[11] *Morning Herald*, 6 Feb. 1844; Palmerston to Russell, 22 Oct. 1843, Russell papers, P.R.O. 30/22/4; Gooch, op. cit. i. 65–7.

[12] Peel to Lord Heytesbury, 1 Aug. 1844, Peel papers, Add. MS 40479, ff. 15–18; Stanley to Peel, 18 Feb. 1844, Peel papers, Add. MS 40468, ff. 132–7.

[13] Peel to Graham, 14 Sept. 1844, Peel papers, Add. MS 40450, ff. 152–3; *Morning Chronicle*, 10 Sept. 1844; *Hansard*, lxxiii. 1352–5.

established, but there were limitations inherent in the plans which were to expose the reforms to much criticism and to lessen their value as a contribution to the solution of the social and political problems of Ireland.[14] In a memorandum which he prepared for the cabinet, early in February 1844, Peel reviewed the whole question of reform in Ireland and the measures which he considered would 'detach a considerable portion of the moderate Roman Catholics' from a defeated O'Connell. To that end he stressed the importance of a franchise reform which would ensure substantial equality between the voting qualifications in England and Ireland. The central issues in his memorandum were education and the provision of better facilities for the voluntary endowment of the Catholic church. Education needs, he believed, could not be met merely by an increased vote for the national schools.[15]

Peel at this time appears to have thought in terms of a commission, similar to the Devon Commission, which would consider the best mode of meeting two Catholic educational problems, Maynooth college and the provision of institutions for higher education. The problem of Maynooth had been with the Governement since it came into office.[16] But now Peel had come to the firm conclusion that, Parliament having once agreed to vote money for Maynooth, it was necessary to see that the college was adequately endowed and put on as satisfactory a basis as possible from the Government's point of view. He put forward the suggestion that the proposed commission might study the question of combined education for Catholic clergy and laity, possibly within an extended Dublin University. In proposing this he found himself in substantial agreement with Lord Stanley.[17]

The Devon Commission, however, remained the only exploratory commission which was established. The problem of higher education was met not by founding combined institutions for clerical and lay instruction but by a less ambitious

[14] Memorandum by Peel, 11 Feb. 1844, Peel papers, Add. MS 40540, ff. 19–25.
[15] Memorandum by Peel, [Feb. 1844], Peel papers, Add. MS 40540, ff. 40–5.
[16] See p. 30.
[17] Stanley to Peel, 18 Feb. 1844, Peel papers, Add. MS 40468, ff. 132–7.

arrangement under which the Maynooth endowment was increased and separate colleges were founded for the higher education of the laity. In substance, however, the projects in Peel's
memorandum remained the policy of the ministry until its fall.

The most significant characteristic of the Government's
whole Irish reform policy was the relatively small part given to
social and economic issues. Maynooth, higher education, church
questions, and a possible revision of the electoral law, were the
subjects which chiefly engaged the attention of the Government.
But in this they were not alone. The same limited approach to
economic problems was shown by many of their opponents inside and outside Parliament as well. Yet it would be wrong to
assume that there was no awareness of Irish economic difficulties. What helps to make this period so interesting, as a transi-
tional phase, is the way in which the social ills of Ireland
gradually come to occupy a more important place in political
developments. The Great Famine was to direct men's attention
to some of these evils and compel the Government to adopt
novel measures. But even before the famine there were signs of
a growing concern about the future of rural society. Sharman
Crawford's persistent efforts to bring the needs of the tenant-
farmers before Parliament and O'Connell's use of agrarian
grievances to fortify his arguments in the summer campaign of
1843 illustrate one aspect of this trend.[18] The Government, too,
in a tentative way, late in 1843, gave some recognition to the
fact that landlord-tenant relations in Ireland constituted a
problem which deserved examination.

The initiative in the matter appears to have lain with Sir
James Graham.[19] He did not disguise his belief that no matter
what a commission of enquiry might uncover, little could be
done by legislative action to alter the Irish land system: 'it will
open a distinct view of the causes of discontent in Ireland; but
alas! I fear, that the remedies are beyond the reach of legislative
power'.[20] He did not rule out the possibility of applying some
palliatives, but he clearly felt that the main value of such an
enquiry would be that 'at all events sympathy with the sorrow
of an entire people will be evinced by the government; and the

[18] *Hansard*, lxxi. 412–18, lxxxii. 622.
[19] Graham to Peel, 6 Sept. 1843, Peel papers, Add. MS 40449, ff. 27–8.
[20] Graham to Peel, 17 Oct. 1843, Peel papers, Add. MS 40449, ff. 93–4.

public mind may be softened and soothed in some degree by kindness of purpose and by the exposure of injustice'.[21]

Graham won the support not merely of Peel, but also of De Grey and Sugden. Even Wellington conceded to Peel that he could no do otherwise than appoint a Commission to enquire into the occupation of land in Ireland.[22] In the selection of the five members of the Commission, Peel was anxious that no political preference should be shown and among those ultimately appointed was Thomas Redington, the future Whig Under-Secretary and a Catholic.[23] The inclusion of Redington did not save the Commission, which had the Earl of Devon as Chairman, from the criticism that it was a Commission of landowners without a single representative of the tenants among its members. Nevertheless, there were no signs of unwillingness in Ireland to help the Commission in its work, and O'Connell and other repealers as well as landlords and tenant-farmers gave evidence before it.[24] But the Devon Commission did not present its report until the beginning of 1845 and even then it remained overshadowed by the political struggle which held so much of the attention of the Government and the opponents of its Irish policy.

The attempt to weaken O'Connell's influence in Catholic church circles really began in earnest in October 1843. Already in the summer of 1843, Metternich, the Austrian Chancellor, concerned at the possibility of nationalist unrest gaining ground within the United Kingdom, had made some representations to Rome on the question of the part taken by the Irish clergy in the repeal agitation, but with no definite results.[25] Following on a suggestion made by De Grey that they might secure some assistance from Rome in controlling the Irish bishops, Peel direc-

[21] Graham to Peel, 21 Sept. 1843, Peel papers, Add. MS 40449, ff. 43-6.
[22] Wellington to Peel, 10 Oct. 1843, Peel papers, Add. MS 40460, f. 268.
[23] Peel to Graham, 28 Oct. 1843, Peel papers, Add. MS 40449, ff. 154-5.
[24] D. O'Connell to P. V. Fitzpatrick, 13 Dec. 1843, Fitzpatrick, *Correspondence of Daniel O'Connell*, ii. 311; *Nation*, 23 Dec. 1843; *Evidence taken before Her Majesty's Commissioners of Inquiry into the State of the Law and Practice in respect to the Occupation of Land in Ireland*, part iii. H.C. 1845 (657), xxi. 939-48.
[25] Peel to Graham, 1 Nov. 1843, Peel papers, Add. MS 40449, ff. 176-7. See also, John F. Broderick, *The Holy See and the Irish Movement for the Repeal of the Union with England, 1829-1847*, pp. 163-71.

ted that a 'nosegay' of the acts, speeches and writings of Irish clerics should be prepared for Aberdeen, the Foreign Secretary, who would transmit it to the Pope, or if that proved impossible, to Metternich.[26] This was duly done and the material was sent to Vienna with the request that it be forwarded to Rome.[27] It was, however, not until almost a year later than Rome did act and then in a way that was as non-committal as possible.[28]

The unwillingness of the Roman authorities to become embroiled in a dangerous conflict on behalf of a Government they regarded with some suspicion did not deter Peel from pressing ahead with his religious policy in Ireland.[29] The first practical measure was the Charitable Donations and Bequests Bill. That such a measure would possibly be introduced had been intimated by Peel early in the Session, but it was not until June 18 that it was read for the first time in the Lords.[30] The bill was a considerable improvement on the existing legislation on charitable and religious trusts, being more liberal in its treatment of Catholic interests. But the Government made a serious tactical error which helped to turn a useful piece of legislation into a fiercely controversial political issue.

Charities in Ireland had been administered by a board established under an act of the old Irish Parliament. This body had fifty members and it was almost exclusively Protestant in composition. The primary purpose of the new Bequests Bill was to abolish this board and replace it by a more compact one of thirteen members. Three of the members were to be *ex-officio* appointments, and of the remaining ten, all Crown nominees, five were to be Catholics.[31] The bill, too, in its final form gave in effect legal recognition to the fact that there were Catholic bishops in Ireland, even though their territorial titles were not recognised.[32] Graham described the bill as being 'framed in the spirit of peace', but at no stage before the measure was intro-

[26] Peel to Graham, 27 Nov. 1843, Peel papers, Add.49, MS 404 ff. 233–4.
[27] Graham to Peel, 29 Nov. 1843, Peel papers, Add. MS 40449, ff. 241–4; Aberdeen to Peel, 30 Dec. 1843, Peel papers, Add. MS 40454, f. 78.
[28] William Petre to Aberdeen, 21 Oct. 1844, F.O. 43/38.
[29] Petre to Aberdeen, 15 Jan. 1845, Aberdeen papers, Add. MS 43151, ff. 208–9.
[30] *Hansard*, lxxv. 1087.   [31] Ibid., lxxvi. 1511–15.
[32] Peel to Graham, 21 Aug. 1844, Graham papers, also a copy in Peel papers, Add. MS 40450, ff. 105–6.

duced did the Government seek the views of the Irish Catholic hierarchy on its provisions. The consequence was that, while the bill as a whole was clearly an advance on the previous legislation, it contained provisions which made even those bishops who were willing to co-operate with the Government uneasy as to what they should do once the attack on the bill gained momentum.[33] The Government's defence was that since the bill was concerned with property rights, it had consulted neither the Protestant nor the Catholic bishops.[34] To bring the law in Ireland closer to that in England, the bill also provided that any devise of real property made for religious or charitable purposes within three months of the testator's death should be invalid. This was regarded by the critics of the bill as a reflection on the honesty of purpose of the Irish clergy, while other clauses, it was feared, would prejudice the position of the religious orders.[35]

In Parliament the bill met with little opposition; outside Parliament it was otherwise. O'Connell had prepared the way with his proposal in March that Irish bishops and parish priests should have the powers of a corporation sole for holding real property in perpetual succession. This would have disposed of the need for trustees or a Charitable Donations Board, but it was John MacHale, the Archbishop of Tuam, who commenced the full-scale ecclesiastical attack on the bill.

In a bitter open letter to Peel, he denounced in particular the three months clause which he declared only 'a deadly hate' of the Catholic faith could have inspired.[36] In opposing the bill MacHale rallied a substantial measure of support. In September, thirteen other bishops joined him in a solemn protest against the measure and many of the lower clergy added their names to it as well.[37] From prison, O'Connell let it be known that he regarded the bill as an insidious attempt by the state to influence 'the doctrine, discipline or usages of the Catholic church', while the parliamentary committee of the Repeal Association gave full support to the complaints of those bishops

[33] Heytesbury to Peel, 22 Aug. 1844, Peel papers, Add. MS 40479, ff. 45–8; William J. Walsh (archbishop of Dublin), *O'Connell, Archbishop Murray and the Board of Charitable Bequests*, pp. 1–17.

[34] *Hansard*, lxxvi. 1530–7.

[35] Ibid., lxxvi. 1527–30, 1780.

[36] MacHale to Peel, 24 July 1844, *Nation*, 27 July 1844.

[37] Heytesbury to Graham, 21, 24 Sept. 1844, Graham papers.

who had openly opposed the new legislation.[38] The opposition was formidable, and Archbishops Murray and Crolly hesitated to take the defiant step of agreeing to join the Board when the Act was passed, for they too disliked the disputed clauses and could secure no undertaking from the Government that they would be amended to suit their wishes.[39] A position almost of deadlock developed in the closing months of 1844, and to break it the Government again sought the assistance of Rome.[40]

Through their newly appointed unofficial representative at Rome, William Petre, an English Catholic, the Government endeavoured to offset the influence of MacHale's friends and to persuade the Holy See that the new Act was a substantial boon, despite what its political opponents might say.[41] Petre was persistent in his efforts, but the most he could secure was a vague memorandum from the Cardinal Secretary of State, giving mild approval to the Act though recognising defects in it.[42] This and a long-sought papal rescript to Archbishop Crolly, of Armagh, on the political activities of the Irish clergy, were as much as the Government could secure.

The rescript, like the memorandum on the Bequests Act, was an extremely cautious document. It conveyed the papal disapproval of clerical intervention in political affairs in the most guarded of terms, for as Cardinal Lambruschini, the Secretary of State, told Petre, stronger action could only 'imbitter instead of softening the animosities of parties'.[43] The *Nation* newspaper was to dismiss it as 'a very harmless homily', and it appears to have had little effect in discouraging the clergy from participating in political affairs.[44] Taken in conjunction, however, with the final if reluctant decisions of Archbishops

[38] *Nation*, 10 Aug., 30 Nov. 1844.
[39] Heytesbury to Graham, 21 Sept. 1844, Graham papers; Peel to Graham, 26 Sept. 1844, Peel papers, Add. MS 40450, ff. 189–90.
[40] Graham to Peel, 26 Sept. 1844, Peel papers, Add. MS 40450, ff. 184–7.
[41] Canning to Petre, 1 Oct. 1844, F.O. 43/38; Peel to Aberdeen, 4 Oct. 1844, Peel papers, Add. MS 40454, ff. 274–5; Graham to Peel, 8 Oct. 1844, Peel papers, Add. MS 40450, ff. 236–43.
[42] Petre to Canning, 29 Nov. 1844, F.O. 43/38.
[43] William Crolly to D. O'Connell, 11 Jan. 1845, *Nation*, 18 Jan. 1845; Petre to Aberdeen, 21 Oct. 1844, F.O. 43/38.
[44] *Nation*, 18 Jan. 1845.

Crolly, Murray and Cornelius Denvir, the Bishop of Down, to join the Bequests Board, the moderately successful negotiations between church and state gave rise to considerable excitement in repeal circles at the beginning of 1845.[45]

The report quickly gained currency that the United Kingdom was on the point of establishing diplomatic relations with Rome and of signing a concordat with the Holy See.[46] There had been, in Government circles, some consideration given to the question of entering into diplomatic relations with Rome in the spring of 1844. Gladstone in particular favoured such a move, though Graham considered that too early a concession to Rome in this issue would mean the loss of a valuable bargaining point for the future.[47] There was, however, no suggestion of a condordat to regulate the position of the Catholic church within the United Kingdom, and indeed Petre was quick to observe that despite a certain measure of goodwill, the papal authorities were unwilling to discuss Irish political affairs in any detail with him.[48]

The report of an impending concordat was soon denied, but the whole agitation against the Bequests Bill, which reached a climax in November and December, had with the federalist issue helped to restore an element of tension and excitement to Irish political life. The ministry had won, it is true, the hesitant support of the two Archbishops for the new Act, and was encouraged to go forward with still further remedial measures. To that extent O'Connell had suffered a set-back, but the main task of breaking O'Connell's influence was still far from completion.[49]

Towards the end of 1844, O'Connell admitted that for some

[45] Daniel Murray, *A Pastoral Address to the Roman Catholic Clergy and Laity of the Diocese of Dublin*; Heytesbury to Peel, 20 Dec. 1844, Peel papers, Add. MS 40479, ff. 216–17.

[46] *The Times*, 4 Jan. 1845; *Morning Chronicle*, 30 Dec. 1844; Repeal Assoc. meeting, 30 Dec. 1844, *Nation*, 4 Jan. 1845; *Morning Herald*, 18 Jan. 1845.

[47] Memorandum by Gladstone, 19 Apr. 1844, Peel papers, Add. MS 40470, ff. 201–11; Graham to Peel, 20 Apr. 1844, Peel papers, Add. MS 40450, ff. 24–5.

[48] Petre to Aberdeen, 21 Jan. 1845, Aberdeen papers, Add. MS 43151, ff. 210–11.

[49] William Crolly to D. O'Connell, 11 Jan. 1845, *Nation*, 18 Jan. 1845; Bessborough to Russell, 10 Jan. 1845, Russell papers, P.R.O. 30/22/4.

months there had been a pause in the repeal agitation.[50] In practice this had been the case from the beginning of the year. The trial of O'Connell and his companions, which finally began in January, rather than repeal, appears to have held the public attention. But if O'Connell perhaps lost something in prestige by having to submit to a conspiracy charge, he won in compensation widespread sympathy. Catholic opinion in both Britain and Ireland was hurt by the exclusion, in a most dubious manner, of Catholics from the jury empanelled to hear the case. Protest meetings were held in many Irish provincial centres. Even Archbishop Crolly, the politically moderate primate, spoke at one such meeting, and when O'Connell was in England, in February and March, many leading Catholic peers, although political opponents of his, attended a London banquet in his honour.[51]

The members of the Government deplored the way in which the proceedings against O'Connell had been mismanaged, but they could not avoid the ill-effects the prosecutions had on English Whig and liberal opinion generally.[52] In Parliament, the Whigs pressed the ministry closely on the conduct of the whole action against repeal from the summer of 1843 onwards. In attacking the Government's Irish policy and the prosecutions, Russell took the lead by opening, on February 13, a debate on the state of Ireland. The debate was an important and a long one, with Russell and the other Whig leaders contending that O'Connell had shown every anxiety to avoid a breach of the peace and urging that only a bold policy of political and ecclesiastical reform could tranquillise the country.[53] The debate was important in another way too. It saw the return of O'Connell to his seat in Parliament after his absence throughout 1843, and a vigorous defence of O'Connell by Sheil, Wyse, David Ross, and other Irish Whigs.[54]

The attack on the Government's policy towards the repealers did not end with the February debate. In March, Wyse

[50] Repeal Assoc. meeting, 11 Nov., *Nation*, 16 Nov. 1844.

[51] *Nation*, 20 Jan., 16 Mar. 1844.

[52] Graham to Peel, 18 Jan. 1844, Peel papers, Add. MS 40449, ff. 304–5; Graham to De Grey, 13 Jan. 1844, Graham papers; Peel to Graham, 22 Apr. 1844, Graham papers.

[53] *Hansard*, lxxii. 683–726, 830–46, 970–92.

[54] Ibid., lxxii. 726–60, 925–36, lxxiii. 71–107, 185–206.

presented a petition from the Repeal Association complaining of the manner in which the trial had been conducted, while in July and August, Wyse, Russell and Sheil resumed the attack on the Government.[55] Outside Parliament, O'Connell was warmly received by Liberals and free traders when he visited London, Birmingham, Manchester, and other English cities, in March.[56] Such demonstrations of sympathy were no doubt also expressions of the Radicals' dissatisfaction with Peel's government, but they showed, too, that O'Connell could still count on much goodwill among English Liberals, a fact O'Connell was quick to emphasise, as when he wrote that, 'the middle-class—the sound substantial middle class of England, appear to me to be strongly impressed with the injustice done to us'.[57]

A variety of factors, therefore, helped to ease the tension between O'Connell and the Whigs. At the beginning of the new session he had resumed his place in the Commons and with a small group of his followers took part to a limited extent in the business of the House. The Whig championing of his cause had impressed him, and the Whigs, in turn, were not slow to notice his avoidance of any emphatic statements on the question of repeal. Lord Clarendon, for example, could observe that with the exception of a tax on absentee Irish landowners 'something might and ought to be done' to meet O'Connell's other practical proposals for reform.[58]

Graham, as early as February, suspected that the Whigs and O'Connell contemplated a new alliance with the destruction of the established church as the common object. He believed that the Whigs would seek to induce O'Connell to forego the repeal agitation until the results of the effort to upset the religious settlement could be ascertained.[59] But though there

[55] Ibid., lxxiii. 1352–5, lxxvi. 830–45, 1956–61, 2006–7.

[56] *Morning Chronicle*, 14 Mar. 1844.

[57] D. O'Connell to T. M. Ray, 4 Mar. 1844, *Nation*, 9 Mar. 1844; *The Times*, 13 Mar. 1843.

[58] D. O'Connell to Richard Sheil, 19 June 1844, Fitzpatrick, *Correspondence of Daniel O'Connell*, ii. 322–4; Repeal Assoc. meeting, 1 Apr., *Nation*, 6 Apr. 1844; Clarendon to Russell, 25 Jan. 1844, Russell papers, P.R.O. 30/22/4, and Gooch, op. cit., i. 69–70; Russell to Monteagle, 24 Nov. 1844, Monteagle papers.

[59] Graham to De Grey, 16 Feb. 1844, Graham papers.

seems to be no substantial ground for thinking that any definite compact existed between O'Connell and the Whig leaders at this time, Russell appears to have been of the opinion in November that O'Connell was no longer anxious to engage in a repeal agitation.[60] Lord Morpeth, in September, had the impression that O'Connell was puzzled as to what course he should follow for the future.[61] But Peel probably put O'Connell's predicament best when he wrote, soon after O'Connell's release from prison: 'I think it probable that the first and immediate object of O'Connell will be to attempt to make the late events the instrument of effecting the overthrow of the present Government—and that for this purpose there will be contact between him and our political opponents. The party behind him in Ireland will not, however, permit him, if they can help it, to limit himself to this—and will persuade him that the best way of effecting the primary object—a change of Government—will be renewed agitation for repeal and as much disturbance of the peace in Ireland as is consistent with safety'.[62]

The success of O'Connell's appeal to the House of Lords and the 'martyrdom' of his imprisonment erased the stigma of the trial. Lord Bessborough, a close observer of developments in Ireland, considered that the victory in the Lords would persuade the people that O'Connell was invincible.[63] In the Repeal Association, his return was the signal for much enthusiasm, and the success of the appeal undoubtedly left Peel and Graham discomfited and not a little alarmed at the prospect of a possible renewal of the old repeal agitation.[64] But O'Connell had learned one lesson: there was to be no repetition of Clontarf. In his very first speech after his release he made this clear by saying that the decision of the Lords had surely made it unnecessary to hold the monster meeting they had abandoned the previous year. The people had demonstrated the legality of

[60] Russell to Monteagle, 24 Nov. 1844, Monteagle papers.
[61] Morpeth to Monteagle, 16 Sept. 1844, Monteagle papers.
[62] Peel to Graham, 14 Sept. 1844, Peel papers, Add. MS 40450, ff. 152–3.
[63] Bessborough to Russell, 20 Sept. 1844, Russell papers, P.R.O. 30/22/4.
[64] Repeal Assoc. meeting, 9 Sept., *Nation*, 14 Sept. 1844; *Morning Chronicle*, 5 Sept. 1844; Peel to Graham, 15 Sept. 1844, Peel papers, Add. MS 40450, ff. 154–5; Graham to De Grey, 21 Sept. 1844, Graham papers.

peaceful agitation and that was enough.[65] The *Nation* newspaper concurred in this opinion.[66] But the rejection of agitation
still left unanswered the question of what course of action
O'Connell and his followers should now pursue.

At the same September meeting, O'Connell did express a
desire to go ahead with his plans for a Council of Three
Hundred, but he warned his listeners that the preparations
would take time and he prudently fixed no date for assembling
the Council.[67] But if the Council, in fact, was never to proceed
beyond this stage, the Bequest Bill dispute did help to maintain
excitement in Ireland, and O'Connell was able to employ it
to some advantage. It was, however, in his turning to federalism
that contemporaries saw a distinct possibility that O'Connell
might embark on a new and formidable political campaign.[68]

Suggestions for some measure of devolution within the United
Kingdom were many, particularly in the second half of 1844.
They ranged from the proposal that the Queen should hold
court and summon the imperial Parliament at least once in
every three years in Dublin to projects for a subordinate
Parliament to deal with Irish affairs.[69] The news that a number
of prominent Irish 'federalists' or advocates of an Irish Parliament with limited powers, had joined the Repeal Association
led Graham to suspect that 'the federal arrangement will be
the middle term on which for the moment opposite parties will
agree: and some scheme of national representation will be devised, to which the Whigs will agree . . .', which would require
that all Irish legislation should originate in Ireland but be
subject to approval by the imperial Parliament. Some such
arrangement he thought would meet O'Connell's aims quite
well.[70] The fact that the proposal favouring occasional sessions
of the imperial Parliament should have been brought forward

[65] Repeal Assoc. meeting, 9 Sept., *Nation*, 14 Sept. 1844; Graham to
Peel, 18 Sept. 1844, Peel papers, Add. MS 40450, ff. 164–7.

[66] *Nation*, 14 Sept. 1845.

[67] Ibid.

[68] Graham to Aberdeen, 20 Sept. 1844, Graham papers; Russell to the
Duke of Leinster, 13 Sept. 1844, Russell papers, P.R.O. 30/22/4, and
Gooch, op. cit., i. 72–3; *The Times*, 17 Sept. 1844.

[69] *Nation*, 28 Sept. 1844; *Edinburgh Review*, lxxix (1844). 189–274; *The
Times*, 28 Sept. 1844.

[70] Graham to Peel, 17 Sept. 1844, Peel papers, Add. MS 40450, ff. 160–3.

in the Dublin Corporation, by a Tory member, confirmed Graham in his apprehensions.[71]

But Graham was not the only one to feel alarmed. Russell considered the issue grave enough to necessitate a formal letter to the Duke of Leinster, the leader of the Irish Whigs, in which he declared his resolve to maintain the legislative Union and rejecting emphatically any federalist solution.[72] His concern was understandable. As early as March, 1844, Lord Charlemont, a leading Irish Whig, took up energetically the plan for occasional parliamentary sessions in Dublin, while, as Gavan Duffy mentions, a number of Irish Whig peers interested themselves in a type of devolution which appears to have been similar to the project mentioned by Graham.[73]

In the circumstances, it is hardly surprising that O'Connell should have seen in federalism distinct possibilities.[74] Already a number of federalists had joined the Association and he had hopes of winning the support of men such as Sharman Crawford and David Ross, the member for Belfast.[75] Again, the concern felt by the Whig and Tory leaders alike was an indication of the significance they attached to federalism or devolution, as a more modest and more dangerous substitute for repeal.

O'Connell, the lawyer, too, seems to have found an obvious attraction in federalism. It suggested a solution for the long unanswered constitutional problem of how Ireland was to share, if at all, in the control of imperial and foreign affairs after the Act of Union had been repealed. O'Connell put his point of view clearly when he stated: 'The federalists . . . appear to me to require more for Ireland than the simple repealers do . . . the federalists require that there should be for questions of

[71] Graham to Peel, 28 Sept. 1844, Peel papers, Add. MS 40450, ff. 195–6.

[72] Russell to the Duke of Leinster, 13 Sept. 1844, Russell papers, P.R.O. 30/22/4, and quoted in part in Gooch, op. cit., i. 72–3; Leinster to Russell, 17 Sept. 1844, Russell papers, P.R.O. 30/22/4.

[73] Charlemont to Monteagle, 14 Mar. 1844, Monteagle papers; Gavan Duffy, *Young Ireland*, pp. 165–6.

[74] D. O'Connell to P. V. Fitzpatrick, 12 Oct. 1844, Fitzpatrick, *Correspondence of Daniel O'Connell*, ii. 332; B. A. Kennedy, 'Sharman Crawford's federal scheme for Ireland', in H. A. Cronne, T. W. Moody and D. B. Quinn (eds.), *Essays in British and Irish History in Honour of James Eadie Todd*, pp. 245–54.

[75] D. O'Connell to William Smith O'Brien, 1 Oct. 1844, Smith O'Brien papers, vol. 434, no. 1245.

imperial concern, colonial, military, naval and of foreign alliance and policy, a congressional or federative parliament in which Ireland should have her fair share and proportion of representation and power . . .'.[76] Even if Ross, Sharman Crawford, Henry Caulfield and other federalists did not join the Repeal Association, O'Connell considered that once they produced a federal plan, the case for an Irish legislature would be substantially strengthened.[77] Though O'Connell left himself a means of escape by putting on the federalists the onus of elaborating a scheme, his rather sudden acceptance of the principle of federalism in preference to simple repeal had not the effect he obviously intended. His action appears to have alarmed a section of the federalists, anxious to preserve their independence of action, but it also disturbed a section of his own supporters.[78]

The men who had gathered around Gavan Duffy and Thomas Davis since the foundation of the *Nation* had, in the two years of that newspaper's existence, strengthened and deepened their concept of nationality. For them it had become something above all divisions: 'we preached a nationality that asked no man's creed . . .'.[79] But it was a nationalism which

[76] Repeal Assoc. meeting, 14 Oct., *Nation*, 19 Oct. 1844.
[77] Daniel O'Connell to W. J. O'Neill Daunt, [Nov. 1844], Fitzpatrick, *Correspondence of Daniel O'Connell*, ii. 345.
[78] *Nation*, 2 Nov. 1844; R. Potter to Smith O'Brien, 16 Oct. 1844, Smith O'Brien papers, vol. 434, no. 1253; *Quarterly Review*, lxxv. 268.
[79] *Nation*, 12 Oct. 1844; Gavan Duffy, *Young Ireland*, pp. 102–16. Charles Gavan Duffy (1816–1903), was a native of Monaghan and worked as a journalist in Dublin and Belfast. The proprietor and editor of the *Nation*, he was one of those tried along with Daniel O'Connell on charges of conspiracy in 1844. He was arrested in July 1848 but the subsequent attempts to secure his conviction for treason felony failed. During his imprisonment the *Nation* newspaper was suppressed. On his release, he re-established the newspaper in Sept. 1849. He was actively associated with the tenant-right agitation from 1849–50 onwards. In 1855 he emigrated to Australia where he quickly won for himself a leading role in state politics in Victoria. He became Prime Minister of Victoria in 1871 and was knighted in 1873. Though he had some influence of a moderating kind on Irish politics in the eighteen-seventies and eighties, the most significant contribution of his later career to Irish affairs was his work on the history of the repeal and tenant-right movements. A reformer rather than a revolutionary, Gavan Duffy was possibly the ablest among the more conservative of the Young Irelanders. He died, in Feb. 1903, at Nice.

from its very nature allowed little scope for manoeuvre or compromise. As the *Nation* put it: 'the aspiration of Ireland is for unbounded nationality'.[80] The preoccupations of the 'repeal year' had left few opportunities for discord to develop. Even in the weeks immediately following the proclamation of the Clontarf meeting there is little evidence of division in the repeal ranks, apart from the slight disagreement on federalism which has already been noticed.[81] It was only gradually, in the indecisive months of 1844, that a number of factors came into play which helped to weaken the old cohesion within the repeal movement. O'Connell's suggestion, immediately after his trial in February, that the Association should be dissolved and re-constituted on a new and legally more secure basis appears to have been the occasion for some disagreement. The proposal was, however, dropped, and it was not until later in the year that the divisions within the movement became really pronounced.[82]

When the Repeal Association criticised the Bequests Bill as being in certain ways objectionable, Davis, in particular feared that the Association might become over-involved in issues which bore no direct relation to the repeal cause. This sense of anxiety was heightened for Davis by the fact that the *Nation* had incurred criticism in some clerical circles because of the liberal character of the views contained in articles published in its pages.[83] For Davis, therefore, the danger, as he saw it, was that religious liberty might be endangered. 'I for one', he wrote, 'will not sacrifice my right to it for any consideration.'[84]

In this campaign to keep the Association outside religious controversy, the position was complicated by the fact that the relations between the Young Irelanders and many of the leading Protestant federalists were friendly and close. Writing from Belfast, at the end of October, Davis said that on the religious

[80] *Nation*, 2 Nov. 1844.

[81] Randall Clarke, 'The relations between O'Connell and the Young Irelanders', in *Irish Historical Studies*, iii (1942–3). 18–30.

[82] Gavan Duffy, *Young Ireland*, p. 164; De Grey to Graham, 13 Feb. 1844, Graham papers.

[83] Thomas Davis to Smith O'Brien, 20 Aug. 1844, Smith O'Brien papers, vol. 434, no. 1291; Gavan Duffy, *Young Ireland*, pp. 224–7.

[84] Davis to Smith O'Brien, 3 Nov. 1844, Smith O'Brien papers, vol. 434, no. 1282.

issue 'the federalist leaders here go entirely with me on it and in fact *now* or never we Protestants must ascertain whether we are to have religious liberty'.[85] The interesting but difficult situation, therefore, emerged that while Davis, Gavan Duffy and their friends shared a common liberalism with the federalists and welcomed them as allies, they could not accept federalism as a final solution to the constitutional problem.[86] In this combination of a liberalism which would have tended to limit Catholic influences on the Association and a nationalism which could not be whittled down, the dual characteristics of Young Ireland made themselves apparent.

In the closing months of 1844, the religious issues remained still in the background, but the disagreement was there, and it made O'Connell's task all the more difficult in the federalist dispute. Before the combined opposition of Smith O'Brien and the Young Irelanders, he seems to have given way on federalism, and indeed, the correspondence which has survived suggests that he went to considerable trouble in soothing Smith O'Brien and in endeavouring to meet Davis's objections and charges.[87] In the case of Davis, O'Connell readily admitted that he did not want to lose him 'by reason of any Protestant monomania'.[88]

On this, as on other occasions, O'Connell was anxious to avoid making the Repeal Association an exclusively Catholic organisation. In describing the repeal agitation as 'a struggle of Irishmen of every sect and persuasion for the attainment of an object which would be of equal benefit to all', he used terms no Young Irelander could quarrel with.[89] But the necessities of political strategy and O'Connell's preference for the immediate and the practical made demands which the men of the *Nation* could not always admit.[90]

[85] Davis to Smith O'Brien, 27 Oct. 1844, Smith O'Brien papers, vol. 434, no. 1296.

[86] *Nation*, 19 Oct. 1844.

[87] D. O'Connell to P. V. Fitzpatrick, 31 Oct. 1844, Fitzpatrick, *Correspondence of Daniel O'Connell*, ii. 340–2; D. O'Connell to Smith O'Brien, 1 Oct. 1844, Smith O'Brien papers, vol. 434, no. 1245; D. O'Connell to Smith O'Brien, 9 Nov. 1844, Smith O'Brien papers, vol. 434, no. 1273.

[88] D. O'Connell to Davis, 30 Oct. 1844, Fitzpatrick, *Correspondence of Daniel O'Connell*, ii 338–40.

[89] Repeal Assoc. meeting, 6 May, *Nation*, 11 May 1844.

[90] *Morning Herald*, 29 Oct. 1844.

O'Connell's virtual abandonment of federalism did help to hide the difference within the repeal movement, but the fundamental questions of what the future policy of the Association should be and what attitude it should adopt to the new reforming measures of the Government remained unanswered at the beginning of 1845. This was a fact which was not lost on contemporaries.[91]

The Bequests Act had made apparent the new trend in Peel's policy and his position was undoubtedly strengthened by the much smoother working of the Irish administration from the summer of 1844 onwards. The sickly and difficult De Grey had resigned and was succeeded, in July, by Lord Heytesbury, an experienced diplomat who was generally content to do what he was instructed to do without endeavouring to elaborate an Irish policy of his own.[92] Equally important, he worked well with Eliot, who ceased to be Chief Secretary at the beginning of 1845, when he succeeded his father as Earl St Germans, and was replaced by Sir Thomas Fremantle.[93] Even Lucas in his last year in office (he retired at the end of July 1845) gave little cause for complaint, being described by Heytesbury as, 'an indefatigable and very efficient servant of the Government', though perhaps he could not 'go cordially with us in our more recent line of policy'.[94] It was another sign of this new line in policy that the Government should have considered appointing a Catholic as Lucas's successor, but finally made a compromise by appointing a Catholic barrister as Chief Clerk in the Chief Secretary's office with the new and more impressive title of Assistant Under-Secretary. A Protestant Under-Secretary it was

[91] *Nation*, 16 Nov. 1844; Heytesbury to Graham, 12 Nov. 1844, Graham papers; *The Times*, 9 Jan. 1845.
[92] Peel to Heytesbury, 1 Aug. 1844, Peel papers, Add. MS 40479, ff. 15–18; Graham to Peel, 16 Sept. 1844, Peel papers, Add. MS 40450, ff. 156–9.
[93] Peel to Graham, 20 Jan. 1845, Peel papers, Add. MS 40451, ff. 21–2; Heytesbury to Peel, 27 Jan. 1845, Peel papers, Add. MS 40479, ff. 272–3. Thomas Francis Fremantle (1798–1890). Baronet 1821. First elected to Parliament in 1830. Secretary of the Treasury, 1834, 1841–4. 1844 Secretary at War. In 1846 he became Deputy Chairman and subsequently Chairman of the Board of Customs. He was created Baron Cottesloe in 1874.
[94] Heytesbury to Peel, 19 July 1845, Peel papers, Add. MS 40479, ff. 397–8.

felt was still necessary, if the Government were to retain any influence with the Irish Tories, particularly at so critical a time.[95]

[95] Peel to Heytesbury, 18 July 1845, Peel papers, Add. MS 40479, ff. 395-6; Heytesbury to Peel, 20 July 1845, Peel papers, Add. MS 40479, ff. 399-402; Peel to Heytesbury, 25 July 1845, Peel papers, Add. MS 40479, ff. 405-6; Peel to Heytesbury, 7 Aug. [1845], Peel papers, Add. MS 40479, ff. 422-3.

IV

MAYNOOTH AND THE
'GODLESS COLLEGES', 1845

EVEN BEFORE THE BEQUESTS ACT dispute had ended, the
Government was giving close attention to Maynooth and the
question of higher education in Ireland. Peel's two original suggestions, which he had put before the cabinet in February
1844, that higher education for the Catholic clergy might be
provided in institutions open to laymen and that the whole
problem be considered by a special commission, were gradually
discarded.[1] A variety of factors contributed to the cabinet's
decision to treat Maynooth and the higher education of the
laity separately. Gladstone was averse to any alteration in the
status of Maynooth, at least until diplomatic relations had been
established with the Holy See, while Graham, influenced by
representations which were made from Catholic sources, came
fairly quickly to the conclusion that Maynooth and the lay
colleges would have to be kept apart.[2]

Though the Government did not conduct direct negotiations
with the bishops on the new Maynooth Bill, it was kept in-
formed of the general attitude of the hierarchy through lay intermediaries, particularly through Anthony Blake, a Catholic
commissioner under the Bequests Act.[3] The general tenor of

[1] Memorandum by Peel, Feb. 1844, Peel papers, Add. MS 40540, ff.
40–55.
[2] Graham to Heytesbury, 26 Nov. 1844, Graham papers.
[3] Heytesbury to Graham, 4 Nov. 1844, Graham papers.

Blake's communications was that since special training of 'a monastic character' was needed for candidates for the priesthood, it would not be possible to provide it in an institution open even to lay Catholics. Blake, however, conceded that changes might have to be made in the system of public visitation of Maynooth.[4] Graham subsequently incorporated these views in a cabinet memorandum and after some further discussions, the new Maynooth Bill was drafted on the lines Graham had recommended, though he did cling to the hope that a place might yet be found for Maynooth in any future university system.[5]

The Maynooth Bill, as introduced by Peel on 3 April 1845, left the college very much as it had been in constitution and discipline. The visitations, by Crown-appointed visitors, were put on an annual instead of a triennial basis, but apart from this no serious effort was made to increase public control over the institution.[6] The purpose of the bill was simply to create goodwill between the Government and the Irish Catholic clergy by endowing their college adequately. To this end the annual grant was raised to £26,360 and put on a statutory basis to avoid controversial annual votes, while £30,000 was made available, as a single grant, to provide proper buildings.[7]

In introducing this bill 'to put the establishment on a liberal footing; so that the reminiscences of Maynooth may no longer be revolting', Peel and his colleagues took a calculated and dangerous risk. In Catholic circles the bill was well received, but the storm it provoked in Britain, especially in non-conformist circles, threatened to break the unity of Peel's own party at a time when the Government's tariff policy was already causing uneasiness among the protectionists. Outside Parliament, the ultra-Protestant anger expressed itself in petitions, pamphlets and meetings; in Parliament the threat to the Government was even greater, with Tories attacking the measure on Protestant principles and Radicals, such as Ward and Bright,

[4] Memorandum by Graham, 16 Nov. 1844, Graham papers.

[5] Graham to Heytesbury, 30 Nov. 1844, Graham papers; Graham to Heytesbury, 9 Jan. 1844, Graham papers.

[6] *Hansard*, lxxix. 18–38.

[7] Ibid.

opposing it because it brought the system of state-subsidised religion a stage further.[8]

Stanley, and Graham even more so, believed that the Maynooth measure, though necessary, would destroy the Government and the unity of the Tory party. Peel, too, was conscious of the risk, but neither he nor any of his closest colleagues showed any inclination to abandon the bill.[9] How grave the crisis was the division lists show. On the first and subsequent readings, the great majority of those voting against the measure were Tories. On the first reading alone, over 100 of them voted against their leader, and though Protestant opposition to the bill was not as vocal in Ireland as it was in Britain, only some 10 Irish Tories could be found to support it on its third reading.[10] Without the support of the majority of the Whigs, the measure might have been lost.[11] If the storm over Maynooth was a remarkable illustration of how far Peel was now prepared to go in defying the conservative wing of his party once he felt a decision had to be taken, it also foreshadowed that more serious crisis of the next year which was to complete the division within the Tory party.

As a measure of reform, the Maynooth Bill was a minor affair. It was significant rather as a gesture, as a suggestion that further concessions in favour of the Irish Catholics might follow. Though Peel did not accept the Whig arguments in support of a state endowment for the Catholic church, he nevertheless refused to pledge himself against endowment at any time in the future. He left it very much an open and unsettled question.[12]

Peel had been prepared in 1845 to face a crisis over a measure which did not bear on the fundamental problems of the Irish

[8] *Hansard*, lxxix. 495; *The Times*, 7 Mar. 1845; *Nation*, 19 Apr. 1845; *Morning Herald*, 11 Apr. 1845; *Morning Chronicle*, 22 Apr., 2 May 1845; H. G. Ward to Russell, 30 Mar. 1845, Russell papers, P.R.O. 30/22/4; *Hansard*, lxxix. 1124–55.

[9] Stanley to Peel, 8 Apr. 1845, Peel papers, Add. MS 40468, ff. 311–12; Graham to Heytesbury, 12 Apr. 1845, Graham papers; Peel to Stanley, 9 Apr. 1845, Peel papers, Add. MS 40468, ff. 313–14.

[10] *Hansard*, lxxix. 108–11, 1042–5, lxxx. 744–8; *The Times*, 7 Apr. 1845; Heytesbury to Peel, 24 Apr. 1845, Peel papers, Add. MS 40479, ff. 333–4.

[11] *The Times*, 7 Apr. 1845; *Morning Herald*, 1 May 1845.

[12] *Hansard*, lxxix. 90–7, 1301–5, 1024–42.

economy, yet he was ready to drop, because of landlord opposition, the moderate proposals contained in Lord Stanley's
tenant compensation bill of the same year.[13] But in making
religious and educational questions, instead of land reform, the
issue, Peel and his colleagues were not alone. In the repeal
movement much the same tendency could be observed. On the
eve of the famine, it was not the Devon Commission's report and
the problem of tenant-right but the Colleges Bill which
provoked most controversy and dissension.

Though the Academical Institutions (Ireland) Bill, which
Graham introduced at the beginning of May, was to encounter
some opposition from Sir Robert Inglis and the ultra-Tories, it
was in Ireland rather than in Parliament that debate on the
measure was sharpest and of most serious consequence.[14] That
the Bill became a subject of contention at all was in a large
measure the fault of the Government. Like the Maynooth and
Bequest Bills, it was intended as another move in the plan to
wean Catholic opinion away from O'Connell. But the Government's unwillingness to become involved with the Catholic
hierarchy produced a situation akin to that which had arisen
in connection with the Bequests Bill the previous year. Once
the ministry had decided not to link Maynooth with a broader
scheme of higher education, the negotiations on the Maynooth
Bill were relatively simple and so the indirect link with the
bishops through men like Blake sufficed. It was otherwise with
the Colleges Bill.

In the course of the debate in the Commons, Peel explained
that the Government had not conferred with the Catholic
bishops because, had it done so, it would also have had to
approach the Protestant bench of bishops, and run the risk of
frustrating the whole plan of opening the new colleges to
students of all persuasions.[15] Though Peel was correct in claim-
ing that there had been no formal negotiations with the bishops
about the bill, the opportunity had been taken during the

---

[13] *The Times*, 19 May 1845; Graham to Stanley, 22 June 1845, Graham
papers.

[14] *Hansard*, lxxx. 345–66. For a full discussion of the problems concerned
with higher education in Ireland at this period see T. W. Moody and J. C.
Beckett, *Queens, Belfast, 1845–1949*, i. 1–103.

[15] *Hansard*, lxxx. 385–91.

discussions on Maynooth to raise with Blake, the Catholic intermediary, the problem of higher education for the laity. In December, Graham was able to tell Peel that the colleges' plan had met with the acquiescence of both the Protestant primate and Blake, and he added: 'we could not have pleased either much without offending the other'.[16] Again, in February 1845, Blake assured Graham 'that a *second* university in Dublin together with the provincial colleges will be accepted as satisfactory . . . anything less than this will be opposed, for the Catholics will not consent to be "relegated to the provinces" '.[17] How far Blake was entitled to speak thus for the Catholic authorities is obscure. One thing is certain; when the bishops met in Dublin, on May 23, what they objected to in the bill was not the actual location of the colleges, but the character of the instruction to be given in them.[18]

Inglis, early in the debate on the bill, described the scheme as a gigantic one of 'Godless education', a phrase O'Connell soon made his own.[19] There is, however, no reason to think that Peel or his colleagues, where higher education was involved, were particularly 'enamoured of the liberal belief in the new religion of secular enlightenment', as a recent writer has suggested.[20] In his original memorandum of February 1844, Peel would appear to have had in mind combined education for the clergy and laity on the pattern of the older English universities, while Lord Stanley, who was even more explicit, contemplated a college in Ulster for the Presbyterians and one in Munster and another in Connacht, principally, though not exclusively, for Catholics, where clerical students might receive a liberal ecclesiastical education in conjunction with general studies. The latter, he considered, they could share with the lay students of the college.[21] In April 1844, Graham for the first time put forward the suggestion that if Trinity College, Dublin, could not be opened more extensively to Catholics, it might instead be useful to establish a new college or university,

[16] Graham to Peel, 18 Dec. 1844, Peel papers, Add. MS 40450, ff. 416–17.
[17] Graham to Heytesbury, 17 Feb. 1845, Graham papers.
[18] *Nation*, 31 May 1845.
[19] *Hansard*, lxxx. 377–80; Repeal Assoc. meeting, 17 July, *Nation*, 19 July 1845.
[20] Fergal McGrath, *Newman's University Idea and Reality*, p. 77.
[21] Stanley to Peel, 18 Feb. 1844, Peel papers, Add. MS 40468, ff. 182–7.

without a denominational character, but providing separate religious instruction.[22]

Having abandoned the suggestions for altering Maynooth or the existing constitution of Dublin University, the Government was left with a plan for provincial colleges which owed much to the pioneering work of Thomas Wyse and the recommendations of the 1838 parliamentary committee on education in Ireland.[23] The Government, however, contemplated establishing institutions more akin to universities than the colleges Wyse appears to have had in mind.[24] The problem of the place of religion in the new foundations remained and Peel stated his attitude clearly when he wrote to Graham, at the end of December: 'I agree with Lord Heytesbury that the attempt to connect chapels with the new colleges would involve us in great embarrassment. Ample means of attending existing places of worship in the neighbourhood of the college and direct encouragement to attend are all I think we can hope to accomplish'.[25]

The Government had to consider not merely Catholic but Presbyterian and Episcopalian interests as well. The problem of even deciding on a site for the Ulster college, as between the Presbyterian case for Belfast and the Catholic and Episcopalian for Armagh, was to illustrate the complexity of the problems which had to be overcome. The Government decided to meet its difficulties as best it could, by providing funds to establish three colleges without religious tests of any kind and leaving the endowment of chairs of theology to private benefactors.[26]

Irish reactions to the bill varied widely. As with the Bequests Act, the Catholic hierarchy were divided. The moderate minority were inclined to favour a conditional acceptance of it, while the others, led by MacHale, firmly resolved to reject

[22] Memorandum by Graham, 12 Apr. 1844, Peel papers, Add. MS 40470, ff. 197–8.
[23] *Copy of a letter to the Right Honourable Lord Viscount Morpeth from Thomas Wyse, esq. relative to the Establishment and Support of Provincial Colleges in Ireland*, H.C. 1843 (446), li, 339–46.
[24] *Hansard*, lxxxi. 500.
[25] Peel to Graham, 27 Dec. 1844, Graham papers.
[26] Peel to Graham, 6 Sept. 1845, Peel papers, Add. MS 40451, ff. 255–6; T. W. Moody and J. C. Beckett, *Queen's, Belfast*, i. 84–98; *Hansard*, lxxxi. 1037–43.

it. The Government's fear that the measure would encounter opposition from the Catholic clergy was soon justified.[27] On May 23, meeting in Dublin under the chairmanship of Archbishop Murray, the bishops adopted an agreed memorial to the Lord Lieutenant asking that a 'fair proportion' of the professors and office holders in the colleges should be Catholics approved of by the local bishops and that instruction of Catholic students in history, logic, metaphysics, moral philosophy, geology, and anatomy should be entrusted to Catholic professors.[28] They required other safeguards too; that there should be paid chaplains appointed to the colleges and that stringent regulations should be made to ensure the dismissal of any teacher or college officer guilty of attempting to undermine the religious faith of any student. But the memorial was essentially a compromise made between the moderates and the friends of MacHale. Its language was ambiguous. It did not reject the scheme but put forward recommendations which if adopted would have made the bill a very different one from what Peel and Graham contemplated.[29]

That this cautious memorial, though its adoption was seconded at the bishops' meeting by MacHale, did not express his viewpoint effectively, is shown by his open letter to Peel of June 7. In it he denounced the Colleges Bill as an 'infidel and slavish and demoralising scheme'.[30] In contrast, Archbishops Crolly and Murray both seemed prepared at least to give the bill a trial if amended.[31] To meet the moderate Catholic objections, Graham introduced amendments enabling residential halls, under religious control, to be established in conjunction with the colleges and provisions were also introduced to ensure that the local Catholic bishop would be included in the board of visitors along with representatives of the other churches.[32] These amendments did not satisfy O'Connell, nor did they satisfy MacHale. In September, MacHale and seventeen other members of the hierarchy issued a fresh protest reiterating their

[27] Graham to Heytesbury, 10 May 1845, Graham papers.

[28] *Nation*, 31 May 1845.

[29] Peel to Graham, 27 May [1845], Graham papers.

[30] MacHale to Peel, 7 June 1845, *Nation*, 14 June, 1845.

[31] Graham to Heytesbury, 4 June 1845, Graham papers; *Hansard*, lxxxi. 630–1; *Morning Herald*, 19 Aug. 1845.

[32] *Hansard*, lxxxi. 1037–43.

belief that the provincial colleges would be dangerous to faith and morals.[33] Archbishop Crolly disassociated himself fully from the new protest, which he said had been prepared by MacHale during Crolly's absence from a meeting at Maynooth. In refusing to adopt MacHale's resolution, Crolly was not alone, for Archbishop Murray and seven other bishops followed his example.[34]

The division within the hierarchy followed, therefore, much the same pattern as in the year previously. But the novel element in the Irish reaction to the bill was the controversy it produced within the ranks of the repeal movement. The Young Irelanders at once welcomed the principle of the bill, indeed, they had long pressed for some such measure.[35] They saw in it a potent means of bringing young Irishmen, regardless of their religious convictions, together: 'whatsoever plan will strengthen the soul of Ireland with knowledge, and knit the sects of Ireland in liberal and trusting friendship, will be better for us than if corn and wine were scattered from every cloud'.[36] They did find fault with the bill, but only with details, particularly the concentration of the power of appointment to professorships in the hands of the Crown and they argued that more could be done to provide religious instruction without any interference with the spirit of the measure.[37]

O'Connell's views on the bill were not lacking in inconsistencies. When the question of university education came under discussion in the Repeal Association in December 1844, he gave as his opinion that in any future college, 'education in literature and religion should not be separated, but each persuasion should have the means of partaking of both . . .'.[38] Again, when he did go to Parliament to speak on the bill, while stressing that religion should be the basis of all education, he admitted that he still thought a system of mixed education in literature and science would be proper, 'but with regard to

---

[33] *Nation*, 27 Sept. 1845.
[34] Fremantle to Peel, 20 Sept. 1845, Peel papers, Add. MS 40476, ff. 448–51.
[35] *Nation*, 3 Aug. 1844.
[36] *Nation*, 17 May 1845.
[37] Repeal Assoc. meeting, 12 May, *Nation*, 17 May 1845.
[38] Repeal Assoc. meeting, 2 Dec., *Nation*, 7 Dec. 1844.

religious education, I think that each denomination . . . should be educated by their respective religious instructors'.[39]

If O'Connell's criticism of the bill, in the Commons, represented his considered opinion, then there was little at issue between him and Davis, Gavan Duffy, John Blake Dillon, and the other Young Irelanders. Yet the Colleges Bill provoked the sharpest dissensions in both the general committee of the Association and at its public meetings.[40] O'Connell's first important reference to the bill, on May 12, was made before the bishops had met. Only the southern, largely Catholic colleges, he argued, would lack adequate facilities for religious instruction. In Belfast, the Presbyterians already had their own independent divinity school and its professors, in receipt of a state subsidy, could easily become associated with the work of the new Ulster college. In Dublin, Trinity College was to retain its Protestant character.[41] Before the end of the month, he had reached the conclusion that 'the Protestants should have one college, that the Prebyterians should have another and that the Catholics should have another . . .'.[42] For O'Connell, however, the greatest practical injustice in the existing scheme was that no provision was made by the Government for the endowment of chairs of Catholic theology in close association with any one of the colleges.

There seems to be some grounds for Gavan Duffy's charges that O'Connell's son, John, did much to create an atmosphere of tension within the Association by sharply criticising all who favoured the bill. In taking an uncompromising stand against the measure, John O'Connell certainly drew upon himself the fire of the equally uncompromising Young Irelanders.[43] Davis, fearful of the creation of a Catholic ascendancy in place of the old Protestant one, was apt to see in the attitude of the O'Connells the beginnings of a priests' party.[44] But the bickerings and

[39] *Hansard*, lxxxi. 1089–98.

[40] Gavan Duffy, *Young Ireland*, pp. 249–59; Denis Gwynn, *O'Connell, Davis and the Colleges Bill*, pp. 58–72.

[41] Repeal Assoc. meeting, 12 May, *Nation*, 17 May 1845.

[42] Repeal Assoc. meeting, 26 May, *Nation*, 31 May 1845.

[43] Gavan Duffy, *Young Ireland*, 249–59; *Hansard*, lxxxi. 1059–63; Davis to Smith O'Brien, 15 June [1845], Smith O'Brien papers, vol. 432, no. 884.

[44] Davis to Smith O'Brien, [Aug. 1845], Smith O'Brien papers, vol. 432, no. 895.

recriminations which culminated in an open clash in the Association, on May 26, had deeper roots than the immediate dispute over the Colleges Bill.

In a letter to Smith O'Brien, in July, Davis indicated what was causing him dissatisfaction: 'between unaccounted funds, bigotry, billingsgate . . . crude and contradictory dogmas and unrelieved stupidity, any course and any system could be ruined'.[45] But there were other minor sources of friction too. O'Connell's criticisms of American slavery, for example, was seen by the Young Irelanders as a needless insult to possible allies in America.[46] Again, while Smith O'Brien strove to keep a middle course in the Colleges Bill dispute, he soon found a grievance of his own when O'Connell brought forward a series of resolutions in the Association in favour of household suffrage and the secret ballot. These suggestions, he feared, would have an adverse effect on any prospective converts to nationalism from the Conservative ranks.[47]

The O'Connells and their supporters, in turn, found the demands and the criticisms of the minority group irritating. Commenting on Smith O'Brien's objections to O'Connell's proposals, the Secretary of the Repeal Association summed up the attitude of O'Connell's close friends on many other issues too when he wrote, 'There is assuredly a difference of opinion on these matters between Mr O'Brien and a majority of the people of Ireland . . . '.[48]

The final division within the Repeal Association was postponed for another year, but the unhappiness and discord of 1845 reflected a growing purposelessness. Between January and the debates of the summer very little happened in the repeal movement. O'Connell remained in Ireland, it is true, and did not attend Parliament until the Colleges Bill came up for debate, but with the abandonment of the federalist plan he had no new policy to offer the nation.[49] Yet there were signs of a growing

[45] Davis to Smith O'Brien, 26 July 1845, Smith O'Brien papers, vol. 435, no. 1371.

[46] Repeal Assoc. meeting, 4 Apr., *Nation*, 5 Apr. 1845.

[47] Smith O'Brien to Davis, 30 July 1845, Gavan Duffy, *Thomas Davis, the Memoirs of an Irish Patriot*, p. 314.

[48] T. M. Ray to Maurice O'Connell, 31 July 1845, N.Lib.Ir.MS, O'Connell papers.

[49] Repeal Assoc. meeting, 3 Feb., *Nation*, 8 Feb. 1845.

unrest among the people, due to distress in the rural areas. In the opening months of 1845, agrarian offences were sufficiently numerous and widespread to cause concern in official circles.[50] In another way, too, the country was uneasy: Peel's policy had irritated the Irish Orange and ultra-Tory connection. In the northern counties, Orange activities were recommenced, with the open support of great landowners such as Lords Roden, Erne, and Enniskillen, while the Tory press complained that the Irish Conservatives were being deserted by the Government.[51] The Repeal Association did little to exploit these developments for its own purposes. An attempt was, indeed, made to organise large public meetings during the summer and autumn, and the grief felt at the unexpected death of Thomas Davis, in September, brought repealers together for a time. But though the Government feared a resumption of the monster meeting agitation, the attempt to rouse popular interest was short-lived.[52]

Attention had been largely concentrated, therefore, on secondary reforms and the controversies they provoked. But at the beginning of 1845, the Devon Commission, which had been constituted, in November 1843, to enquire into the law and practice relating to the occupation of land in Ireland, finally submitted its report. It was a rather timid statement offering few constructive suggestions on which effective legislative action could be taken. The recommendations were, for the most part, concerned with minor points in the land law and in the financing of drainage and land reclamation schemes, but in one or two of their recommendations the commissioners touched on more vital and controversial matters. They suggested that compensation for permanent improvements should be paid to tenants on the termination of their interests in the land. This they felt would preserve the best features of tenant-right while avoiding the creation of a kind of co-proprietorship in a farm, which,

[50] Heytesbury to Peel, 6 Feb. 1845, Peel papers, Add. MS 40479, ff. 285-6; Peel to Graham, 26 Mar. 1845, Peel papers, Add. MS 40451, ff. 49-50.

[51] Peel to Graham, 21 Aug. 1845, Peel papers, Add. MS 40451, ff. 211-12; Graham to Peel, 8 Sept. 1845, Peel papers, Add. MS 40451, ff. 263-6; *Nation*, 16 Aug. 1845; *Dublin Evening Mail*, 6 Oct. 1845.

[52] *Nation*, 27 Sept. 1845; Graham to Peel, 30 Sept. 1845, Peel papers, Add. MS 40451, ff. 327-30.

they feared, unrestricted tenant-right might imply.[53] If the report was something of an anti-climax, the great body of evidence on social conditions which the commissioners collected and published did achieve some good. By drawing attention to the miserable plight of the labourers and cottiers, the evidence helped to make it clear that much more was involved in any solution of the Irish land question than merely the task of giving some security of possession to the tenant farmers.[54]

Irish opinion was, however, disappointed with the Commission's report. The *Nation* commented that it proposed 'little measures for a mighty end', and the Tory *Dublin Evening Mail* felt that it did not give enough attention to the problem of agrarian outrages.[55] In Britain, *The Times* considered that the commissioners could have been bolder in recommending action that might be regarded by some as interfering with the landlords' rights and the *Economist* complained that while the Commission made some useful suggestions, there was none 'that could not have been made before the Commission began to sit as well as now'.[56]

The response of the Government to the report was prompt but cautious. Early in June 1845, Lord Stanley introduced in the Lords the Compensation to Tenants (Ireland) Bill, which was to have been the first of a number of measures based on the recommendations of the Commission. Stanley told the Lords that, 'none of the recommendations went so much to the root of the social condition of the people of Ireland as the providing greater security for the industrious tenant'.[57] He, therefore, proposed that dispossessed tenants should be compensated, at a rate diminishing over a period of 20 to 30 years, for permanent improvements to farm buildings or lands. The bill contemplated, in the case of a dispute, compensation only for such improvements as had been sanctioned by special commissioners. These would have powers to assess the value of unexhausted improvements when a tenant was evicted.

[53] *Report from Her Majesty's Commissioners of Inquiry into the State of the Law and Practice in Respect to the Occupation of Land in Ireland,* H.C. 1845 (605), xix. 1–56.
[54] Ibid.
[55] *Nation,* 22 Feb. 1845; *Dublin Evening Mail,* 26 Feb. 1845.
[56] *The Times,* 24 Feb. 1845; *Economist,* iii (22 Feb. 1845). 178.
[57] *Hansard,* lxxx. 226–7.

The bill was a minor measure which gave no guarantee of any security of possession to the tenant, for, as the Marquis of Clanricarde pointed out, unless the landlord consented to the improvements, the service of an improvements notice by the tenant 'would be a notice to quit'.[58] Yet the limited compulsory powers in the bill aroused some anxiety among the Irish peers, a number of whom joined in a remonstrance against the principle of the measure.[59] Criticism of the bill cut across party divisions. Clanricarde and Londonderry, for example, both opposed it, while in the Commons, Russell considered it extraordinary that a Government valuation commission should be interposed between landlord and tenant.[60] The Lords showed their dissatisfaction by sending the bill to a committee, and the Government, faced with the possibility of sustained opposition to the bill, decided not to go on with it, Peel promising that another bill 'growing out of the report' would be brought in early in the next session.[61]

Though the bill was dropped with little resistance on the Government's part Lord Stanley's speech introducing it nevertheless remains an important survey of the economic position in Ireland on the eve of the famine. For Stanley the source of much of the evil in the Irish social system lay in the under-capitalised state of Irish agriculture. The best way to overcome this, he believed, was to encourage the tenant-farmers to improve the land. Unfortunately, neither his own bill nor that introduced by Lord Lincoln in 1846, made any serious contribution to curing the ills he so ably exposed.[62]

[58] Ibid., lxxxi. 1195–9.
[59] Graham to Stanley, 22 June 1845, Graham papers.
[60] *Hansard*, lxxxi. 1195–9.
[61] Ibid., lxxxii. 1454–81.
[62] Ibid., lxxxi. 211–29.

V

THE THREAT OF FAMINE
1845–6

IN THE AUTUMN OF 1845 came the first reports of a potato
blight in Ireland. Already in early September the disease had
been observed in many districts in the east and south-east, and
by the end of October the official returns indicate that the
blight had established itself firmly in at least eleven counties.
From the outset, however, there was considerable difficulty
experienced in estimating the true extent of the disease, since
potato losses were not uniform even within relatively limited
areas.[1]

Nationalists and reformers in Ireland came to see in the
potato failure yet another and more disastrous demonstration of
the fundamental defects in the national economy. In time the
successive potato failures and the hardships that accompanied
them brought new and radical complications into Irish
politics. The most immediate political consequence of the
partial failure of 1845–6 was to be observed, however, in Britain
rather than in Ireland. In Britain, the Irish food crisis quickly
brought into question the whole future of agricultural protection.

By the autumn of 1845, Peel appears to have been satisfied

[1] Graham to Peel, 18, 28 Sept. 1845, Peel papers, Add. MS 40451, ff.
286–7, 318–9; P.R.O.I., Relief Commission papers (Constabulary Reports),
20–5, 28 Oct. 1845; *Dublin Evening Post*, 7, 23 Sept. 1845.

that the restrictions on the importation of grain had little to recommend them in practice. The decision he came to in the closing months of 1845 represented the final maturing of a conviction which had led him away from the rigid protectionist position first to advocate, and then to implement a reduced import duty on grain, and in the end virtually to sweep away the remaining duties on grain in the early summer of 1846. That final decision to abandon agricultural protection was, however, taken at the cost of serious division within the ranks of Peel's own supporters.[2]

The partial failure of the Irish potato crop proved a factor of critical importance in the formulation of Peel's plans in the closing months of 1845. Peel argued that, if the failure proved to be so extensive as to require a suspension of the Corn Laws even for a short period, then it would be politically impossible to restore the duties in an unmodified form, or to resist their final extinction in the near future.[3] It was important, therefore, for Peel to know what was the true position in Ireland. The constabulary were directed on September 16 to report on the state of the potato crop and in October a scientific commission was established to discover the causes of the disease and to suggest practical remedies.[4] Any immediate moves that might complicate the political situation were, however, avoided. Peel rejected, for example, Lord Heytesbury's proposal that the export of potatoes should be prohibited, and at a cabinet meeting, on October 31, he contended that it would be wrong to advance public funds for relief works while refusing to allow the duty-free importation of food.[5]

Despite strong opposition from the landed interest in the

[2] Graham to Heytesbury, 15 Oct. 1845, Peel papers, Add. MS 40479, ff. 499–506; H. Goulburn to Peel, 27 Nov. 1845, Peel papers, Add. MS 40445, ff. 276–9.

[3] Peel to Fremantle, 7 Nov. 1845, Peel papers, Add. MS 40476, ff. 530–1; Peel to Goulburn, 18 Oct. 1845, Peel papers, Add. MS 40445, ff. 228–31; Memorandum by Sir Robert Peel, 26 Nov. 1845, *Memoirs by . . . Peel*, ii. 182–4.

[4] Graham to Peel, 18 Sept. 1845, Peel papers, Add. MS 40451, ff. 410–13; P.R.O.I., Relief Commission papers (Constabulary Office), 16 Sept. 1845; Graham to Peel, 20 Oct. 1845, Peel papers, Add. MS 40451, ff. 410–13; Heytesbury to Peel, 24 Oct. 1845, *Memoirs by . . . Peel*, ii. 133–4.

[5] Ibid., ii. 141–8.

cabinet, Peel persisted in his efforts to secure approval for an Order in Council remitting the duty on grain to a nominal sum. This temporary expedient was to have been followed by a substantial modification of the protective system in the New Year.[6] As late as the end of November, Peel was still seeking for some basis of unity within his cabinet, but the opinion was widely held that he would fail in his attempt. Such a view seemed justified when, unable to satisfy Lord Stanley, the Duke of Buccleuch and the protectionists, Peel requested Queen Victoria to relieve him of office. This she did with 'marks of confidence and approbation' on December 5.[7]

The way was now open for Lord John Russell to take office with a minority ministry, but circumstances, for the moment, defeated his expectations. He encountered serious difficulties in reconciling conflicting claims to office among his own supporters, while powerful Whig magnates like Melbourne and Bessborough were still inclined to favour the old Whig policy of a moderate fixed duty rather than a full repeal of the Corn Laws. In the circumstances it was not surprising that Russell made it quite clear that he could not undertake to form a government without very explicit assurances of support from Sir Robert Peel. These assurances Peel was not prepared to give.[8] The protectionists having indicated that they did not contemplate forming a ministry, that could only be short lived, it was inevitable that Queen Victoria would recall Peel. Recalled on December 19, he formed the government which was to carry the repeal of the Corn Laws at the cost of the unity of the party he had led to power.[9]

The early reports of the potato blight had produced few indications of alarm in Ireland. It was only slowly, almost imperceptibly, that what proved to be the famine came to occupy anything like a central place in Irish politics. Except

[6] Ibid., ii. 158–9; Peel to Stanley, 5 Nov. 1845, ibid., ii. 162–3; *The Times*, 4 Dec. 1845.

[7] *Memoirs by . . . Peel*, ii. 221–2, 223–6.

[8] Graham to Lord John Russell, 12 Dec. 1845, ibid., ii. 226–8; Lord John Russell to Queen Victoria, 16 Dec. 1845, ibid., ii. 238–40; Lord Grey to Russell, 19 Dec. 1845, Russell papers, P.R.O. 30/22/4; *The Greville Memoirs* (2nd part), ii. 393–4.

[9] Peel to Queen Victoria, 17 Dec. 1845, *Memoirs by . . . Peel*, ii. 240–1; Parker, *Sir Robert Peel*, iii, 248–9.

for the half-hearted espousal of the anti-Corn Law cause, very largely as a gesture to English reformist opinion, and the demand for the closing of the ports to the export of food, the remedies put forward by nationalists were simply the economic medicines they had long prescribed as cures for the ills of the country. The potato failure they regarded, quite correctly, as a social evil that owed its real importance to the poverty of the people and the bankrupt condition of Irish agricultural society. The political crisis in Britain did, however, have some political repercussions in Ireland. O'Connell, for example, saw in the events there a sure sign that the Whigs would inevitably return to power, while the Irish Tory opposition to Peel became increasingly vocal, especially as it had now, on the protection issue, a common grievance to share with a large section of the English Conservative party.

Another symptom of uneasiness in Ireland was the decision of Dublin Corporation, on October 21, to set up a special committee to enquire into the causes of the potato failure. Though this committee was subsequently enlarged to represent the liberal elements among the citizens of the city, it was from the outset very much under Daniel O'Connell's influence. It was, for example, on his suggestion that it was decided to send a deputation to Lord Heytesbury to urge on him the necessity of restricting the use of grain in brewing and distilling, and of putting some control on the export of foodstuffs.[10]

The Lord Lieutenant could not very well refuse to receive such a deputation but in agreeing to meet them he put himself in a somewhat difficult position. He had been instructed by Graham to say nothing beyond promising to refer the deputation's proposals to the Government. He was to assure them, too, that the Government was anxious to help the people in any way it could.[11] With the cabinet divided on the Corn Laws, this cautious attitude was not surprising, but it left the deputation of citizens dissatisfied. O'Connell made good use of the opportunity to transform what had been a mere *ad hoc* committee into a permanent and, in theory, non-political organisation, to be known as the Mansion House Committee.[12]

[10] *Nation*, 25 Oct. 1845.
[11] Graham to Heytesbury, 31 Oct. 1845, Graham papers.
[12] *Dublin Evening Post*, 4 Nov. 1845.

This committee, in practice, remained essentially liberal and reformist in character, and so provided, for a time at least, a convenient meeting place for Whig and repealer.[13]

The Mansion House Committee was not destined to achieve any great political significance, but it served as a useful clearing house for information relating to the spread of the potato blight, and it helped to contradict the protectionist claim that there was no serious food crisis in Ireland. Its opportunities for political action were limited, since by December it was only too evident that Peel was quite determined to act on the assumption that there was danger of a famine in Ireland.

O'Connell clearly counted on an early general election and on a victory for the Whigs. This possibility and the fear of a serious food shortage had the effect of reinforcing O'Connell's realistic attitude. 'If I had only the alternative of keeping the people alive or giving up the repeal, I would give up the repeal . . .', he declared. He was, however, careful to add that the Whigs had not asked him to make any such choice.[14] O'Connell argued that nothing could be expected from Peel and the Tories, while in contrast much could be 'squeezed out' of the Whigs.[15] Speaking at a meeting of the Repeal Association on December 15, he rejoiced at what appeared to be the final collapse of the Peel ministry, because, at last, the people's food would be safeguarded. In substance, O'Connell's argument had changed little since 1841.[16]

An alliance with the Whigs seemed to offer an escape from the political deadlock of 1845. An understanding between O'Connell and his lifelong opponent, Peel, still remained impossible, and the famine danger intensified rather than diminished the suspicion between them. In association with the Whigs O'Connell might exercise some influence, isolated he was lost. A franchise reform had to come before he could be assured of a reasonably large parliamentary following. From Peel, as experience had shown, he could expect little in this respect, from the Whigs he might reasonably hope for some

[13] *Nation*, 8 Nov. 1845.
[14] Ibid.
[15] Daniel O'Connell to Smith O'Brien, 20 Dec. 1845, Smith O'Brien papers, vol. 435, no. 1445.
[16] *Nation*, 20 Dec. 1845.

concessions.[17] It was hardly surprising, in the circumstances, that O'Connell, in outlining the conditions for co-operation with the Whigs, should have placed particular stress on the importance of franchise reform and the need for improvement in the structure of municipal government in Ireland.[18] Except on the issue of the repeal of the Act of Union, O'Connell was confident that he could make some progress with Lord John Russell.[19]

This question of O'Connell's future relations with the Whigs thus became the dominant theme in political discussions in the winter of 1845–6. The problem was almost as old as the repeal movement itself, and co-operation with Whigs or federalists not pledged to repeal had already led to more than one passage of arms between O'Connell and his followers.[20] Now, to meet the threat of a Whig alliance, the Young Irelanders advocated a policy of frank defiance towards the Tories and studied aloofness towards the Whigs.[21]

O'Connell's answer to his critics was that the feeding of the people was the most urgent immediate task and it could best be accomplished by ousting Peel from power. Cooperation with the Whigs to achieve this end was possible, he argued, without endangering the repeal cause.[22] In the circumstances, O'Connell's approach had the advantage of appearing to be a positive one, unlike the Young Irelanders' policy of non-cooperation, which could only have been effective politically if the repeal representation in Parliament had been much stronger and better disciplined than it actually was in 1845–6. The likelihood of a food crisis, and the imminence of Peel's downfall, strengthened O'Connell's hand, especially when it seemed that the radical free traders were about to secure a victory in Britain.[23]

Though Gavan Duffy suggests that disagreement within the Repeal Association, at this time, extended beyond the question of cooperation with the Whigs to the issue of what should be

[17] D. R. Pigot to Russell, 15 Dec. 1845, Russell papers, P.R.O. 30/22/4.
[18] *Nation*, 10 Jan. 1846.
[19] Repeal Assoc. meeting, 15 Dec., *Nation*, 20 Dec. 1845.
[20] See p. 73.
[21] *Nation*, 29 Nov., 6, 20, Dec. 1845.
[22] Repeal Assoc. meeting, 15 Dec., *Nation*, 20 Dec. 1845.
[23] Repeal Assoc. meeting, 8 Dec., *Nation*, 13 Dec. 1845.

done to avert a famine, there is little evidence to sustain such a view.[24] In practice there appears to have been widespread agreement on the kind of measures needed to help the people. To contrast the *Nation*'s policy on such matters as the need for public works and embargoes on food exports with that put forward by O'Connell seems artificial in the extreme.[25] The issue of what was to happen when the Whigs took office dominated the political controversies within the repeal movement.

In Irish Tory circles the alleged treachery of Peel profoundly disturbed landlord opinion. The Irish landlord's position was not an easy one; he could expect little support or goodwill from the impoverished and exploited tenant-farmers and he received but scant sympathy from the English Whigs and Radicals. The natural allies of the Irish Tories were the protectionists, but in practice they could do little to help the Irish landlords, especially as the Irish Tories in Parliament did not speak with a united voice.[26] Some nine Irish Tories were castigated by the *Dublin Evening Mail*, the Orange journal, for supporting Peel, and on the basis of an analysis made after the general election of 1847 there were fifteen supporters of Peel returned for Irish constituencies and some twenty-five protectionists.[27]

Just as the possibility of the Whigs returning to power had increased the tension within the Repeal Association, so also the break-up of Peels' party weakened the bonds which had secured the body of Irish landlord opinion to English Conservatism. The crisis did not destroy their Conservatism, but it turned many of them temporarily adrift and so introduced yet another disturbing factor into the uncertain political scene of 1846.

Peel's task was a difficult one when he came to face Parliament in February 1846. His majority, if one were to exist, depended on the goodwill of the Whigs, while the protectionists were both strong and determined. To neutralise his enemies as far as possible, Peel resolved to proceed with three questions which he regarded as inter-related and forming a compact whole, namely, the substantial repeal of the Corn Laws, famine

[24] C. Gavan Duffy, *Four years of Irish history*, pp. 43–4.
[25] Duffy, op. cit., p. 17; *Freeman's Journal*, 16 Dec. 1845; *Nation*, 6 Dec. 1845.
[26] *The Times*, 19 Feb., 2 Apr. 1846.
[27] *Dublin Evening Mail*, 2 Mar. 1846; *Dublin Evening Post*, 24 Aug. 1847.

relief measures for Ireland, and a bill to ensure the preservation of public order in Ireland.

For Peel and Graham the maintenance of peace and order in Ireland became a rather uncertain and alarming problem towards the end of 1845. Apart altogether from the possibility of a food shortage provoking widespread unrest in rural areas, Peel feared that O'Connell, encouraged by the attempts to revive the repeal agitation in September, might embark on a new popular campaign.[28] To complicate matters, the Ulster Orangemen were showing greater signs of restlessness and of dissatisfaction with the Government's religious policy. The possibility of clashes between Orangemen and repealers, and the embarrassing question of what should be done with Conservative magistrates who participated in Orange demonstrations, filled Graham with despondency.[29] Though neither the Prime Minister nor Graham was prepared to go as far as the Duke of Wellington in urging strong measures, Peel believed that it was necessary to take timely action to meet any increase in agrarian crimes, and to prevent clashes at meetings and during processions between Orange supporters and the repealers.[30] But while the task of drafting an effective processions bill proved technically impossible, the Protection of Life Bill was finally included in the Government's legislative programme.[31] Peel hoped to integrate Irish and British needs, and to make the Irish coercion bill a logical concomitant of the other measures he intended to bring forward. Throughout the protracted debates of 1846, he constantly insisted that the state of Ireland and the success of his earlier tariff reforms justified in themselves the virtual abolition of agricultural protection, but that relief measures would be of little value if lawlessness prevailed in Ireland.[32]

The unrelenting protectionist opposition to the repeal of the

[28] Peel to Graham, 28 Sept. 1846, Peel papers, Add. MS 40451, ff. 318–19; Graham to Peel, 3 Oct. 1845, Peel papers, Add. MS 40451, ff. 350–1.

[29] Graham to Peel, 2 Oct. 1845, Peel papers, Add. MS 40451, ff. 339–42; Graham to Peel, 14 Nov. 1845, Peel papers, Add. MS 40452, ff. 15–22.

[30] Graham to Peel, 3 Oct. 1845, Peel papers, Add. MS 40451, ff. 350–1; Peel to Graham, 5 Oct. 1845, Graham papers; Peel to Graham, 3 Dec. 1845, Peel papers, Add. MS 40452, ff. 46–51.

[31] Graham to Heytesbury, 6 Jan. 1846, Graham papers.

[32] *Hansard*, lxxxiii. 1–5, 81.

Corn Laws dominated the debates in Parliament. The Whigs, embarrassed at having to support a measure not their own, remained largely silent while the Irish Liberal and O'Connellite members took little interest in any measure except the coercion bill. This measure, the Protection of Life (Ireland) Bill was by no means unique, though its provisions were severe. The Government spokesmen argued that the bill was necessary because of the decided increase in crime in Ireland. In 1845 the total number of crimes against property and the public peace had amounted to 5,281 offences, as compared with 3,103 in 1844. Both St Germans in the Lords and Graham in the Commons agreed that the primary source of these crimes in Ireland was agrarian unrest directly connected with the unsatisfactory system of land tenure.[33] It is an interesting comment on the character of Irish society that the counties responsible for the increase in agrarian crime were not those along the poverty-stricken western seaboard but counties such as Limerick, Tipperary, Roscommon and Cavan, where the people were still sufficiently spirited to resist the efforts of the landlords to resume possession of the better land.[34]

The authorities evidently feared that the partial failure of the potato crop would be followed by a widespread refusal to pay rents on the part of the small farmers. The bill was, however, an admission at a critical time that no immediate improvement could be expected in the social state of Ireland. Under the Protection of Life (Ireland) Bill, additional police could be drafted into proclaimed areas, a rigid curfew could be imposed, and collective fines levied to compensate victims of outrages.[35] The provision that aroused most dissatisfaction in Ireland was that providing the punishment of fifteen years' transportation for breach of the curfew. In the Lords the bill encountered little opposition. In the Commons it was otherwise.

In contrast to the indifference displayed by the Irish repeal members towards the actual relief measures, the coercion bill seemed to galvanise the Repeal Association into a new activity.

[33] Ibid., lxxxv. 333–60.
[34] *Evidence taken before Her Majesty's Commissioners of Inquiry into the State of the Law and Practice in respect to the Occupation of Land in Ireland*, pt. ii, H.C., 1845 (616), xx. 636, 788–9.
[35] *Memoirs . . . by Peel*, ii. 302–5; *Hansard*, lxxxv. 333–60.

A meeting of Irish members of Parliament was held in Dublin, on January 23, and O'Connell indicated that he would oppose any coercive measures unless they were accompanied by remedial legislation.[36] This firm attitude complicated Russell's position. The Whig peers favoured the bill, and Russell himself appears to have considered that some new police legislation was needed, though along different and more moderate lines than the Government's bill.[37] The strongest weapon the Irish repealers had was their ability to impede the passage of the Corn Importation Bill, by prolonging the debate on the coercion bill and thereby intensifying the general feeling of uncertainty.

Russell did not want to create, in March or April, if he could possibly avoid it, a situation in which he would have to form a government dependent on Radical and Irish support for its existence.[38] He therefore hesitated to cultivate any close association with the protectionists lest he forfeit Peel's goodwill.[39] But he could not at the same time afford to ignore the Irish attitude, for in opposing the bill the repealers were joined by the other Irish Liberal members.[40] Russell's solution of his difficulty was to agree to the first reading of the coercion bill, though he was careful to reserve to himself the right to raise objections to some aspects of the bill at a later stage.[41] The Irish, however, disliked any compromise arrangement which would allow the Corn Laws to be disposed of first, because they feared that, with the Corn Laws out of the way, Peel would be in a far stronger position to press his coercion measure through the House.[42]

At a meeting of Irish repeal and Whig members, on April 4, O'Connell strongly denounced the English Radicals for not playing a more effective part in resisting coercion in Ireland, and he went so far as to say that, if the English free traders did

[36] *Nation*, 24 Jan. 1846.
[37] Lord Clarendon to Russell, 11 Mar. 1846, Russell papers, P.R.O. 30/22/5; Marquis of Clanricarde to Russell, 11 Mar. 1846, Russell papers, P.R.O. 30/22/5; Arbuthnot to Peel, 5 Apr. 1846, Peel papers, Add. MS 40484, ff. 292–7.
[38] Russell to Lord Duncannon, 11 Apr. 1846, Russell papers, P.R.O. 30/22/5; Arbuthnot to Peel, 22 Apr. 1846, Parker, *Sir Robert Peel*, iii. 346.
[39] Arbuthnot to Peel, 2 May 1846, Peel papers, Add MS 40484, ff. 311–12.
[40] *Nation*, 28 Mar. 1846; *Hansard*, lxxxv. 289–331.
[41] Ibid., lxxxv. 547–57.
[42] *Nation*, 28 Mar. 1846.

not come forward and oppose the coercion bill, they could expect no further support from him in the struggle against the
Corn Laws.[43] So far as O'Connell was concerned, the Corn Laws
were of secondary importance compared with the coercion
bill.

Even more emphatic was Smith O'Brien's reaction to the
manner in which his country was being used in the Corn Law
dispute. As a nationalist, he felt that Irish interests were being
forgotten; to bring the interminable debates to an end, and to
take Irish affairs out of the realm of party controversy, he wrote
to Lord George Bentinck, the protectionist leader, seeking his
support for a bill which would permit the duty-free importation
of foreign grain until the end of August. This letter had its sequel
in the House of Commons, on April 24, when, in reply to a
question from Smith O'Brien, Bentinck assured the House that,
if the Government and the Irish members considered such a
suspension of any value, he would not oppose it.[44] Coming as it
did so soon after O'Connell's criticisms of the English Radicals,
Smith O'Brien's proposal and Bentinck's answer naturally gave
rise to some speculation. Peel, however, dismissed Smith
O'Brien's suggestion as unacceptable, and O'Connell showed
no disposition to encourage Smith O'Brien in his efforts to
reach some understanding with the Tory protectionists.[45]

With the Irish Liberals and repealers uneasy and rebellious,
Russell might well have found himself in an unpleasant position,
but circumstances favoured him. The Irish had, at least, been
partially successful in their parliamentary tactics. They did not,
it is true, halt the progress of the Corn Law measure, but they
had prolonged the debate on the first reading of the coercion
bill. This in practice meant that if sufficient time were to be
made available for the great Corn Law debate, the discussion on
the coercion bill would have to be postponed. The resulting
delay robbed the bill of that quality of urgency which Peel had
been at pains to emphasise.[46] With the Corn Importation Bill

[43] *Dublin Evening Post*, 4 Apr. 1846.
[44] Smith O'Brien to Lord George Bentinck, 19 Apr. 1846, Smith O'Brien
papers, vol. 436, no. 1551; *Hansard*, lxxxv. 980–90.
[45] *Greville memoirs* (2nd part), ii. 384–5; *Hansard*, lxxxv. 1014–15.
[46] Normanby to Russell, 6 June 1846, Russell papers, P.R.O. 30/22/5;
Arbuthnot to Peel, 7 June 1846, Peel papers, Add. MS 40484, ff. 315–16.

safe, Russell on May 25 opposed the second reading of the coercion bill, which he criticised as being excessively harsh in its provisons.[47] The protectionists, bent on revenge, resolved to vote with the Whigs and the Irish repealers against the bill, on the ground that, if Peel really considered the Irish situation so dangerous, he should have sacrificed the repeal of the Corn Laws to the coercion measure.[48] On June 25, the free trade bill was passed by a House of Lords unprepared for a struggle, and on the same day, the Government was defeated in the Commons on the second reading of the Protection of Life Bill by the substantial majority of 73 votes.[49]

These closely interwoven debates on the Corn Laws and coercion are important because they determined the setting in which the social problems of Ireland were considered. In the tense, acrimonious months between February and June there was little objective discussion of these problems. Instead, the question of the reality and the extent of the potato failure became almost a side-issue in a political contest which had little to do with fundamental Irish needs. Yet, despite the surrounding circumstances, the relief measures adopted by Parliament to meet the short-term problem created by the partial failure of the potato crop were reasonably successful. Because he linked the urgent problem of Irish relief with a highly controversial English question, Peel may have deserved much of the criticism levelled against him by the protectionists. It must, however, be recognised that his government acted with reasonable promptness in bringing forward relief measures despite the distractions of the Corn Law debate.

Already in November a Government relief commission had been established in Dublin. The Public Works (Ireland) Bill was introduced late in January and three other measures, the County Works Presentments (Ireland) Bill, the Drainage (Ireland) Bill, and the Fishery Piers and Harbour (Ireland) Bill followed in the succeeding weeks. The general scheme envisaged by these measures was to provide relief partly from local sources and partly from the imperial Exchequer. From the outset, the opinion was strongly maintained in official circles that the cost of relieving the exceptional distress in Ireland

[47] *Hansard*, lxxxvi. 1201.   [48] Ibid., lxxxvii. 29–37.
[49] Ibid., lxxxvii. 959–61.

should not be met in full from the revenue of the United Kingdom. The assumption was made that the relief of famine victims was analogous to the relief of casual paupers under the Poor Law code, but the Government resisted any temporary extension of the Irish Poor Law to authorise outdoor assistance by the Poor Law guardians lest it became a permanent feature of the Irish relief system. The money advanced by the Treasury was administered by the Special Relief Commission and was made available to local committees.[50]

The Irish reaction to Peel's relief measures was to be critical of their narrow scope and of their lack of generosity in the matter of imperial grants.[51] Among nationalists, there was already a strong feeling that Ireland should not be compelled to seek favours from the British Exchequer. The Treasury, it was considered, should be prepared to employ the tax revenue from Ireland solely to meet Irish needs.[52] Apart, however, from such general criticisms, it is difficult to distinguish any really fundamental objections to the schemes introduced by Peel to meet the first season of famine. O'Connell still sought an absentee tax, but though Peel could not agree to this there was a remarkable degree of unanimity between men so divergent in outlook as O'Connell, Peel and Smith O'Brien in urging the Irish landlords to do their duty.[53]

Apart from the purely emergency legislation to meet the potato failure, Peel had little to offer Ireland in the way of remedial legislation. He had carried through his modest schemes to placate Catholic opinion in 1844 and 1845, but there was no indication that he was prepared, in 1846, to go further and deal with the critical problem of the relations between landlord and tenant in a really comprehensive way. The failure of Peel to find some solution to the Irish land question was just as conspicuous in 1846 as it had been in the previous year.[54] A tenant compensation bill was introduced, but it was

[50] C. E. Trevelyan to Sir R. Routh, 22 Jan. 1846, *Correspondence Explanatory of the Measures adopted by Her Majesty's Government for the Relief of Distress arising from the Failure of the Potato Crop in Ireland*, H.C. 1846 (735), xxxvii. 14–18; *Hansard*, lxxxiv. 780–4; Graham to Heytesbury, 15 Dec. 1845, Graham papers; E. Twisleton to Graham, 21 Dec. 1845, Graham papers.
[51] *Hansard*, xciv. 49–72.   [52] *Nation*, 7 Feb. 1846.
[53] *Hansard*, lxxxiii. 1050–68, lxxxiv. 987–8.
[54] Ibid., lxxxviii. 283–4.

little better than the much criticised measure Lord Stanley had brought forward in 1845. A tenant could secure compensation for improvements he had made in his holding only on the determination of his tenancy, and since no security of tenure was to be given to the tenant he would still remain at the mercy of the arbitrary decisions of his landlord. This feeble bill made its appearance late in the session, and amid the distractions of the time, received scant consideration.[55] When Russell came into office the measure was dropped, and nothing took its place.[56]

Despite the obvious defects in his policy, Peel showed some foresight in his handling of the Irish food question. Though he strove to keep state intervention at a minimum, he did not make the mistake of assuming, as his successors did, that private traders could meet the needs of the people.[57] The importation of Indian corn on the Government's account and the sale of the meal through local relief committees, at a moderate price, did much to check any attempt to exploit the market in the spring and summer of 1846.[58] Despite food riots in April, the indications are that the relief measures and the public works fulfilled their immediate purpose in preventing exceptional suffering during the traditionally 'hungry months' of the summer.[59] Even the *Nation* admitted that the Government had done its best within the framework of the existing social structure.[60]

The food shortage remained a relatively minor issue throughout the summer of 1846, but if expedients had neutralised, for a time, the challenge of famine, Peel went out of office without having accomplished anything to make the Irish people better

[55] Ibid., lxxxvi. 11–17, lxxxvii. 279–94.

[56] Ibid., lxxxviii. 283–4.

[57] Russell to the Duke of Leinster, 17 Oct. 1846, Russell papers, P.R.O. 30/22/5 and G. P. Gooch, *The Later Correspondence of Lord John Russell*, i. 155–8.

[58] *Correspondence explanatory of the Measures adopted by Her Majesty's Government for the Relief of Distress arising from the Failure of the Potato Crop in Ireland*, H.C. 1846 (735), xxxvii. 148–9.

[59] *Nation*, 18 Apr. 1846; Lt. Gen. Blackeney to Lord Somerset, 4 June, 9 June, 5 Sept. 1846, Kilmainham papers, vol. 238, pp. 23, 28, 33.

[60] *Nation*, 15 Aug. 1846. 'I have nothing but gratitude from Ireland for *our* measures of relief' (Peel to Graham, 2 Sept. 1846, Graham papers).

able to meet the calamity that lay ahead of them. In his educational measures and religious policy, in the Devon Commission, and in some of his appointments, he had shown the power of the new spirit in British Conservatism. He had succeeded in narrowing the gap between Whig and Tory where reform in Ireland was concerned. But the great administrator and his lieutenant, Graham, were unable to advance much further. Old enmities and the prejudices of an age remained. And while Peel might regret the rigid economic orthodoxy of his successor's famine policy, in 1846–7, it is significant that Peel and his followers were well content to accept the Government's Irish measures with the minimum of criticism.[61]

[61] Peel to Graham, 30 Dec. 1846, Graham papers.

VI

A SEASON OF CRISIS, 1846–7

∿∿∿∿∿∿∿∿∿∿∿∿∿∿∿∿∿∿∿∿

(1)

IN JULY 1846, the growing unrest within the Repeal Association gave rise to a protracted and at times bitter public controversy between O'Connell and those repealers who saw in nationalism an absolute ideal which should not be the subject of political compromises. The disagreements over federalism and higher education, in 1844–5, had shown how easily disputes on matters of principle could imperil the unity of the repeal movement. From 1844 onwards, it became increasingly obvious that the members of the Young Ireland group were unwilling to trust O'Connell fully in any negotiations with the Whigs or other non-repealers. To defeat any possibility of a compromise with the Whigs, they were resolved to build up an independent force within the Association. By acting together and by resisting O'Connell when necessary, they hoped to lessen Catholic clerical influences and counteract the growing political power of O'Connell's sons.[1] In the circumstances, it is difficult to see how a serious conflict could have been avoided.

While the Young Irelanders were denouncing the folly of a new Whig alliance, O'Connell had made up his mind that some understanding with the Whigs was essential, if he were to exercise any effective influence on state policy.[2] Though there

[1] See p. 88.
[2] D. R. Pigot to Russell, 15 Dec. 1845, Russell papers, P.R.O. 30/22/4.

had been some difficult moments in the Corn Law and coercion bill debates, they did not have any lasting effect on O'Connell's attitude to the Whig alliance, and O'Connell made no secret of his satisfaction at the prospect of the return of the Whigs to power.[3] He may have believed, as he wrote to Smith O'Brien, that Parliament was not particularly well disposed towards passing 'any measure really efficacious for Ireland'; but he nevertheless believed that the chances of good legislation were greater under Russell than under Peel.[4] In this, as events were to prove, O'Connell erred on the side of optimism.

The Young Irelanders did not want to be expelled from the Repeal Association. As long as they were members of it they could at least seek to influence the policy of the one political movement which commanded the support of the Catholic masses of the people. They used their position within the Association, for example, to challenge O'Connell's decision to allow Sheil, the new Master of the Mint in the Russell ministry, to be returned unopposed to Parliament for the Borough of Dungarvan. But such a resistance was precisely the kind of political embarrassment O'Connell was anxious to be rid of in the summer of 1846.[5]

An abortive and long-delayed prosecution of Gavan Duffy, as editor of the *Nation*, for seditious libel in an article published in November 1845, provided O'Connell with the opportunity he required. Following on the prosecution, O'Connell proposed that the Repeal Association, as a legal precaution, should sever all connections with newspapers. More important, he went on to propose that the Association should reassert in definite terms its complete reliance on peaceful and constitutional methods and, as a matter of general principle, its rejection of the use of force for the attainment of political objectives in Ireland or elsewhere.[6]

The universality of O'Connell's proposition was quite unacceptable to his opponents, who argued that the interests of a

[3] Arbuthnot to Peel, 7 June 1846, Peel papers, Add. MS 40484, ff. 315–16.
[4] D. O'Connell to Smith O'Brien, 30 June 1846, Smith O'Brien papers, vol. 437, no. 1648.
[5] D. O'Connell to D. R. Pigot, 8 July 1846, Fitzpatrick, *Correspondence of Daniel O'Connell*, ii. 379.
[6] Minutes of adjourned committee meeting (Repeal Association), 11 July 1846, Smith O'Brien papers, vol. 437, no. 1660.

nation might well require a more militant policy than one of mere constitutional agitation. O'Connell, however, was determined to force the issue and he did not hesitate to make clear his intention. 'I drew up this resolution', he said, 'to draw a marked line between Young and Old Ireland . . . I do not accept the services of any man who does not agree with me both in theory and in practice.'[7] Faced with a choice between submission and withdrawal from the Association, the Young Irelanders decided to reject O'Connell's leadership. Though some of those involved in the secession did not, at first, regard the breach as a complete one, it was, in practice, to mark the end of nominal unity within the repeal movement until the short-lived Irish League was founded in 1848.[8]

The secession had come about for political reasons and throughout the closing years of the repeal movement's history the division between the Repeal Association and the Young Irelanders remained primarily political in character though social developments were to bring new and important factors to beat on the dispute. Contemporaries saw in the events of July 1846 a victory for O'Connell. The Catholic church leaders, when they spoke, made it clear that their sympathies were still with O'Connell, and in the Ireland of the mid-nineteenth century the opinion of the clergy carried much weight among the people of the countryside. This strong O'Connellite feeling among the clergy helped to ensure that support for the Young Irelanders would, in practice, be largely confined to the urban areas.[9] *The Times* summed up the position tersely when it stated that 'Old Ireland has beaten its young rival. The priests have done it'.[10]

Had there been no failure of the potato crop for a second time in the autumn of 1846, the course of political development in Ireland might well have confirmed the victory O'Connell appeared to have won in 1846. But that second and, as it proved, total failure of the crop had a most disturbing effect on

[7] *Nation*, 18 July 1846.

[8] D. O'Connell to Smith O'Brien, 18 July 1846, Smith O'Brien papers, vol. 437, no. 1663; Smith O'Brien to Gavan Duffy, 12 Oct. 1846, N. Lib. Ir. MS 2642, no. 3444; Repeal Assoc. meeting, 17 Aug., *Nation*, 22 Aug. 1846.

[9] C. Gavan Duffy, *Four Years of Irish history*, p. 101.

[10] *The Times*, 13 Aug. 1846.

political calculations. It soon became apparent that little beyond promises and inadequate expedients could be expected from the Russell administration. By early December, as a consequence, O'Connell found himself in the unhappy position of having to denounce in bitter terms the meagreness of the measures adopted by the ministry he had welcomed a few months previously. The folly of division within the repeal movement at such a time seemed only too evident and the demand for reunion among the ordinary supporters of the repeal cause began to assume significant proportions, especially in the larger towns.[11]

After their breach with the Repeal Association, the Young Irelanders, at first, were quite content to accept Smith O'Brien's suggestion that they should concentrate their attention on literary matters. A special section of the *Nation* was, therefore, devoted to articles for the instruction of 'their fellow countrymen in that intellectual and moral discipline that best fits men for freedom'.[12] The pressure to organise, to build up a new political movement, came from outside the inner councils of the Young Irelanders.[13]

In the towns, especially Dublin, Cork and Limerick, where rising food prices and unemployment caused much discontent among the artisan class, opposition to the policy of the Repeal Association, from September onwards, assumed a more concrete form.[14] From Cork came demands for a reunion of the repeal party but it was in Dublin, in October and November, that this new opposition was most formidable. There the majority of the repeal wardens, the keymen of the repeal organisation, adopted a remonstrance protesting against not only the peace resolutions but the Whig alliance as well.[15] These developments challenged the inactivity of the Young Irelanders and though some of them, including Smith O'Brien, were inclined to hang back and merely watch the proceedings in Dublin, others, like Thomas Francis Meagher and Richard

[11] *Nation*, 12 Dec. 1846.
[12] Ibid., 31 Oct. 1846.
[13] Smith O'Brien to Gavan Duffy, 12 Oct. 1846, N. Lib. Ir. MS 2642, no. 3444.
[14] *Freeman's Journal*, 23 Sept. 1846.
[15] *Nation*, 7 Nov. 1846.

O'Gorman, realised the dangerous implications of inactivity.[16] They feared, as O'Gorman wrote, that O'Connell, annoyed by the paucity of the Government's relief measures, might take up more vigorously the national cause while they stood by and did nothing but write newspaper articles.[17]

It was not surprising that several prominent Young Irelanders took part in a meeting, on December 2, organised by the Dublin remonstrants, as the critics of the official policy of the Association were called. The meeting was apparently well supported by working men and the arguments put forward were the familiar ones criticising the policy of the Repeal Association and denying that the Young Irelanders had sought to involve the repeal movement in unconstitutional activities. One important decision, however, was taken. It was resolved

[16] 'I do not consider the present as a favourable moment for inviting the public at large to co-operate with us. The public mind is not yet prepared for such an effort . . .' (Smith O'Brien to Gavan Duffy, 11 Nov. 1846, N. Lib. Ir. MS 2642, no. 3451). R. O'Gorman to Smith O'Brien, 27 Nov. 1846, Smith O'Brien papers, vol. 437, no. 1710. Thomas Francis Meagher (1825–67) was a native of the city of Waterford. His father Thomas Meagher was a wealthy merchant, a repeal M.P. for the city for many years and a former mayor. In the Repeal Association Thomas Francis Meagher won the reputation of being the most effective orator among the Young Irelanders. When a vacancy occurred in the parliamentary representation for Waterford city, in Feb. 1848, Meagher, as a Confederate, contested the seat. It was, however, won by a local Liberal candidate. By inclination attached to the more conservative wing of the Young Ireland party, Meagher nevertheless took a very active part in the events of 1848. He was a member of the Confederate mission to Paris and after his return to Ireland worked hard to organise support for the Young Irelanders in the southeast of the country. After the rising of 1848, he was sentenced to death for high treason, but was subsequently transported to Tasmania. In 1852, having surrendered his ticket-of-leave, he escaped to the United States. During the American Civil War, Meagher served with distinction in the Union forces and rose to the rank of brigadier-general. After the war he was appointed Secretary of Montana Territory, and in 1866 temporary Governor. In July 1867, he was drowned while travelling by boat on the Missouri. The circumstances of the happening are obscure. Richard O'Gorman (1826–95) was a native of Co. Clare, and the son of a prosperous merchant who had been closely associated with the Catholic emancipation agitation. O'Gorman took part in the revolutionary activities of 1848 and subsequently escaped to New York where he set up in practice as a lawyer. He later became a New York state judge.

[17] R. O'Gorman to Smith O'Brien, 27 Nov. 1846, Smith O'Brien papers, vol. 437, no. 1710.

to hold another meeting early in January, when such measures as might prove necessary to recommence the repeal agitation could be adopted.[18]

The Dublin remonstrance meeting produced an immediate reaction in the Repeal Association. At a meeting of the Association, on December 7, Daniel O'Connell dwelt in detail on the sufferings of the people, the want of food and employment and the failure of the Government to deal with famine and distress in an effective way. In order to press the claims of the community on the British Government and Parliament, he argued that two things were necessary. The Irish gentry should join with the urban middle-classes in a great national conference and repeal unity should be restored. For unity's sake he was willing to let a representative committee go into the whole question of the disputed peace resolutions.[19] This friendly gesture on O'Connell's part was well timed. No matter what the outcome of the negotiations might be, the fact would remain that the great Liberator had acted in a magnanimous manner towards his critics.[20]

A conference was arranged between O'Connell and the secessionists who had received his offer with rather mixed feelings. John Blake Dillon, one of the founders of the *Nation*, for example, was particularly anxious for a reconciliation on 'good and honest' terms, particularly as even the Young Irelanders' own supporters regarded O'Connell's gesture as a friendly one made in defiance of his closest advisers.[21] In

---

[18] *Nation*, 5 Dec. 1846.   [19] Ibid., 12 Dec. 1846.

[20] Smith O'Brien to Gavan Duffy, 15 Dec. 1846, N. Lib. Ir. MS 2642, no. 3464.

[21] J. B. Dillon to Smith O'Brien, [Dec. 1846], Smith O'Brien papers, vol. 434, nos. 1298–9. John Blake Dillon (1814–66) was a native of Co. Mayo and a barrister by profession. He took part in the rising of 1848 having satisfied himself that there was no honourable alternative. After the rising he escaped to the United States, but subsequently returning to Ireland, he was elected M.P. for Tipperary in 1865. A man of ability and very much a political realist, he was active in the efforts to resolve the differences between Young Ireland and Daniel O'Connell. On his return to Ireland from America, he opposed extreme courses, especially Fenianism, and in the eighteen-sixties he supported the ultra-moderate National Association which had been founded with the encouragement of Cardinal Paul Cullen, the Archbishop of Dublin. John Blake Dillon's son John was one of the leading figures in the Home Rule movement.

contrast, Smith O'Brien refused even to consider reopening the question of the theoretical validity of using physical force and stayed away from the Dublin conference.[22]

When the representatives met, on December 15, O'Connell soon made it clear that he could not abandon the peace resolutions, though he was quite prepared to restrict their scope to Anglo-Irish relations alone. The Young Irelanders, for their part, wanted such issues as place-hunting, cooperation with the Whigs, and the finances of the Association discussed as well as the peace resolutions. O'Connell, however, contended that such specific questions could only be discussed after the Young Irelanders had accepted the peace resolutions in their modified form and had returned to the Repeal Association.[23] Such a course the Young Irelanders refused to adopt and by demanding a virtual capitulation, when some compromise might have been secured, they let O'Connell win whatever credit there was to be gained.[24] Never again, in 1846–7, did the opposition to the Repeal Association assume among the urban population so threatening a form as it did in November and December 1846.

The year ended with the repeal movement still divided and unprepared to meet the problems created by the famine. Despite the encouragement given to them by the remonstrance meeting in Dublin, the Young Irelanders, even late in December, were still rather hesitant about launching a new political movement. With the foundation, early in January 1847, of the Irish Confederation, they did provide themselves with an organisation, but it was perhaps characteristic of the mood prevalent at the time that Smith O'Brien was doubtful about the wisdom of accepting the leadership of any new movement.[25] O'Connell, for his part, had to admit that the Whigs had

[22] Smith O'Brien to Gavan Duffy, 13 Dec. 1846, N. Lib. Ir. MS 2642, no. 3463; J. B. Dillon to Smith O'Brien, [Dec. 1846], Smith O'Brien papers, vol. 434, no. 1299.

[23] *Nation*, 15 Dec. 1846.

[24] Smith O'Brien to Gavan Duffy, 24 Dec. 1846, N. Lib. Ir. MS 2642, no. 3468.

[25] J. B. Dillon to Smith O'Brien, 19 Dec. [1846], Smith O'Brien papers, vol. 434, no. 1301; Smith O'Brien to Gavan Duffy, 24 Dec. 1846, N. Lib. Ir. MS 2642, no. 3468; Gavan Duffy to Smith O'Brien, 26 Dec. [1846], Smith O'Brien papers, vol. 434, no. 1303; *Nation*, 2 Jan. 1847.

brought with them not an era of generous measures for Ireland, but only one of inadequate expedients and humiliating pauper relief.

(II)

Lord John Russell's return to office was received with satisfaction in Ireland, at least in Whig and moderate repeal circles. O'Connell, despite some privately expressed fears, expected to gain concessions from the Whigs, while the repeal press, excepting the *Nation*, welcomed the formation of the new administration.[26] The Prime Minister, however, assumed office under distinctly unfavourable circumstances. Russell had helped to force Peel out of office, but he remained very much under the shadow of his predecessor. Peel's striking tribute to Cobden in his last speech as Prime Minister and his decision not to go to the country helped to strengthen Peel's prestige as a man who could rise above narrow political considerations. He remained the acknowledged champion of the anti-Corn Law cause while Russell had to contend with the fact that the new government's own supporters were in a minority in the commons. The survival of the ministry depended on a continuance of hostilities between the two sections of the Conservative party. Prudence demanded of the Government a legislative programme involving no very startling or controversial measures.[27] Russell had, therefore, to watch carefully the attitudes of both Houses, a situation which helped to strengthen his natural caution and hesitancy.

Though little progress was made with Irish affairs in the first month of the new administration, the Prime Minister's statement in the Commons, on July 18, is of some importance since it does help to illustrate the kind of reforms on which the Government hoped to base its Irish policy. Russell readily acknowledged the need for remedial legislation having a long term rather than an immediate effect on the Irish social system. He promised a landlord and tenant bill to take the place of the unwieldy measure introduced by the previous government. The franchise was to be so reformed as to put

[26] Repeal Assoc. meeting, 6 July, *Nation*, 11 July 1846; *Freeman's Journal*, 17 July 1846; *Pilot*, 29 June 1846; *Dublin Evening Post*, 7 July 1846.
[27] E. Halévy, *The Age of Peel and Cobden*, pp. 130-42.

England and Ireland on a basis of equality and he wanted
something done to encourage the reclamation of waste land in
Ireland.[28] These cautious proposals, however, avoided such
controversial topics as the extension of the Ulster tenant-right
to the whole country and O'Connell's favourite scheme for the
taxation of absentee landlords. Again, Russell's refusal to
continue the temporary relief measures after August 15,
despite O'Connell's plea that the early potato crop was seriously damaged by blight, was an early indication of that
parsimony which was to characterise the approach of the Whig
administration to the Irish famine.[29]

As early as May 1846 there had been reports of the widespread
recurrence of the blight. By mid-July the general opinion in
Ireland was that the disease had even spread to areas which had
escaped the previous year.[30] The winter of 1846–7 was to show
that the faliure of the potato crop was for all practical purposes
a total one. Even had the crop not been destroyed, 1846–7
would have been a hard year for the small farmers and labourers.
Because of the partial failure in 1845–6, seed potatoes were in
short supply with the result that the total area under potatoes
fell by at least 250,000 acres. Without reserves to fall back upon,
the poor of the countryside were already defenceless when the
blight struck for the second time.[31]

At the beginning of August, Russell laid down the principles
on which his government would act in the event of a serious food
crisis in Ireland. It could not become, he argued, an established
practice for the state to supply the people with food at un-
economic prices. It was contrary to the real interests of the community to do so and impossible for the Government to undertake the task of feeding a nation. Supplying the market with
food was primarily a matter for private enterprise, though the
Government might have to intervene in very remote areas.
Russell expected that the law of supply and demand, if permitted to function freely, would solve the problem of getting the

[28] *Hansard*, lxxxviii. 283–4.   [29] Ibid.
[30] *Dublin Evening Post*, 5 May 1846.
[31] *Correspondence explanatory of the Measures adopted by Her Majesty's Government for the Relief of Distress arising from the Failure of the Potato Crop in Ireland*,
H.C. 1846 (735), xxxvii. 208, 109–10; P.R.O.I. Relief Commission
papers (Constabulary Reports), 20 May 1846.

food to the people. Though the private trader was to be left in control of the market, the cost of the relief schemes was to be met by loans advanced by the Treasury at the request of special baronial or county sessions. The loans were to be repaid by the levying of a local rate.[32] Fortified by the scientific orthodoxy of his views, Russell made the Poor Employment (Ireland) Act, the basis of his famine relief policy.

Though Russell was not altogether blind to the danger of a serious food shortage, his comments later in the year suggest that he, in common with other observers, both British and Irish, seriously underestimated the extent of the failure and the complexity of the administrative problems involved in providing even a minimum amount of employment for the poor.[33] The *Freeman's Journal* commenting on Russell's August speech, could say: 'now . . . that Indian meal has become an article of general consumption . . . it is wiser to derive the supply through the ordinary channels of private speculation, checked by the declaration of Lord John, that circumstances might arise to warrant the commissariat officers in furnishing food'.[34]

The rigid doctrinaire principles laid down by Russell did not in fact provoke an unfavourable reaction in Ireland except among those unwilling to work with the Whigs. Like the *Freeman's Journal*, O'Connell expressed his confidence in the Government's measures if they were energetically applied.[35] It was hardly surprising, therefore, that the Poor Employment (Ireland) Bill passed virtually undebated through Parliament in August. But though the bill passed silently into law it was destined soon to become a source of controversy and bitterness. From the outset, the Russell administration made the mistake of assuming that a well-organised competitive retail trade in foodstuffs was established in Ireland, when, in fact, such a trade could hardly be said to have existed outside the towns. The Poor Employment Act helped to provide some work for the people; it did little to get food to them at a price they could pay

[32] *Hansard*, lxxxviii. 766–78.
[33] Sir R. Routh to Lord Monteagle, 22 Oct. 1846, Monteagle papers.
[34] *Freeman's Journal*, 20 Aug. 1846.
[35] D. O'Connell to T. Ray (Sec. Repeal Assoc.), 17 Sept. 1846, Repeal Association papers.

or to control the virtual monopoly enjoyed by the few merchants in rural areas.[36] Even the local relief committees, which received some assistance from the state, were required to sell food at the price prevailing in the nearest market towns with the cost of transportation added to it.[37]

The complete destruction of the potato crop, in 1846–7, made the disaster a national one but the Government, fearful of tampering with economic laws and convinced that the Irish landlords were not doing their duty, endeavoured through the Poor Employment Act, to keep famine relief on a strictly local basis. It hoped to compel the landlords, through the payment of rates, to bear a substantial share of the burden. The intention of compelling the landlord to do his duty was praiseworthy. But without some effective scheme to check speculation in foodstuffs the Poor Employment Act remained an inadequate protection for all those who had no other resources to support them except their small earnings from the relief works.[38]

About the middle of September, the first serious attacks were voiced on the Poor Employment Act, better known as the Labour Rate Act. At that time the baronial and county sessions were convened to recommend relief schemes to the Irish Board of Works. The schemes had to be of a public nature benefiting no particular individual, but presumably of value to the community as a whole. This in practice, meant that the loans raised under the act were to be expended on unnecessarily elaborate road works, or in the completion of schemes commenced under the earlier relief measures. The landlords, in the sessions, showed themselves willing enough to vote relief schemes, but the realisation that these costly undertakings would be largely unproductive in character caused widespread dissatisfaction.[39] The demand was, at once, raised for productive works, which in effect meant the improvement of private estates to increase the output of agricultural produce.[40] The demand was not an unreasonable one, for one of the worst

[36] Bessborough to Russell, 19 Jan. 1847, Russell papers, P.R.O. 30/22/5.

[37] T. P. O'Neill, 'The organisation and administration of relief, 1845–1852', in *The Great Famine*, pp. 227–9.

[38] Labouchere to Russell, 16 Dec. 1846, Russell papers, P.R.O. 30/22/5.

[39] 9 and 10 Vic. c. 107; *Nation*, 26 Sept. 1846.

[40] *Dublin Evening Mail*, 21 Sept. 1846.

problems of Irish society was the undercapitalised condition of agriculture. If the land were to be taxed, it seemed but natural that the money so raised should be expended in such a way as actually to improve the productivity of the soil. It is significant, too, that this protest was taken up by repealers of both camps, and the new demand for productive works became one of the principal factors linking the landed class with the nationalists during the critical months of 1846–7.[41]

The plea for state advances to aid agricultural improvements rather than unproductive works, was by no means confined to repealers and disgruntled country gentlemen. Lord Monteagle and Lord Devon were active in urging the need for schemes to improve Irish agriculture, and they found in Lord Bessborough, the Whig Lord Lieutenant, an able ally in stressing the need for a broader approach to the Irish crisis.[42] Russell, however, continued to maintain firmly that 'it was fair to call upon the property of Ireland to repay the sums which should be advanced by the state for the relief of the present distress'. Any substantial grant for the relief of the Irish poor from the United Kingdom Exchequer would he considered be disastrous.[43] In coming to this conclusion he had the full support of the Chancellor of the Exchequer, Charles Wood.[44]

In their resistance to the demands for state aid on a large scale, the ministers were able to act in the knowledge that the principal civil servants entrusted with the administration of relief were firmly opposed to any additional intervention by the state in what they deemed to be the sphere of private economic effort. In the shaping of Government policy in relation to public investment in Ireland, Charles Trevelyan, the Assistant Secretary at the Treasury and the virtual head of that Department,

[41] *Dublin Evening Post*, 3 Oct. 1846; *Nation*, 3 Oct. 1846.

[42] John William Ponsonby (1781–1847), fourth Earl of Bessborough. He was known, until his succession to the earldom in Feb. 1844, by the title of Lord Duncannon. An extensive Irish landowner, he supported both Catholic emancipation and parliamentary reform. He first entered Parliament in 1805 and was Home Secretary, 1834, under his brother-in-law, Lord Melbourne. A personal friend of Daniel O'Connell, he was considered to be a man of tact and good sense.

[43] Russell to Earl of Devon, 24 Aug. 1846, Monteagle papers.

[44] Sir Charles Wood to Monteagle, [Sept. 1846], ibid.

played a particularly important rôle.[45] His great industry and sense of duty found full scope during the famine period, but though he worked hard to co-ordinate public relief measures, his narrow, doctrinaire approach to state intervention had undoubtedly an inhibiting influence on public investment in Ireland. He was ever ready to urge that 'the bolstering and cockering system has been carried to the utmost, people under it have grown worse rather than better'.[46] His approach to economic policy was, however, possibly best summed up in his declaration that 'for the Government to undertake by its own direct agency the detailed drainage and improvement of the whole country, is a task for which the nature and functions of government are totally unsuited'.[47] In the circumstances, it was not surprising that the administration in London should have looked upon the landlords and, indeed, the Irish people as a whole as being primarily responsible both the for tragic conditions existing in Ireland and for the task of improving them. Men like Russell and Trevelyan saw the British Government as a great humanitarian force striving to do all it could, within the permissible limits, for the Irish poor, while the gentry and others hung back and failed to perform their duties.[48]

Between the ministers in London and the Irish executive in Dublin, there was, however, an obvious and at times sharp divergence of opinion on how the emergency should be met. It reflected the difference in outlook between those who had to deal with an immediate problem, close at hand, and those who were removed from the direct impact of the disaster. Bess-

[45] Charles Edward Trevelyan (1807–86), Assistant Secretary at the Treasury, 1840–59. He was closely associated with the civil service reforms of the eighteen fifties. Governor of Madras, 1859. Finance Minister in India 1862. Author of *The Irish Crisis* (1848). See, Jenifer Hart, 'Sir Charles Trevelyan at the Treasury' in *English Historical Review*, lxxv, no. 294 (Jan. 1960). 92–110.

[46] Jenifer Hart, op. cit., p. 99.

[47] Trevelyan to Labouchere (copy), 5 Sept. 1846, Monteagle papers. Such opinions were, of course, also held outside the public service at this time. '. . . . . Under such a calamity what can a Government do to alleviate it? Extremely little. A government may remove all impediments which interfere to prevent the people from providing for themselves, but beyond that they can do little' (*Economist*, (30 Jan. 1847), v. 113–17).

[48] Russell to the Duke of Leinster, 17 Oct. 1846, Russell papers, P.R.O. 30/22/5; Sir C. Wood to Russell, 2 Dec. 1846, Russell papers, P.R.O. 30/22/5.

borough, the Lord Lieutenant, was prompt in advising that large stocks of meal should be purchased on the state's account since 'the smaller merchant here certainly at present is not providing a sufficient quantity of meal at any wage' for the poor people.[49] It was pointed out to the Treasury that the rules of political economy were 'wholly inapplicable' to the existing state of affairs in Ireland, and Bessborough pressed for a relaxation of the provisions of the Labour Rate Act, in order to assist private land-improvement schemes, on the ground that Irish agriculture was very short of capital.[50] Russell and the Treasury firmly resisted the request at first and only gave way when Labouchere, the Chief Secretary, and the Under-Secretary, Thomas Redington, joined in support of the Lord Lieutenant.[51] Even then advances were only permitted on such terms as drastically curtailed the value of the concession.[52] The new rules, made public in a circular letter from the Chief Secretary, had, at least, the immediate effect of helping to ease the political tension in Ireland and preventing a public rift between the London and Dublin administrations which the cabinet was naturally anxious to avoid.[53] Irish questions, nevertheless, continued to disturb the relations between the members of the Government, with the result that the only policy Russell could afford to press was one which gave the minimum offence to any interest, but which proved quite inadequate for the needs of Ireland.[54]

Russell, rightly, conceived the famine to be a period of transition in the social history of Ireland, but there, in effect, he stopped.[55] He chided Wood for regarding the potato failure as

[49] Bessborough to Russell, 13 Sept. 1846. Russell papers, P.R.O. 30/22/5.
[50] Bessborough to Russell, 30 Sept. 1846, Russell papers, P.R.O. 30/22/5; Sir G. Grey to Russell, 28 Sept. 1846, Russell papers, P.R.O. 30/22/5.
[51] Memorandum of the Irish Government, 27 Sept. 1846, Russell papers, P.R.O. 30/22/5; Labouchere to Russell, 24 Sept. 1846, Russell papers, P.R.O. 30/22/5.
[52] Wood to Russell, 14 Oct. 1846, Russell to Bessborough, 4 Oct. 1846, Russell papers, P.R.O. 30/22/5; *Final report from the Board of Public Works, Ireland, relating to Measures adopted for the Relief of Distress in July and August, 1847*, H.C. 1849 (1047), xxiii. 725–36.
[53] Monteagle to Russell, 4 Oct. 1846, Wood to Russell, 14 Oct. 1846, Russell papers, P.R.O. 30/22/5.
[54] See p. 130.
[55] Russell to Bessborough, 6 Nov. 1846, Russell papers, P.R.O. 30/22/5.

no extraordinary calamity, yet he was unable or unwilling to assert sufficient authority in his cabinet to silence the advocates of parsimony and established interests.[56] Though Russell judged the Irish landlords severely, they were not without influence in the Whig councils. Before a determined assault by Lansdowne, himself a great Irish landlord, Russell abandoned a plan to extend the income tax to Ireland as a means of raising additional revenue for Irish needs, and Lansdowne's and Clanricarde's objections to permanent provision being made for outdoor relief prevailed over Bessborough's advocacy of such an arrangement.[57]

It was easy for Lord John Russell to deplore the delinquencies of the Irish landlords, just as it is comparatively easy for us to detect the weak points in a relief system based on the Labour Rate Act and uncontrolled food prices. But the tragedy of the famine remains. The Whigs had long realised the need for reform in Ireland, but the task demanded braver hearts than could be found in the ranks of the aristocratic Whigs of the mid-nineteenth century. They should, perhaps, have risen above the economic prejudices and beliefs of their day, but they did not, and the consequence was that much unnecessary suffering was inflicted on the poor of Ireland during the long months of 1846–7.

'I know all the difficulties', wrote Lord Bessborough to Russell, in January 1847, 'that arise when you begin to interfere with trade, but it is difficult to persuade a starving population that one class should be permitted to make 50 per cent. by the sale of provisions, while they are dying in want of them'.[58] The Lord Lieutenant's words help to emphasise an unfortunate consequence of the Government's food policy, namely, that it left the poor at the mercy of a relatively small body of traders and speculators. Despite the virtual monopoly enjoyed by these merchants, the local relief committees were instructed not to undersell the traders but to follow the general movement of

[56] Russell to Wood, 15 Oct. 1846, G. P. Gooch, op. cit., i. 154.

[57] Landsowne to Russell, 30 Nov. 1846, Russell papers, P.R.O. 30/22/5; Russell to Lansdowne, 2 Dec. 1846, Gooch op. cit., i. 162–3; Bessborough to Russell, 29 Dec. 1846, Bessborough to Russell, 19 Jan. 1847, Russell papers, P.R.O. 30/22/5; Clanricarde to Russell, 8 Jan. 1847, Russell papers, P.R.O. 30/22/5.

[58] Bessborough to Russell, 23 Jan. 1847, Russell papers, P.R.O. 30/22/6.

prices.[59] The pressure on food prices at the time was further strengthened by the fact that the grain harvest of the previous year had been a rather poor one throughout Europe. The shortage of grain resulted in exceptionally heavy buying in 1846–7. At the end of August 1846, wheat sold for 50/4d per quarter in London. By 6 February 1847 the price had risen to 76/4d per quarter and other commodity prices tended to follow the movement of prices in the grain markets.[60]

Throughout the winter months, the poor were largely dependent, therefore, on the Government's inadequate relief measures. Employment on the relief works reached a maximum figure of 734,792 in March 1847.[61] But while the numbers employed were considerable, it became increasingly obvious to the authorities that the schemes were much too wasteful and open to abuse. A much more serious objection to these schemes was that the most distressed among the poor, the sick and the aged, were in effect excluded from the benefits unless they had able-bodied relatives still capable of doing some manual labour and willing to share their small earnings with them.[62] For those without such support there only remained, as a final refuge, the overcrowded workhouses. The reports from these workhouses told a terrible story. In April 1847, for example, the weekly death rate among the inmates had reached 25 per 1000. A few months later, in August 1847, when the revised relief measures had had time to prove themselves, the death rate fell to 8 per 1000.[63]

In January 1847, the Lord Lieutenant had to inform Russell, rather regretfully, that the food merchants '. . . . I am assured have done as little as they could have done even if the Government had entered on the trade'.[64] With food prices rising and

[59] Trevelyan to Monteagle, [Oct. 1846], Monteagle papers; *Economist* (23 Jan. 1847), v. 85–6.

[60] Ibid. (1 Aug. 1846), iv. 998 and (6 Feb. 1847), v. 159.

[61] *A Return showing the Average Daily Number of Persons Employed on Relief Works in Ireland, during the Week ending the 6 March 1847.* H.C. 1847 (185), liv. 23–4.

[62] Bessborough to Russell, 8 Jan. 1847, Labouchere to Russell, 8 Jan. 1847, Russell papers, P.R.O. 30/22/6.

[63] *First Annual Report of the Commissioners for administering the Laws for Relief of the Poor in Ireland,* H.C. 1847–8 (943), xxxiii. 377–580.

[64] Bessborough to Russell, 23 Jan. 1847, Russell papers, P.R.O. 30/22/6.

the public works proving so inadequate, the Government came to the belated and reluctant conclusion that something more radical would have to be attempted in Ireland. 'If we can get relief committees and soup kitchens established everywhere', Russell wrote, at the end of January, 'we shall do better.'[65] The Government's new approach in practice represented an abandonment of the Labour Rate Act on which so much reliance had been placed. Now, as a temporary measure, arrangements were made, in the spring and summer of 1847, for the free distribution of food to the poor. This step undoubtedly helped to check the worst evils of the famine, but it came too late to save many small farmers and cottiers from a winter of hunger and death.[66]

The state, in the mid-nineteenth century, was struggling to adjust itself to the demands of a new world, which was anxious to throw off the bonds of state paternalism and yet was slowly becoming conscious of the social obligations of the community to its members. Lord John Russell found a compromise that could satisfy few, and it left behind it a bitter legacy. It was out of the sufferings of 1846–7, and its aftermath, that a new and harsher attitude towards the British Government found its way into the thoughts of Young Ireland, and thence into the common fund of Irish nationalism.

[65] Russell to Bessborough, 27 Jan. 1847, Russell papers, P.R.O. 30/22/6.
[66] *Fifth, Sixth and Seventh Reports of the Relief Commissioners constituted under the Act 10 Vict. c. 7, and Correspondence connected therewith with Appendix*, H.C. 1847–8 (876), xxix. 27–206.

VII

FAMINE AND POLITICS
1847 (1)

~~~~~~

THE GOVERNMENT'S FAILURE to satisfy the immediate
needs of the people, in the winter of 1846–7, had an unsettling
effect on Irish politics. Criticism of the Whigs became more
widespread and in mid-September, O'Connell made the
suggestion that a council representing all Irish interests should
be established to induce the Government to take effective action
to save the country from ruin.[1] The *Nation* newspaper approved
of this suggestion and even in landed circles it was sympatheti-
cally received. Already many landlords were coming to believe
that the Government's relief measures would have to be
resisted because they imposed too heavy a burden of taxation
and added little to the economic wealth of the country.[2]

Both the Repeal Association and the Young Irelanders hoped
that the landlords in significant numbers would now show an
interest in nationalism. An effort was to be made to bring them
into the repeal movement but the events of 1847 were to show
that, as a class, though angry with the Government, they were
not prepared to abandon their allegiance to the Union.[3] The
landowners were, however, in a determined mood and in

[1] *Nation*, 26 Sept. 1846.
[2] *Dublin Evening Post*, 26 Sept. 1846; *Nation*, 3 Oct. 1846.
[3] Repeal Assoc. meeting, 7 Dec., *Nation*, 12 Dec. 1846; John Mitchel to
Smith O'Brien, 30 Dec. 1846, Smith O'Brien papers, vol. 437, no. 1747.

December 1846 a number of them came together to form the Reproductive Works Committee. The Committee won widespread support. Daniel O'Connell and his son John supported it, as did some Tories like Frederick Shaw, the member for Dublin University.[4] The Committee had as its first task the convening of a meeting of landed gentry and Irish members of Parliament to deliberate on the issue of what should be done to avert a social disaster.

The meeting, which was attended by a number of peers, 26 members of Parliament and many landowners and professional men, was held in Dublin on 14 January 1847. Coming together on the eve of the reassembly of Parliament, this gathering made it appear as if a real sense of national solidarity was about to assert itself, but there was no real confidence between the various interests to make any union a lasting one in the troubled months of 1847.[5]

The resolutions passed at the January meeting and the speeches reflected well the passing mood of compromise and goodwill. The Government's policy of depending on private enterprise to supply the starving people with food was deplored. The famine, it was urged, should be treated as an 'imperial calamity' and in consequence the emergency employment schemes should be regarded as a charge on the imperial Exchequer alone. But though the meeting showed little sympathy with those who favoured a rigid observance of the laws of political economy, its proposals dealing with long-term social changes were cautious in tone.

It was agreed that any permanent relief system, if it were to meet Irish needs, should do more than merely provide workhouses. The relief funds, it was argued, should be made available to increase the economic capacity of the country through land reclamation, the construction of harbours, drainage works and better housing for the agricultural labourers. More important socially than these recommendations was the meeting's recog-

[4] Frederick Shaw (1799–1876) held the office of recorder of Dublin for some 48 years. He favoured, in 1840, municipal reform and though an opponent of the repeal of the Corn Laws, he was regarded as being a representative of moderate Tory opinion in Ireland and a man of some political influence. *Dublin Evening Post*, 26 Sept. 1846; *Dublin Evening Mail*, 16 Dec. 1846.
[5] *Nation*, 16 Jan. 1847.

nition of the tenant-farmer's right to a reasonable, though undefined, measure of compensation for improvements made
during the term of his tenancy.[6] This gesture to the tenant-
farmers was taken as an indication of a new spirit of cooperation between the landed class and the rest of the community
and this impression appeared to be further strengthened by the
willingness with which 83 Irish peers and members of Parliament agreed to act in concert as an Irish parliamentary party.
The object of the 'party', which included Whigs and Tories
as well as repealers, was to bring before Parliament the proposals which had been adopted at the Dublin meeting. By May
1847, however, the bold decision to act together had lost most
of its meaning. Even at the time of the Dublin meeting and the
launching of the Irish party, Lord Bessborough, the Lord
Lieutenant, could assure the Prime Minister that, if he met the
Irish members in a friendly way, '. . . I am sure they will do
everything that is right'. The O'Connells, he added, were
particularly well inclined towards the Whig ministry, and John
O'Connell, especially, was 'very sensible to any little civility'.[7]
In the circumstances it is not surprising that Lord John Russell
should have taken a rather favourable view of the landlords
deliberations.[8]

The Young Irelanders naturally saw in the landlords'
discussions a hopeful sign because, in the same week as the
landlords had come together, they had held the first meeting
of their new Irish Confederation.[9] The Young Irelanders,
having abandoned for the moment the prospect of a settlement
with O'Connell, after the failure of the negotiations in early
December, decided to establish their own organisation. The
final decision to set themselves up in formal opposition to the
Repeal Association was hurriedly taken in the closing days of
December. Throughout November, Smith O'Brien had been
pessimistic about the possibility of the Young Irelanders forming a successful, independent political party, and as late as

[6] Ibid.

[7] *Freeman's Journal*, 1 May 1847; Bessborough to Russell, 16 Jan. 1847,
Russell papers, P.R.O. 30/22/6.

[8] Russell to Bessborough, 18 Jan. 1847, Russell papers, P.R.O. 30/22/6.

[9] Gavan Duffy, *My life in two hemispheres*, i. 239; D. O'Connell to T. Ray,
13 Feb. 1847, Fitzpatrick, *Correspondence of Daniel O'Connell*, ii. 405–7.

December 8 he was still debating whether or not it would be proper for him to attend Conciliation Hall in the event of his returning to Dublin from his estate in County Limerick.[10] In the end he did agree to assume the leadership of a new movement, but only under pressure from Gavan Duffy and his friends.[11]

The Young Irelanders left themselves little time to draw up a clearly formulated programme before they held their first meeting on 13 January 1847, but there could be few doubts as to their ultimate aims. Believing the nation to be someting superior to all sectional interests they saw in nationality a force which in some undefined way could resolve the many conflicts of Irish society. The necessity for a comprehensive national movement, including Catholics and Protestants, gentry and farmers, figured largely in their discussions in December and January. In urging Smith O'Brien to accept leadership Gavan Duffy, for example, could tell him that 'the Protestant and landed gentry must be won', and Smith O'Brien was of the opinion that a large part of the Irish landed gentry had been frightened away from repeal by 'the ultra-democratic and ultra-Catholic tendencies' of a portion of the old repeal movement.[12] At the first meeting of the new Irish Confederation, the Young Irelanders were at pains to emphasise the fact that their cause was not that of demoncracy or sect, but Ireland. The landlords were urged to reform their ways and embrace the cause of repeal. Even John Mitchel, the future critic of landlordism, was strong in the belief that the landlords had a mission to perform and it was to take a bold part in the nationalist movement.[13] But the in

[10] Smith O'Brien to Gavan Duffy, 11 Nov., 8 Dec. 1846, N. Lib. Ir. MS 2642, nos. 3333, 3460.

[11] Gavan Duffy to Smith O'Brien, 26 Dec. 1846, Smith O'Brien papers, vol. 434, no. 1303; Smith O'Brien to Gavan Duffy, 28 Dec. 1846, N. Lib. Ir. MS 2642, no. 3469.

[12] Gavan Duffy to Smith O'Brien, 26 Dec. [1846], Smith O'Brien papers, vol. 434, no. 1303; Smith O'Brien to Gavan Duffy, 24 Dec. 1846, N. Lib. Ir. MS 2642, no. 3468.

[13] *Nation*, 16 Jan. 1847; John Mitchel to Smith O'Brien, 30 Dec. 1846, Smith O'Brien papers, vol. 437, no. 1747. John Mitchel (1815–75) was the third son of Rev. John Mitchel of Newry, a minister of the dissident or remonstrant section of the Presbyterian church in Ulster. For a period Mitchel practised as an attorney at Banbridge, Co. Down, and joined the Repeal Association in 1843. A friend of both Thomas Davis and Gavan

bitter months ahead it proved increasingly difficult for some Young Irelanders to cling to the view that political nationalism alone was a sufficient basis on which to build a vigorous national movement. In January and February 1847, however, such occurrences as the landlords' meeting in Dublin and the formation of an Irish parliamentary party encouraged the Young Irelanders to hope that the Irish would be able, at last, to present their immediate demands to Parliament with a substantial measure of agreement between themselves. Their confidence was hardly lessened by Lord John Russell's virtual admission, when Parliament met in January, that the measures the Government had taken to meet the famine had not succeeded.

As early as the end of September the question of recalling Parliament in November had been discussed in official circles.[14] Whether a November session would have made much practical difference is doubtful. Both Bessborough and Lansdowne were of the opinion that an early meeting of Parliament would only provoke needless debate and controversy over what they felt were still untried measures, while Russell believed that Parliament would be in no mood to sanction large advances for relief in Ireland.[15] Nevertheless, for a time it seemed that Parliament would have to be recalled to satisfy a strong plea from the Dublin administration to have the Labour Rate Act modified.

It was urged that the rigid provisions of the Act should be relaxed sufficiently to permit advances to be made for the improvement of private agricultural land. The Government was not enthusiastic about tampering with the Act, but in the end a compromise solution was found. Some limited schemes of land drainage were to be permitted immediately and, when Parliament met in the new year, the Government promised to introduce an indemnity bill to cover any possible irregularities.[16] Instead of having to acknowledge the failure of its relief measures in November or December, the Government was able to post-

[14] Russell to Bessborough, 29 Sept. 1846, Russell papers, P.R.O. 30/22/5.
[15] Bessborough to Russell, 3 Oct. 1846, Lansdowne to Russell, 15 Oct. 1846, Russell to Bessborough, 6 Nov. 1846, Russell papers, P.R.O. 30/22/5.
[16] Russell to Bessborough, 30 Sept. 1846, Labouchere to Russell, 25 Nov. 1846, Russell papers, P.R.O. 30/22/5.

Duffy, he removed to Dublin, in 1845, when he joined the editorial staff of the *Nation*, as a close associate of Gavan Duffy, the proprietor of the newspaper. For a further biographical note see p. 205, n. 140.

pone that unhappy task until January. Reluctantly Russell and his colleagues came to accept the fact that the starving poor of the Irish countryside could best be helped by a free distribution of food to those in need. In October 1846 Russell could still write: 'It must be thoroughly understood that we cannot feed the people . . . we can at best keep down prices where there is no regular market or established dealers from rising much beyond the fair price with ordinary profits'.[17] Again, as late as December, Labouchere, the Chief Secretary, complained to Russell that 'we are violently assailed for not providing depots and feeding the whole country, but this is so absurd that it will not stand discussion in Parliament'.[18] A few months later over 3,000,000 persons daily were in receipt of free food rations in Ireland.[19]

When Parliament met in January, Lord John Russell sought to justify what his government had done to meet the needs of a famine-stricken people. His arguments were the familiar ones. The object of the public works, he explained, was not so much to achieve something useful as to enable the poor to earn enough to live on and to help them to retain their industrious habits so that they would be encouraged to seek private employment as soon as possible.[20] Though the Prime Minister still attempted to justify the theoretical soundness of the Government's approach to famine relief, he went far towards admitting that the labour rate system had failed in practice. He told Parliament that the relief works would be gradually abandoned and that the Government would propose instead that free food should be distributed to the poor through local relief committees. This new arrangement was to be financed by a local rate, government donations and private subscriptions. The free distribution of food, it was stressed, could only be regarded as a temporary and dangerous expedient to be abandoned as soon as a revised permanent Poor Law came into operation, as was hoped by the Government, in the autumn of 1847.[21] Under the revised Poor Law, the

[17] Russell to Bessborough, 11 Oct. 1846, Russell papers, P.R.O. 30/22/5.
[18] Labouchere to Russell, 23 Dec. 1846, Russell papers, P.R.O. 30/22/5.
[19] See p. 140.
[20] *Hansard*, lxxxix. 138–49.
[21] Ibid., lxxxix. 76–84; T. P. O'Neill, 'The organisation and administration of relief, 1845–52' in R. D. Edwards and T. D. Williams (eds.), *The Great Famine, 1845–52*, pp. 235–46.

full burden of supporting the poor would fall on the Irish Poor Law unions alone; a far from encouraging prospect both for the poor and for those in Ireland who had put their trust in the Whig alliance.

The Government's meagre emergency measures and the bleak proposals for a revision of the Poor Law gave rise, not surprisingly, to critical comment in Ireland.[22] There was, however, a more constructive side to the Government's programme. Russell told Parliament that more would be done to facilitate land drainage, the Irish property law was to be revised so that leaseholds renewable for ever could be converted into freeholds, and most striking of all, the Government would ask that £1,000,000 should be made available to finance the reclamation of waste land in Ireland. Compulsory powers would be sought, Lord John Russell said, to obtain the necessary land from uncooperative landowners. When the land had been reclaimed it would then be sold or leased to small farmers. And though he made no specific proposals on the great issue of compensating tenant-farmers for improvements made by them, he assured the House that tenant compensation and the problem of how heavily encumbered Irish estates could be sold free of encumbrances were being given every consideration by the Government.[23]

The legislative programme would have had an even more ambitious character were it not for the conservative influences which prevailed in the cabinet. The proposal had come from the Dublin administration that the Irish county franchise should be established on the basis of an £8 poor-law rating.[24] But the cabinet inclined to Lansdowne's view that a £10 rating and a £5 freehold franchise should be taken in preference, to avoid the creation of too large an electorate in Ireland.[25] Labouchere, the Chief Secretary, however, found the £5 freehold franchise particularly unsuitable, and argued that it would simply result in a class of squatters totally dependent on their landlords'

[22] D. O'Connell to T. M. Ray, 6 Feb. 1847, Fitzpatrick, *Correspondence of Daniel O'Connell*, ii. 401–2; *Freeman's Journal*, 22 Jan. 1847.

[23] *Hansard*, lxxxix. 426–54.

[24] Bessborough to Russell, 20 Nov. 1846, Labouchere to Russell, 25 Nov. 1846, Russell papers, P.R.O. 30/22/5.

[25] Russell to Bessborough, 19 Nov. 1846, Russell to Labouchere, 24 Nov. 1846, Russell papers, P.R.O. 30/22/5.

goodwill.[26] Faced with this conflict of views, Russell decided not to include franchise reform in his immediate proposals, much to the disappointment of O'Connell and the repealers. Again, though Russell had considered the possibility of extending either the income tax or the English Poor Law to Ireland, and Bessborough had recommended permanent legislation for the employment of the poor, the cabinet would only agree to some minor changes in the Irish Poor Law.[27] Here, too, the restraining influence of Lansdowne was an imporatant factor.[28]

Russell's whole approach to Irish issues displayed a distinct unwillingness to come to grips with the fundamental realities. From a purely political point of view Russell's reluctance was understandable. Any measures likely to curtail the rights of Irish landowners were bound to meet strong opposition in the Lords and in the Commons, too, the landed interest was influential and vocal on both sides of the House. Under sustained pressure from a united Irish party, Parliament and the Government might have been jolted into activity, but in practice even the few worthwhile measures in the Government's programme were quietly dropped on one pretext or another. The obvious contrast between Russell's earlier proposals and the achievement of his Government was a measure of the failure of the Irish parliamentary party. Lacking cohesion and an agreed policy, the party was not to survive the contest provoked by the Government's new Poor Relief Bill and Lord George Bentinck's bold proposals for railway development in Ireland.

Although the Tory protectionists had, at first, questioned the seriousness of the potato failure in 1845–6, in practice they showed a greater willingness to accept state intervention in economic and social affairs than either Peel or Russell, and they rightly saw in the emergence of the Irish party evidence of the

[26] Labouchere to Russell, [Dec. 1846], Russell papers, P.R.O. 30/22/5. Henry Labouchere (1798–1869). First elected to parliament in the Whig interest in 1826. 1832, Lord of the Admiralty. 1835, Master of the Mint, and Vice-President of the Board of Trade. President of the Board of Trade, 1839. Chief Secretary for Ireland, 1846. President of the Board of Trade, 1847. Colonial Secretary, 1855–8. Created Baron Taunton in 1859.

[27] Lansdowne to Russell, 30 Nov. 1846, Russell to Lansdowne, 2 Dec. 1846, Bessborough to Russell, 15 Dec., 28 Dec. 1846, Russell papers, P.R.O. 30/22/5.

[28] Bessborough to Russell, 29 Dec. 1846, Russell papers, P.R.O. 30/22/5.

failure of the Government's relief measures. It is clear, too, that the political implications of the creation of an Irish parliamentary party were not lost on the protectionists who saw that, with the aid of the discontented Irish members, they might well upset the existing political balance at Westminster.

In opening the debates of 1847, Bentinck and his friends attacked the useless public works that had been undertaken in Ireland. The principles put forward to justify the Government's attitude, Bentinck contended, might be reasonable enough in normal times, but they were of little value in the face of a famine. Anticipating his railway proposals, he said that if the Government did not introduce really comprehensive measures for Ireland, he and his supporters would most certainly do so.[29] Bentinck made good his warning in the form of a railway bill which he brought forward at the beginning of February. This measure did not contemplate state railways in Ireland, but proposed that some £16,000,000 should be advanced by the Treasury to finance Irish railway projects. The advances were to be repaid over a period of not less than thirty years.[30] This generous proposal was well received in Dublin, since it represented the kind of capital investment that had long been advocated in Ireland. Young Irelanders and Conservatives joined in praise of the bill and on February 2, Bentinck addressed the Irish parliamentary party on his railway plan. The fifty members present voted their unanimous approval of the scheme.[31] Bentinck was, however, destined to be disappointed if he expected sustained support from the Irish parliamentary party.

Bentinck sought to stress the non-controversial character of his bill when introducing it, but since the whole principle of the measure involved a direct criticism of the Government's relief and financial policy, Russell could not permit it to go unchallenged.[32] The Prime Minister indicated that he would oppose the bill on its later stages, arguing that such a heavy outlay on the Irish railways would inevitably involve a reduction of expenditure on the ordinary relief measures. To streng-

[29] *Hansard*, lxxxix. 101–9.
[30] Ibid., lxxxix. 773–802; *Nation*, 13 Feb. 1847.
[31] *Dublin Evening Mail*, 5, 8, Feb. 1847; *Nation*, 13 Feb. 1847.
[32] Russell to Bessborough, 14 Feb. 1847, Russell papers, P.R.O. 30/22/6; *Hansard*, xc. 86–116.

then his position, Russell summoned a meeting of the Irish Liberal and repeal members and he made it quite clear to them that, if the bill were given a second reading, the ministry would be forced to resign.[33] This decision put the Irish members in a very difficult position. Politically they had little in common with the Tory protectionists, and the Russell ministry, despite its defects was regarded by them as preferable to an ultra-Tory one. Again, there was the danger that a major political crisis would hold up those famine relief measures the people so urgently needed.[34]

In an effort to gain time, a deputation of 34 Irish members pressed Bentinck to seek a postponement of the second reading of his bill. He was agreeable to this. This undertaking was of little practical value to the Irish since he told the House that although he was quite prepared to postpone the measure, he was also ready to go ahead with it should the Government prefer him to do so. Faced with this challenge, Russell replied that he was willing to let the bill be dealt with at once. With the life of the ministry at stake, the Irish party could no longer postpone the hour of decision by inadequate expedients.[35]

In the debates, the Irish Conservative opponents of Peel supported Bentinck and considerable efforts appear to have been made to secure a strong attendance of protectionist members at the debates. The Irish repealers, however, in so far as they took part in the contest, expressed only tepid support for the principle of the measure.[36] Gone was the fine unanimity with which the Irish party had welcomed the proposals. Peel, though he might from time to time criticise the Government's policy, firmly supported Russell on the Irish railways' question. He concentrated his attack on the financial risks involved in Bentinck's scheme. Too great a sum, he argued, would have to be advanced over too short a period, and he saw in the bill an ill-advised incursion by the state into the sphere of private business.[37] Almost from the outset the bill had little prospect of success and the defeat of the measure on the second reading, by 332 votes to 118, was the best proof that there was no likeli-

[33] *Nation*, 13 Feb. 1847.   [34] *Hansard*, xc. 85–116.
[35] Ibid., lxxix. 1216–18, 1211–13, 1220.
[36] Ibid., lxxix. 1388–96, 1404–6.
[37] Ibid., lxxix. 157–64, xc. 65–86.

hood of a formidable alliance between the Tory protectionists and a resolute Irish party.[38] Of the 70 Irish members who voted in the division, on February 16, only 37 of them supported the bill. The *Nation*, with considerable justification, could say: 'thirty-seven only acted as they spoke . . . thirty-three voted against Ireland for the Whigs . . . many stayed away'.[39] In helping to split the Irish party's vote, the repeal members must bear some of the blame. Of the repealers who took part in the division, seventeen supported Bentinck while six voted with the Government.[40]

The defeat of Bentinck's railway bill was a serious blow for the Irish parliamentary party, but the party might have survived were it not for the Government's measure to revise the Irish Poor Law of 1838. The Irish landlords generally had tended to resist local taxation to finance employment schemes unless it could be shown that the work to be done might help to increase the actual value of their estates. Any extension of the Irish Poor Law system, that would involve increased local taxation and bring with it no obvious economic advantages, was bound to meet with a great deal of opposition in landed circles. The spokesmen of the landed class viewed with particular suspicion any suggestion that public relief, apart from the emergency measures the famine had made necessary, should be given outside the walls of the workhouses.[41]

The Government's Poor Relief (Ireland) Bill was a rather limited measure of administrative reform, but it did contain some innovations. A separate Irish Poor Law Board was constituted and the bill placed the Poor Law guardians, in contrast to the 1838 Act, under an obligation to grant relief to all destitute poor in their union areas. In addition outdoor relief could be given to the sick and the aged and in exceptional circumstances to the able-bodied poor as well.[42] In bringing forward this bill, the Government acted on the assumption that famine conditions would not continue indefinitely in Ireland. To have assumed, however, that a Poor Law based on the English pattern and supported exclusively out of local funds could have successfully come into operation in the autumn of

[38] Ibid., xc. 123–6.　　[39] *Nation*, 27 Feb. 1847.　　[40] Ibid.
[41] *Dublin Evening Mail*, 1 Feb. 1847; *Hansard*, lxxxix. 631.
[42] T. P. O'Neill, op. cit., pp. 246–54; *Hansard*, xc. 1244–61.

1847, was to seriously underestimate the degree of economic and social collapse in Ireland.[43]

The 1838 Poor Law had never been popular in Ireland or really successful in relieving a distress which, even in the pre-famine years, was too deep-rooted in its causes and too general to be remedied by pauper relief. A mere revision of the 1838 Act was not likely, in the cruel circumstances of 1847–8, to lessen greatly the poverty of the Irish small farmers and cottiers. But the very fact that the bill brought with it the possibility of some change placed the repeal members of Parliament in a difficult situation. They could not afford to allow the bill to be endangered by a Tory opposition angered by the prospect of outdoor relief and the threat of a growing burden of local taxation. Both sections of the Irish party were dissatisfied with the new bill but for very different reasons.

The Conservative members opposed the bill with the argument that heavy additional taxation would drive the Irish landed classes out of existence.[44] John O'Connell, in contrast, said he would support the bill in the hope that it might save a few lives, and, his father, in his pathetic last speech in Parliament, told the House he would accept anything that might help the poor, though he had ceased to believe, as he told a correspondent, that really generous aid would be given since there existed 'an unwillingness to place upon the British people the burdens absolutely necessary to give efficient relief to Irish misery'.[45] In these circumstances, it was not surprising that the Poor Law issue became a critical and fatal one for the Irish party, and of the 105 Irish members of both Houses who subscribed to a resolution attacking the provisions of the bill, only 4 were repealers.[46] In view of the hostile attitude of the majority of the Irish party members to the bill, John O'Connell and his followers ceased to attend the meetings of the party, though Smith O'Brien continued to be associated with it in the belief that in the end it might achieve some good.[47]

[43] Ibid., xci. 245–50. See pp. 160–3.

[44] *Hansard*, lxxxix. 631.

[45] Ibid., xc. 1367–76; D. O'Connell to T. M. Ray, 6 Feb. 1847, Fitzpatrick, *Correspondence of Daniel O'Connell*, ii. 401–2.

[46] *Nation*, 13 Mar. 1847.

[47] *Hansard*, xc. 1397–9; Irish Confed. meeting, 7 Apr., *Nation*, 10 Apr. 1847; *Freeman's Journal*, 1 May 1847.

The landlords' agitation against the Poor Law bill had one rather paradoxical result: it enabled the Government to give some practical evidence of its goodwill towards the Irish land-lords. Though Radicals, like John Arthur Roebuck and Poulett Scrope, might thunder against the Irish landlords, the Government still had a healthy respect for the rights of property and the interests of the landed class as a whole.[48] The bitter taste of the new Poor Law was, therefore, sweetened by the Government's acceptance of a Conservative amendment which required that an applicant for poor relief should surrender his holding of land, if it exceeded a quarter of an acre in extent. This amendment, the 'Gregory Clause', was frankly expected to facilitate the removal of the famine-stricken small holders, and it in fact proved a convenient aid for the landlords in the clearances of 1847–8.[49] The Poor Relief (Ireland) Bill became law, but little else of Russell's ambitious scheme found its way to the statute book.

The Irish party interlude, though of short duration, is of some importance in the history of Irish nationalism. Middle-class nationalists saw in the Irish party the kind of organisation which would ultimately win the landowners for the repeal cause. In the conditions of the mid-nineteenth century such a party seemed to offer the only possible way of mobilising Irish political influence, and though this Irish party failed, the ambition to create one was not readily abandoned. The difficulties to be overcome were, however, too many. It was impossible to disguise for long the fact that the interests of the landowners and the tenants were not the same, just as it was difficult to ignore the fact that any lasting political settlement had to involve the overthrow of a political ascendancy which it had taken centuries to create.

The collapse of the Irish party marked, too, the end of any really serious effort to compel Russell to honour the promises he had made at the beginning of the session. The Destitute Poor (Ireland) Act, better known as the Soup-Kitchen Act, fulfilled its modest role of tiding the people over the months of acute shortage, but no grand scheme took shape to raise the standard of living of the stricken multitude. The ambitious waste land measure was abandoned on the plea that the

---

[48] *Hansard*, lxxxix. 10–22, 473–5, xci. 171–5.   [49] Ibid., xci. 583–93.

compulsory clauses were bound to prove unacceptable to the House of Lords. The pressure of other business was offered as an excuse for not attempting to deal with the long delayed question of compensation to tenants for agricultural improvements.[50] The Government did, however, agree to advance £620,000 by way of loans for railway development and £40,000 for harbour works, but these concessions alone could not hide the inadequacy of the Government's Irish policy.[51]

The desperate plight of the people and the feebleness of the Government's measures did not stir the Repeal Association into renewed activity, because the once great movement had little real strength left in it. The leader was obviously dying and that in itself gave rise to speculation and a feeling of uncertainty about the future of repeal as a political force. Bessborough, who had known O'Connell personally for very many years, feared that, with O'Connell's death, a violent contest for leadership in Irish politics would take place between Old and Young Ireland. In any such struggle, he believed, John O'Connell would have the goodwill of the Catholic clergy.[52]

Bessborough considered, too, that the Young Irelanders might even try to make some preparations for a rebellion and so should be closely watched. Russell accepted this possibility but felt that the first thing which would happen 'on the political extinction of O'Connell' would be the foundation of a strictly Catholic party. In this party John O'Connell would be only one of several leaders, some of whom might well be priests recruited from Maynooth College. The Prime Minister suggested that in the event of such a party emerging, the Government should work to establish direct contact with the new men and not depend merely on the influence of John O'Connell and Archbishop Murray of Dublin.[53]

Bessborough confidently expected the early break-up of the Repeal Association, but though the weekly repeal rent fell to the very small sum of £18:11:5 at the beginning of March, his expectations were not fulfilled in 1847.[54] The famine, it is true,

[50] *Freeman's Journal*, 1 May 1847; *Hansard*, xciii. 636–8, 632–3.
[51] Ibid., xci. 1420–4, xcii. 213–98, xciii. 1019–44.
[52] Bessborough to Russell, 24 Feb. 1847, Russell papers, P.R.O. 30/22/6.
[53] Russell to Bessborough, 26 Feb. 1847, Russell papers, P.R.O. 30/22/6.
[54] Bessborough to Russell, 3 Mar. 1847, Russell papers, P.R.O. 30/22/6.

had seriously disorganised the disciplined following on which O'Connell had relied, but the Association survived, in form at least, for a time after O'Connell's death. Little, however, was needed to bring about its final collapse. Without funds, effective leadership or a spirited population to support it, the Repeal Association could only hope to exercise some political influence by clinging to the English Whig connection.

From the autumn of 1846 onwards, Daniel O'Connell and his sons had given the Government the benefit of their advice and were on friendly terms with the Lord Lieutenant. In a cautious way the authorities were grateful for their help, but Russell was quite clear in his directions to the Chief Secretary, on the question of rewarding docile repealers with public employment. 'I do not see myself', he wrote, 'that much is given to O'Connell, but at all events I myself prefer non-repealers to repealers.'[55] Not counted as being in opposition and yet not quite fully trusted by the Whig Government, the official repeal movement was destined to play out its existence in an atmosphere of futile indecision.[56]

The Young Irelanders, too, had their difficulties, for while they clung fiercely to their objective of national independence, they never seemed able, or perhaps, never had the opportunity, in the short lifetime of their Confederation, to clarify their methods and give definition to their secondary aims. In the winter of 1846–7, it seemed possible that many landlords might seek refuge in repeal, but the Young Irelanders' efforts to win their support proved fruitless.[57] Despite these disappointments the majority of the Confederate leaders were unwilling to depart from their belief in a nationalism which rejected social revolution as a means of achieving political independence. A minority among them, however, influenced by the sufferings of the people during the famine months and the failure of the landlords to accept repeal, were drawn towards agrarian agitation and the bold plan of appealing directly to the interests of the peasant population by advocating a tenant-right campaign

[55] Labouchere to Russell, 13 Nov. 1846, Russell to Labouchere, 24 Nov. 1846, Russell papers, P.R.O. 30/22/5.
[56] Russell to Bessborough, 26 Feb. 1847, Clanricarde to Bessborough, 16 Mar. 1846, Russell papers, P.R.O. 30/22/6.
[57] *Nation*, 16 Jan. 1847.

and resistance to the exactions of the landlord and tax collector.[58]

It was difficult to organise a vigorous political movement on a national basis in the spring and summer of 1847, since the country was in a state of social collapse. By the beginning of July, some 3,000,000 persons were estimated to be in receipt of food rations from the relief committees and though the exact figures may never be known, thousands of poor people had already died of hunger and disease by the summer of 1847.[59] Yet it was against this background of disaster and suffering that the leaders of the the two sections of the repeal movement began to consider once more the possibility of reunion.

The initiative was taken by John O'Connell, but the conference of 4 May 1847 between the representatives of the Association and the Confederation proved a failure. O'Connell was prepared to make concessions on certain points. He admitted that the Whig alliance had been a failure in many ways. He agreed that no repealer should take public office under a government not pledged to repeal the Act of Union and he conceded that the principle of peaceful agitation was not of universal applicability. On one fundamental issue O'Connell refused to accept the Young Irelanders' proposals. He would not agree to their proposition that both the Repeal Association and the Confederation should be dissolved and a new repeal organisation be established in their place.[60] O'Connell still thought of reunion in terms of the Young Irelanders returning to the Repeal Association. In the circumstances of the time, for him to have given way to the Young Irelanders would have been to recognise them as the victors in a struggle where there were no victors at all. On the grounds that he could not reach any final decisions while his father was abroad, John O'Connell brought the negotiations to an end.[61]

Though the negotiations for reunion failed, other attempts were made to mobilise Irish opinion in the spring and sum-

[58] See pp. 148–51.

[59] *First Annual Report of the Commissioners for Administering the Laws for Relief of the Poor in Ireland*, H.C. 1847–8 (963), xxxiii. 377–580; Sir William P. MacArthur, 'Medical History of the Famine', in R. D. Edwards and T. D. Williams (eds.), *The Great Famine*, pp. 308–12.

[60] *Nation*, 17, 24 Apr. 1847.

[61] Ibid., 8 May 1847; *Freeman's Journal*, 5 May 1847.

mer of 1847. Early in May John O'Connell urged the Irish members of Parliament to withdraw from Westminster and meet in Dublin as a council of national distress, and the *Nation* newspaper, too, made a similar plea. But apart from a short lived Irish Council, which endeavoured to revive the spirit of the Irish party, nothing concrete emerged from such calls to action.[62]

In the midst of these disappointments and failures Daniel O'Connell died at Genoa, on May 15, while journeying to Rome, leaving behind him no leader capable of meeting the enormous challenges of a period of social and political collapse. Gavan Duffy was to claim that O'Connell, from 1844 onwards, had been in a state of mental decline, but the evidence to support this claim is weak. As late as the summer of 1846, O'Connell was still forceful and skilful enough to drive the Young Irelanders out of an organisation they were reluctant to leave, though Lord John Russell, some months later, in February 1847, could observe that O'Connell was 'failing fast' in health.[63] The famine and the issues it involved proved too great a task for a man who had lived long and fought, at times, nobly. The great expedient—the Whig alliance—which he had hoped would tide Ireland over the difficult years, had failed. In any assessment of his achievements, it must be recognised that he had to contend with a hopeless inheritance of misgovernment and past oppression. It was not easy to secure adequate political and social reforms by the means men considered reasonable and moderate in the mid-nineteenth century. In the immediate context of the year 1847 his death made little difference politically, but he did leave to the Repeal Association the legacy of a great name.

In the midst of the tribulations of 1847, the general election of the summer came as a rather incongruous interlude. The activity it provoked and its results were very remote from the realities of Irish life. The general election did not come as a surprise. The break-up of the Tory party, in 1846, had made an election almost inevitable, and it produced few unexpected results. Russell came back into office, but his Government still

[62] See p. 152.
[63] Gavan Duffy, *Young Ireland*, p. 197; Russell to Bessborough, 26 Feb. 1847, Russell papers, P.R.O. 30/22/6.

needed the goodwill of the Peelites and the Radicals to survive.[64] With some 453 members of free-trade sympathies as against 202 protectionists, Russell's position was reasonably safe so long as he avoided dangerous innovations.[65] Political necessity again helped to strengthen the Prime Minister's natural caution and indecision. The circumstances clearly demanded a resolute and disciplined Irish representation, but the elections of 1847 signally failed to send such a group to Parliament.

In the election campaign of 1847 the Young Irelanders were able to exercise comparatively little influence, indeed in most areas they were regarded as men who had hastened, by their disloyalty, the death of the Liberator.[66] In contrast, the Repeal Association showed more vitality and determination than its critics had expected.[67] The Young Irelanders sought to persuade the candidates to take a pledge against place-hunting. In practice, only two successful repeal candidates were prepared to profess full agreement with the Irish Confederation. One was Smith O'Brien, the other a curious Tasmanian protégé of his, and a champion of political decentralisation, Chisholm Anstey. Anstey was returned for Youghal, but abandoned repeal in 1848 in favour of a strange political career which, for a time, brought him a judicial post in India.[68]

John O'Connell, from the beginning of the campaign, emphasised that under no circumstances would he take the pledge against place-hunting. To take the pledge, he argued, would simply mean giving the Orange connection a virtual monopoly of public offices in Ireland. He was, however, careful to add that little in the way of comprehensive reforms could be expected from any English party.[69] Despite the apparent vigour of the Association during the election contest, John O'Connell was in an even more difficult position than the Young Irelanders. They, it is true, had no coherent plan of action, but the Repeal

[64] H. Goulburn to Peel, 24 Aug. 1847, Peel papers, Add. MS 40445, ff. 404-6.

[65] Halévy, *The Age of Peel and Cobden*, pp. 155-61.

[66] *Freeman's Journal*, 1 June 1847; *Nation*, 12 June 1847.

[67] Richard O'Gorman to Smith O'Brien, 14 July 1847, Smith O'Brien papers, vol. 438, no. 1932; Goulburn to Peel, 24 Aug. 1847, Peel papers, Add. MS 40445, ff. 404-6.

[68] *Nation*, 14, 28 Aug. 1847; *D.N.B.*, i. 512-13.

[69] Repeal Assoc. meetings, 7, 21 June, *Nation*, 12, 26 June 1847.

Association had tried one plan and it had failed. Petty con-cessions, in the matter of public offices, were all that John O'Connell could now expect and they were all he was to get.

On the surface, all the formalities of a well fought election were preserved. The Whigs were successfully opposed in five constituencies by repealers.[70] The Attorney-General for Ireland was defeated and even Sheil was challenged in Dungarvan. In all, the repeal party secured 39 seats, though the allegiance of some of the members was rather doubtful.[71] The weakness of the party could not be disguised. They made no progress in the en-trenched Tory constituencies of the north, and the failure of the majority of the repeal members to remain free of Whig influ-ences undermined their effectiveness as an independent force in Parliament. Again, it seems clear that some prospective candidates found it wise to declare themselves to be repealers or to subscribe to the Repeal Association for the first time on the eve of the elections.[72] The number involved, however, does not appear to have been as large as Gavan Duffy suggests.[73] Of the 39 repealers elected some 19 had sat in the previous Parliament, while 14 more were listed as decided supporters of repeal even by the *Nation* newspaper.[74] The weakness in the repeal rep-resentation lay as much in the old members as in the new-comers.

Though there was little coherence or firmness of purpose in the repeal movement in the summer of 1847, the election speeches show that in all sections of the movement men were becoming increasingly aware of the importance of social issues. The conventional political demands were still made but the arguments in favour of tenant-right, of greater security of possession for the tenant-farmer, were given much more attention than in the past. The *Freeman's Journal*, the principal organ of moderate repeal opinion, insisted that 'tenant right should be elevated into an election test'.[75] Though few were

[70] *Dublin Evening Mail*, 9 Aug. 1847; *Nation*, 4 Sept. 1847.
[71] Ibid.
[72] *Dublin Evening Post*, 20 July 1847; Repeal Assoc. meetings, 12, 19 July, *Nation*, 17, 24 July 1847.
[73] Gavan Duffy, *Four Years of Irish History*, p. 148.
[74] *Nation*, 4 Sept. 1847; McGee to Smith O'Brien, 1 Sept. 1847, Smith O'Brien papers, vol. 439, no. 1974.
[75] *Freeman's Journal*, 1 June 1847.

prepared to press this demand to anything like its logical conclusion, the increased interest in the plight of the small farmers was, perhaps, the most significant development in 1847, for it pointed to the emergence of a new approach to Irish nationalism.

VIII

FAMINE AND POLITICS
1847 (II)

THE GREAT SOCIAL PROBLEM IN IRELAND in the first half
of the nineteenth century was that of the land. It was a problem
which expressed itself in agrarian unrest and in the unsatisfactory relations between landlord and tenant. The Government of Sir Robert Peel had endeavoured to do something
about the Irish land question. It set up the Devon Commission,
in 1843, to examine, as we have seen, the working of the land
system and again Peel's was the first British Government to
introduce measures, in 1845 and 1846, to compensate Irish
tenant-farmers for permanent improvements made by them,
should their interests in their holdings be terminated by the
landowners. But the two compensation bills, though quite
inadequate from the tenants' point of view, were still too
advanced to win much support among the landlords and they
never became law.[1] The doctrine of the inviolability of property
rights and the great influence of the landed class were to ensure
that the Irish land system would remain unchanged in the
eighteen-forties despite the attempts to better it.[2]

Though the land problem constituted the fundamental
material grievance of the masses of the Irish people, economic

[1] See pp. 91–2, 105–6.
[2] R. D. Collison Black, *Economic Thought and the Irish Question, 1817–1870*,
pp. 15–44.

and social issues were generally treated by the Irish leaders as being, in practice, subordinate to the claims of political nationalism and religious equality. Despite his ambitious political demands, O'Connell, for example, was no radical reformer in relation to land. He did not advocate a new social order but rather sought limited changes in the existing land system which would give the tenant-farmers some security against eviction. O'Connell, like many of his contemporaries was a friend of 'tenant-right'. This was a vague term subject to many interpretations, but for O'Connell it seems to have signified the right of an evicted tenant-farmer to compensation for all improvements made by him during his tenancy. He would also have permitted a tenant to sell his interest in the land to the highest bidder. O'Connell did not favour full peasant proprietorship but urged the Government to introduce legislation which would virtually have compelled the landlords to grant 21 or 31 year leases.[3]

The tragic circumstances of the winter of 1846–7 helped to focus attention on agrarian issues, especially as the Government failed to introduce the long-awaited tenants' compensation bill. Instead of taking up the land question, it permitted the much criticised 'Quarter Acre Clause' to be included in the new Poor Law bill and so made easier the removal of many impoverished small farmers and cottiers from their holdings.[4]

The impact of the 'Quarter Acre Clause' was most obvious in the distressed areas, but even in the more prosperous parts of Ulster dissatisfaction with the existing agrarian system gained ground noticeably in 1847–8. The northern farmer had, by the early nineteenth century, won in many areas a grudging recognition from his landlord that he had a customary, though not a legal, right to go on occupying his farm so long as he paid the agreed rent or to receive fair compensation for his interest in the land should he be required to surrender his holding to the landlord. This 'Ulster custom', which usually permitted the tenant to dispose of his interest to a suitable purchaser,

---

[3] *Hansard*, lxxxv. 492–527; Repeal Assoc. meetings, 15, 22 June, *Nation*, 20, 27 June 1846; *Evidence taken before Her Majesty's Commissioners of Inquiry into the State of the Law and Practice in respect to the Occupation of Land in Ireland*, part iii, H.C. 1845 (657), xxi. 939–48.

[4] See p. 219.

was, however, looked upon with no enthusiasm by many
Ulster landlords and not a few of them tried to interpret the
tenant-right in a very narrow way, as the evidence given before
the Devon Commission shows.[5]

Sharman Crawford, the persistent advocate of the tenants'
interests in Parliament, had again sought, in 1847, to induce
the Commons to accept measures which would have given to
all Irish tenants and not merely those of Ulster most of the
advantages of the Ulster custom in a legal form. Neither the
Government nor the influential Irish landed connection in
Parliament showed themselves responsive to his efforts and
Sharman Crawford made no more progress with his proposals
than he had in previous years.[6] The resistance of the Irish landlords and the growing fear that some meagre compensation
bill would be brought forward by the Whig Government as a
legal substitute for tenant-right strengthened the sense of
watchfulness in Ulster and elsewhere in the country.[7]

In Cork, a tenant-right league was established in February
1847, the organisers urging the importance of getting up similar
associations throughout the country.[8] Efforts were made to
organise the farmers in Wexford, and in the north the movement rapidly became strong and influential. Meetings were
held at Coleraine and Derry, and the legal recognition of
tenant-right was demanded, not merely for Ulster, but for the
rest of Ireland as well.[9] This recognition of the common economic interest of the farmers of the north and south anticipated
to some extent the ideas which were to animate the great
tenant-right movement of the eighteen-fifties, but the repeal
movement and all it implied had to be swept away before an
essentially social agitation could emerge on a nation-wide basis.
Though the tenant-right agitation lay in the future, the new
interest in the claims of the impoverished peasantry was,

[5] *Evidence taken before Her Majesty's Commissioners of Inquiry into the State of the Law and Practice in respect to the Occupation of Land in Ireland; together with Appendix and Plans*, H.C. 1845 (606), xix. 735–6.

[6] *Freeman's Journal*, 22 July 1847; *Hansard*, xciii. 632–3.

[7] *Northern Whig*, 2 Mar. 1847; *Hansard*, xcix. 974–6.

[8] *Nation*, 6 Feb., 27 Feb. 1847; Trenwith to J. Fintan Lalor, 5 May 1847, Lalor papers, N. Lib. Ir. MS 340.

[9] *Northern Whig*, 2 Mar. 1847; *Nation*, 10 Apr. 1847; Gavan Duffy, *My Life in Two Hemispheres*, i. 203.

nevertheless, of considerable significance; it made all the more attractive the proposition that the repeal agitation and the demand for tenant-right could be brought together in an effective combination which would rouse the people from their torpor.[10]

'Tenant-right' was, then, a much discussed issue in 1847, though, in the absence of a clear legal definition, the meanings given to the term were numerous. John O'Connell, like many other tenant-righters, regarded the tenant farmer as having, in effect, a property right in the land itself, once he paid his rent. In taking this view John O'Connell seems to have accepted a more advanced interpretation than either his father or Sharman Crawford. However much they may have differed among themselves, all advocates of tenant-right saw in that system an effective answer to the problem of insecurity of tenure.[11]

It was against this background that one of the few original thinkers on social issues in Ireland in the first half of the nineteenth century entered into communication with the Young Irelanders. He was James Fintan Lalor.[12] Fintan Lalor had for long given his attention to the problem of the relations between landlord and tenant. His father's active part in the anti-tithe agitation of the eighteen-thirties may well have encouraged this physically frail man to challenge both the theoretical and practical justifications of the existing social order in Ireland and to put forward his views in vigorous, passionate terms.[13] Fintan Lalor's entry into active politics was rather sudden. At the beginning of 1847, he was highly critical of the whole repeal movement and its methods. He refused to accept Daniel O'Connell as his leader because, as he put it in a characteristi-

[10] *Nation*, 31 July, 20 Aug. 1847.

[11] Ibid., 12 June 1847; *Abstract of all Notices served upon Relieving Officers of Poor Law Districts in Ireland by Landowners and Others under the Act 11 and 12 Vict.*, H.C. 1849 (517), xlix. 279–314.

[12] Lalor papers, N. Lib. Ir. MS 340. Lalor (b. 1807) was the eldest son of Patrick Lalor of Tenakill, Abbeyleix, a prominent supporter of Daniel O'Connell and M.P. for Queen's County. A cripple, Fintan Lalor nevertheless edited the *Irish Felon* newspaper in 1848, and was arrested when the Habeas Corpus Act was suspended. Released because of ill-health, he took part in the fruitless revolutionary schemes of 1848–9 and died in Dublin, December 1849. See L. Fogarty, *James Fintan Lalor*, pp. ix–xlx and, in Irish, Tomás Ó Néill, *Fiontán Ó Leathlobhair*, passim.

[13] Gavan Duffy, *Four Years of Irish History*, p. 167.

cally biting phrase, O'Connell was a 'forsworn traitor at the helm'.[14] The Young Irelanders he was prepared to work with if they would accept him. But in his first letter to Gavan Duffy he was quick to point out: 'I will never act with, nor aid any organisation limiting itself strictly to the sole object of dissolving the present connection with Britain and rigidly excluding every other . . .'.[15] Fintan Lalor stressed from the outset the danger of political nationalism monopolising the attention of Irish nationalists, for, as he declared, 'A mightier question is in the land, one beside which repeal dwarfs down into a petty parish question'.[16]

Lalor, in his early correspondence with Gavan Duffy in 1847, revealed an acute realisation of the weakness of the newly founded Irish Confederation on the crucial question of a coherent programme and plan of action. Lalor's outspoken criticisms and his advocacy of a policy, which would combine a radical land agitation with the demand for repeal, were received with considerable interest by the Confederate leaders though the more conservative among them, including Gavan Duffy, were to become increasingly uneasy about both the methods Lalor urged should be adopted and the implications of his theories.[17] Though Gavan Duffy and the majority of the leading Young Irelanders grew sceptical, Lalor's theories had a direct and lasting influence on an important group which included John Mitchel, his friend Devin Reilly and Michael Doheny.[18]

Lalor's analysis of the Irish land system and of the role of the land agitation in a national movement, is, perhaps, best developed in his early letters to the *Nation*, before he became involved in the disputes and the activities of the succeeding months. Lalor was by no means opposed to a social system based on private property. He accepted private ownership in land to almost the same extent as it was recognised by English

[14] Fintan Lalor to Gavan Duffy, 11 Jan. 1847, L. Fogarty, *James Fintan Lalor*, p. 1.

[15] Ibid., p. 2.   [16] Ibid., pp. 2–3.

[17] Gavan Duffy to Fintan Lalor, [Jan. 1847], Gavan Duffy to Fintan Lalor, 24 Feb. 1847, Lalor papers, N. Lib. Ir. MS 340; Gavan Duffy, *Four Years of Irish History*, pp. 167–8.

[18] D'Arcy McGee to Fintan Lalor, 20 Mar. 1847, Lalor papers, N. Lib. Ir. MS 340.

law. It was rather in his views on the origins and moral implications of land ownership that he departed from the accepted
legal propositions. He acknowledged the English legal principle
that there could be no absolute ownership in land, but in
contrast to the English system, he insisted that the ultimate
proprietor was not the Crown but the whole community. All
titles to land derived from the people. Lalor was prepared to
allow the existing landlords to retain possession of their estates
provided they 'now combine and co-operate with that people
from whom for long ages' they had stood apart as 'aliens and
enemies'. Allegiance to Ireland and a full recognition of the
tenants' just claims were the best guarantees of the landlords'
survival under a new social order.[19]

Turning to the immediate position in Ireland, Lalor argued
that the famine and the widespread economic collapse represented 'a dissolution of the social system . . . a clear original
right returns and reverts to the people—the right of establishing and entering into a new social arrangement'. The people
could confer new and valid titles to the land of Ireland, but they
would grant them only to those landlords who were willing to
give the tenant-farmers security of tenure.[20] With society, as he
conceived it, in a state of dissolution, the time had obviously
come to link the demand for political independence with the
even more pressing demand for economic security.[21]

Though Lalor never fully clarified the question of the relative
importance that should be attached to political and agrarian
aims, his bold policy of linking political nationalism with
agrarian grievances was nevertheless of significance in the
development of that radical group within the Irish Confederation which was led by John Mitchel. It would, however, be
wrong to assume that Mitchel accepted Fintan Lalor's opinions
without reservation. As late as the summer of 1847, Mitchel
was still prepared to give the landlords a last chance to redeem
themselves. Lalor, in contrast, grew increasingly impatient
with them because of their failure to make any concessions to

[19] Fogarty, *James Fintan Lalor*, pp. 7–25, texts of the *Nation* letters.
[20] Ibid.
[21] D'Arcy McGee to Fintan Lalor, 20 Mar. 1847, Fintan Lalor to Gavan
Duffy, 11 Jan. 1847, Lalor papers, N. Lib. Ir. MS 340; Fintan Lalor to
John Mitchel, 21 June 1847, Fogarty, *James Fintan Lalor*, pp. 1–6, 42–6.

the tenant-farmers. He resolved, therefore, to press ahead with an ambitious plan to rouse the rural population against their masters.[22] In practice, Lalor did not seek, even at this point, the complete destruction of the existing landed class, but argued that the tenants could force the landlords to make a fair settlement by withholding all rents.[23]

To that end, Lalor sought to organise a militant tenant-right movement in Tipperary, King's County, Queen's County, and Kilkenny, and a meeting he held at Holy Cross, County Tipperary, on September 19, attracted a great deal of attention, but only one prominent Young Irelander, Michael Doheny, took part in this demonstration and he did so with considerable misgivings.[24] Mitchel, for his part, still hoped, with diminishing confidence, in September, that the landlords, faced by the threat of a radical agitation would concede a just scheme of tenant-right and 'take the people out of the hands of Lalor and of all revolutionists'.[25]

The months between January and September 1847 were characterised by a growing awareness of social and economic issues as practical, immediate political factors. Policies, however, tended to remain ill-defined in all sections of the nationalist movement. In the Repeal Association, as among the Young Irelanders, there was considerable enthusiasm for the tenant-right cause. John O'Connell was prepared to assert that tenant-right was as essential as the repeal of the Union.[26] Neverthless, efforts continued to be made to influence landlord opinion in favour of nationalism and O'Connell was careful to stress that there was an essential harmony of interests between landlords and tenants.[27] Again, O'Connell, rejecting a class struggle, urged that a body representative of all interests should be formed in an attempt to force Parliament to deal with Irish problems.[28] The belief in an Irish party died slowly.

[22] Michael Doheny to Smith O'Brien, 7 Sept. 1847, Smith O'Brien papers, vol. 439, no. 1980.

[23] J. Mitchel to Smith O'Brien, 8 Sept. 1847, Smith O'Brien papers, vol. 439, no. 1983.

[24] *The Times*, 22 Sept. 1847; *Freeman's Journal*, 20 Sept. 1847; Michael Doheny to Fintan Lalor, [Sept. 1847], Lalor papers, N. Lib. Ir. MS 340.

[25] J. Mitchel to Smith O'Brien, 8 Sept. 1847, Smith O'Brien papers, vol. 439, no. 1983.   [26] *Nation*, 30 Oct. 1847.

[27] Ibid., 20 Nov. 1847.   [28] Ibid., 11, 16 Sept. 1847.

Among the Young Irelanders the hope of winning the land-lords' goodwill was not willingly abandoned. The leaders of the Confederation, for example, were closely associated with the foundation of the Irish Council in the early summer of 1847. This new organisation it was thought would help to bring together the more enlightened among the property owners. The Council, however, met with only very indifferent success.[29] Beyond hinting at what might be done if men would only combine for the good of the country, it proved powerless to achieve any lasting results.

There were some short-lived rumours that Protestant opinion in Ireland was on the point of swinging over to national-ism, but the mass conversion never took place.[30] The continued failure of the attempts to win landlord support and the persis-tence of famine conditions had an important political conse-quence. They helped to accentuate the growing differences of opinion on policy matters within the Irsh Confederation, especially when the efforts to achieve a union of all interests in Ireland reached a sorry anti-climax in November.

John O'Connell's exertions resulted in a much publicised assembly of Irish members of Parliament which met at the beginning of the month.[31] Though O'Connell secured the support of Smith O'Brien for his meeting, he failed to interest the Irish Tories in his project.[32] Apart from two or three Whigs, all of the 33 Members who attended the meeting were repea-lers.[33] Ignored by the Conservatives and the bulk of the Irish Whig members, the meeting went into private session from which it never emerged. Two days later, in another effort to rally Irish public opinion, the Irish Council, which had maintained a feeble existence through the summer, staged a public conference in Dublin. Again nothing was achieved though the proceedings of the conference did help to show that membership or non-membership of the Repeal Association no

[29] *Freeman's Journal*, 2 June 1847.

[30] Goulburn to Peel, 24 Aug. 1847, Peel papers, Add. MS 40445, ff. 404–6.

[31] *Nation*, 30 Oct. 1847; *Freeman's Journal*, 7 Nov. 1847.

[32] Henry Grattan to Smith O'Brien, 16 Sept. 1847, Smith O'Brien papers, vol. 439, no. 1994; William Fagan, M.P., to John O'Connell, 8 Sept. 1847, *Nation*, 18 Sept. 1847.

[33] *Nation*, 6 Nov. 1847.

longer indicated the only serious divisions within the ranks of the nationalists. It was hoped that the conference would be a representative gathering like the great January meeting of landlords.[34] The expectations of its organisers were not realised. Only two peers, both with nationalist sympathies, attended and the remainder of the thin attendance was composed of Young Irelanders, the Liberal enthusiasts from the Irish Council, John O'Connell and a few other repeal members of Parliament.[35] The four-day conference, as was to be expected, concerned itself with such topics as the encouragement of Irish industries and the difficult issue of the financing of the famine relief schemes, but it was in the discussions on the agrarian question that the strongest conflicts of opinion among those taking part were revealed.

The Irish Council presented a report to the conference on the relations between landlord and tenant. It was an eminently cautious document which avoided dealing with the major controversial question of the legal recognition of the Ulster tenant-right custom and its extension to the rest of Ireland. The report simply recommended that tenant-farmers should receive compensation for certain substantial improvements to their holdings in the event of their tenancies being terminated by the landlords. A system of registering recognised improvements was suggested and the Council further proposed that a landlord should be released from any obligation to pay compensation for registered improvements by offering to his tenant a lease for 21 years of the lands he occupied.[36] Smith O'Brien probably best expressed the opinion of the moderates present when he urged the acceptance of the Irish Council's cautious recommendations as the wisest compromise solution under the existing circumstances. Smith O'Brien, however, added that he personally tended to favour wider concessions to the tenant-farmers.[37]

The tenant-right question was long and vigorously debated with the more radical elements seeking to win approval for a definition of tenant-right which would have made the tenant a virtual co-owner of the land with the legal proprietor. The debates showed, too, that John Mitchel had now little patience

---

[34] See p. 126.   [35] *Freeman's Journal*, 4 Nov. 1847.
[36] *Nation*, 6 Nov. 1847.   [37] Ibid.

left with compromise solutions, though he did not yet speak in openly revolutionary terms. Tenant-right, he urged, in amendments to the resolutions based on the Irish Council's report, should be recognised at once as the valid custom and law of Ireland and as such should be enforced by common consent in every part of the island without waiting for parliamentary approval of any kind. According to Mitchel, tenant-right did not arise because of improvements made by a tenant to his farm, but was a definite property right which entitled the tenant to sell 'the bare tenancy or occupancy of that farm'. He further argued that under the Ulster custom, rents could not be arbitrarily raised by the landlords and that a tenancy could not be determined by ejectment except on such terms as would allow the farmer to sell his tenant-right interest in the open market, 'the immediate landlord in every case having the right of pre-emption'.[38]

Mitchel's challenging thesis was given a very mixed reception and the debate which followed showed how little real agreement existed among reformers on the exact implications of the tenant-right system. It was pointed out, for example, that in many parts of Ulster, landlords could and did increase rents and through the exercise of pressure were able to ensure that, when a tenant put his holding up for sale, none but a landlord's nominee would get it. Again, while Sharman Crawford regarded tenant-right as a claim 'which is never extinguished by time', he argued, in contrast to Mitchel, that it only arose when a tenant made worthwhile permanent improvements to the land.[39]

In the circumstances, it was not surprising that moderate opinion was opposed to the adoption of Mitchel's amendments and that the opposition should include both Smith O'Brien and Gavan Duffy's close supporter, D'Arcy McGee, the Secretary of the Irish Confederation. In November 1847, the Young Irelanders had no common policy on the land issue and in the months that followed no such policy was, in fact, devised. By the narrow margin of two votes, Mitchel's amendments were defeated. The defeat in itself, in an unrepresentative gathering of 40 people, did not signify much, but the futility of proceedings of this kind was not lost on the radicals in the

[38] Ibid., 13 Nov. 1847.   [39] Ibid.

Irish Confederation. Members of the radical tail may have differed among themselves as to how the agrarian agitation might best be integrated with repeal, but both Mitchel and Lalor were at one in the belief that they should press forward with the agrarian struggle regardless of the feelings of the landed class.[40]

A clear statement of the policy of the Irish Confederation was obviously necessary, but unfortunately the tentative efforts that were made to draft a programme only helped to increase the discord within the movement. Already in September, on Gavan Duffy's suggestion, the task of drawing up a programme had been entrusted to Smith O'Brien and he appears to have presented his draft towards the end of the month.[41] It was subsequently published in the *Nation*, but its terms satisfied neither Gavan Duffy nor Mitchel. This was hardly surprising since Smith O'Brien did little more than to emphasise the importance of close cooperation between all classes in a campaign to secure the return of courageous and independent members to Parliament.[42] This was little better than stating, as Mitchel put it, 'the mode of bringing up the public mind to a state of preparedness', but it did not give a rational answer 'to practical but timid people who asked how we mean to repeal the Union'.[43]

Gavan Duffy rather than Smith O'Brien proved to be the most effective opponent of any attempt to give the Confederation's policy too radical a character. To strengthen the moderate influences, he was even prepared to admit federalists to membership of the Confederation without requiring them to take a repeal pledge. It was he who urged Smith O'Brien to bring Sharman Crawford and other landlords with federalist sympathies into the movement, since 'He [Sharman Crawford] and Mr Monsell would be invaluable both to the Confederation and for the purpose of bringing the gentry to see their duty as

[40] John Mitchel to Gavan Duffy, 7 Jan. 1848, *Nation*, 8 Jan. 1848; Gavan Duffy, *Four Years of Irish History*, p. 153; *Nation*, 20 Nov. 1847.

[41] McGee to Smith O'Brien, 7 Sept. 1847, Smith O'Brien papers, vol. 439, no. 1985; Mitchel to Smith O'Brien, 30 Sept. 1847, Gavan Duffy, *Four Years of Irish History*, pp. 173.

[42] *Nation*, 13 Nov. 1847; Gavan Duffy, *My Life in Two Hemispheres*, i. 240–1.

[43] Mitchel to Smith O'Brien, 30 Sept. 1847, Gavan Duffy, *Four Years of Irish History*, p. 173.

Irishmen'.[44] Shortly after Smith O'Brien had submitted his proposals, the Council of the Confederation entrusted its committee with the task of preparing an additional report. Both Mitchel and Gavan Duffy were among the members of the committee, but the final report appears to have been largely the work of Gavan Duffy and represented essentially his point of view. The work of this committee marked the end rather than the beginning of any serious attempt to produce an agreed policy. By December 20, both Mitchel and his friend Devin Reilly had resigned from the committee. The differences between them and the moderate majority were now too great to be hidden behind an agreed formula and the sharp personal disagreements of the time between Gavan Duffy and Mitchel made the dispute still more bitter.[45]

At the end of January 1848, a substantial majority of the Confederate Council accepted in principle Gavan Duffy's recommendation that they should base their policy on peaceful agitation though there was disagreement about the details of his scheme. In the end, Gavan Duffy withdrew his report and a series of studiously moderate resolutions were drafted for submission to the general body of the Confederation. Not surprisingly, the resolutions were to encounter the stern opposition of Mitchel and his followers.[46] The evidence before them of famine, destitution and death strengthened their will to pursue a radical course. Already before the end of 1847, the agony of the people had become for men such as Mitchel a terrible condemnation of the way in which Ireland was governed.

As early as the month of August the question of food exports was raised in the Irish Confederation, by Rev. John Kenyon, Mitchel's friend, and one of the few active supporters of the Confederation among the Catholic clergy. He said that exploitation by the British had resulted in the export of crops from an impoverished country: 'year after year our plentiful harvests of golden grain, more than sufficient—even since the

[44] McGee to Smith O'Brien, 1 Sept. 1847, Smith O'Brien papers, vol. 439, no. 1974; Gavan Duffy to Smith O'Brien, [late 1847], ibid. vol. 441, no. 2244.

[45] Doheny, *The Felon's Track*, pp. 120–6; R.I.A. MS 23 H. 44 (minute book of the Irish Confederation).

[46] See p. 172. Gavan Duffy, *Four Years of Irish History*, p. 175.

potato blight—to support and support well our entire population—are seen to disappear off the face of the land'.[47] Mitchel
took this argument a step further when he suggested that if an
impartial examination were made of the mutual indebtedness
of the two countries, it would be found that Britain was, on the
balance, very much Ireland's debtor. He, therefore, pleaded that
since Ireland was experiencing a famine, she was under no
obligation to repay the loans advanced by the Government to
meet the emergency.[48] This contention involved a clear rejection of the official practice of treating Britain and Ireland as a
fiscal unit for most purposes since the fusion of the British and
Irish exchequers in 1817.

The attack on the Government for permitting the export of
food from Ireland was also taken up by Mitchel's friend Thomas
Devin Reilly. In an open letter to the Irish Council, Reilly
stated bluntly that the object of all the Government's schemes
was the extermination of the Irish people. Even the poor relief
system had been introduced to ensure that a nation 'which once
numbered nine millions may be checked in its growth and coolly,
gradually murdered'.[49] Early in the New Year, Mitchel was to
put the same point of view in a somewhat different way when
he declared: 'the country is actually in a state of war—a war of
"property" against poverty—a war of "laws" against life . . .'.[50]
From being a visitation of an inscrutable providence, the famine
was becoming the greatest act of vengeance ever perpetrated
against the Irish nation by its enemies, internal and external.

Mitchel and Reilly expressed themselves in much more
radical terms than most of their contemporaries, but like them
they drew to a considerable extent on the one common fund of
bitterness and dissatisfaction. The resistance, spasmodic but
widespread, to the payment of rates and rent, left little doubt
as to the attitude of a famine-tried people, but this discontent
took more coherent shape as well. In the Repeal Association
criticism of the land system was coupled increasingly with
vigorous attacks on the unrestricted export of food from the
country.[51] The Catholic hierarchy, too, presented a strongly

[47] Irish Confed. meeting, 26 Aug., *Nation*, 28 Aug. 1847.
[48] Irish Confed. meeting, 16 Sept., *Nation*, 18 Sept. 1847.
[49] *Nation*, 9 Oct. 1847.   [50] Ibid., 8 Jan. 1848.
[51] Repeal Assoc. meeting, 27 Sept., *Freeman's Journal*, 28 Sept. 1847.

worded memorial to the Lord Lieutenant deploring the fact that 'the sacred and indefeasible right of life are forgotten amidst the incessant reclamation of the subordinate rights of property'. The bishops saw in the seizure of the farmers' crops for non-payment of rent or rates and in the harsh treatment of the evicted tenants tragic acts of injustice against a stricken and impoverished nation.[52] Still stronger words were used by John MacHale, the Archbishop of Tuam, when he wrote to the Prime Minister that, 'the cruelties committed in Ireland on the starving people are scarcely equalled under the sun'.[53]

The radicals among the Young Irelanders condemned the Irish landlords as the enemies of the people, as members of a class which ignored the common claims of humanity, but expected the British Government to maintain it in its full property rights and privileges. But though the landlords, as a class, displayed no particular generosity, their economic position was by no means enviable. They had to bear a heavy burden of taxation at a time when their lands were often encumbered with mortgages and onerous rent charges.[54] The accumulated problems of the Irish rural economy demanded a comprehensive solution, and, whatever were the faults of the Irish landowners, they alone and unaided could hardly have found, even if willing, such a solution in the midst of a famine.

[52] Memorial of the Catholic hierarchy to the Lord Lieutenant of Ireland, 21 Oct. 1847, *Nation*, 30 Oct. 1847.

[53] MacHale to Russell, 17 Dec. 1847, O'Reilly, *John MacHale, archbishop of Tuam*, ii. 21.

[54] *Evidence . . . Part 1* (Devon commission), H.C. 1845 (606) xix.

IX

THE WHIGS' IRISH POLICY
1847–8

~~~~~~~~~~~~~~~~~~~~~~~~~~~~~~~~~~~~~~~

THOUGH THE MEASURES TAKEN by the authorities to meet
the famine became the subject of much criticism in Ireland, they
also provoked adverse comment of a different kind in Britain.
The amount spent in Ireland during the famine years was
considerable by the standards of the time. Already in 1847–8
there were those inside and outside the cabinet who could argue
that the British taxpayer should not be expected to go on meeting the cost of Irish relief.[1] The £3,635,000 advanced by way of
loans, it was urged, ought to be repaid and Irish property made
primarily responsible for the support of all further destitution.
At a time, therefore, when the potato crop had failed once
again, it seemed as if Ireland would be compelled to repay a
great deal of money to the Exchequer and find from her own
limited resources the funds necessary to support the poor in

---

[1] Russell to Clarendon, 17 Nov. 1847, Russell papers, P.R.O. 30/22/6.
Between 1845 and 1848 some £9,536,000 was provided from public funds
to meet the cost of famine relief, including drainage, in Ireland. In 1853,
the Government accepted imperial responsibility for the balances outstanding on the loans advanced for Irish relief. See, *Account of Public Monies
expended or advanced by way of Loan in the Years 1845, 1846, 1847, and 1848,
for the Relief of Distress in Ireland*, H.C. 1847–8 (723), liv. 5–26; *Return of
all Sums of Money granted or advanced on account of the Distress and Famine, or in
aid of the Administration of the Poor Law in Ireland during the Years 1846, 1847,
1848 and 1849, with Amount of Repayments*, H.C. 1848 (352), xlviii. 5–6.

1847–8. It was hardly surprising that resistance to the payment of rates caused serious unrest in many rural areas. It was one of the ways the people of an impoverished countryside could express their sense of discontent.[2]

In November and December 1847, troops had to be called out to protect the rate collectors and popular pressure was often exerted on farmers to induce them not to pay their rates. The campaign against the poor rates was, however, only one aspect of agrarian discontent.[3] The attempts by landlords and their agents to recover arrears of rent and the growing fear of eviction brought the land system increasingly under attack.

The successive failures of the potato crop and the general disruption of farming activities made the payment of rent just as heavy a burden for the small farmer as the payment of the poor rate. It was a situation in which some generous concessions by the landlords would have eased the plight of the farmers, but the Irish landlords, like their tenants, were engaged in a hard struggle for survival. The temptation was there to evict the small holders and replace them by more substantial tenants working larger farms and better able to pay the rent. The provisions of the Poor Law also acted as an inducement to landlords to clear their estates of tenants occupying tiny sub-divided holdings, since, under the law as it stood, landlords were directly responsible for the full rates on occupied properties with a poor law valuation of less than £4.[4]

The deterioration in the relations between landlord and tenant and the clearances, which continued throughout 1847–8, brought a further element of fear and uncertainty into Irish life.[5] The evictions and their cruel consequences helped to provide still more evidence for those who were coming to regard the famine as essentially artificial, prolonged by the indifference

[2] *Dublin Evening Post*, 18 Sept. 1847; *Tables showing the number of Criminal Offenders committed for Trial or bailed . . . in the Year 1848, and the Result of the Proceedings*. H.C. 1848 (1067), xliv. 129–228.

[3] Returns of military parties furnished in aid of the civil power, Kilmainham papers, vol. 226.

[4] W. Stanley (Sec. Poor Law Commissioners), to Rev. T. Costello (of Castlebar), 18 Dec. 1847, *Dublin Evening Post*, 6 Jan. 1848.

[5] *Abstract of all Notices served upon Relieving Officers of Poor Law Districts in Ireland by Landowners and Others . . . .* H.C. 1849 (517), xlix. 279–314; Bernard O'Reilly, *John MacHale, Archbishop of Tuam*, ii. 26.

of the British Government and Parliament and by the selfishness of the Irish landed class.[6]

In August 1847, Sir James Graham wrote to Peel that Ireland 'will be the principal domestic difficulty for Russell'.[7] Events were to prove the accuracy of Graham's prophecy and they were to reveal, too, the Government's inability to reach the kind of courageous decisions the crisis demanded. The Whig ministers either shied away from the challenge of substantial reform or were content to go on applying to Ireland those expedients which apparently satisfied the precepts of economics but left the fundamental problems unresolved. Even immediate questions such as poor relief were handled in an inconclusive fashion. With the existing relief schemes due to end in September 1847, some action had obviously to be taken to feed the people at a time when the potato crop had again failed.[8] It was known, too, that many Poor Law unions in Ireland were already in a bankrupt state.[9] It was a situation that only emphasised the utter inadequacy of the revised Poor Law and the position was made no easier by the determination of the Treasury to secure repayment of the earlier advances made to Ireland under the relief acts.[10] In a memorandum drafted in July, Russell set down his views on the issue of giving further aid to Ireland. He considered that no public works should be undertaken or free rations distributed, because, even were England prepared to continue such schemes, which he felt she was not, their effect would be to turn a large proportion of the Irish population into permanent paupers. 'In short', he wrote, 'Ireland would be as Rome during the reign of the later emperors.' The only concession he felt prepared to make was to sanction donations from public funds to aid local subscriptions and to keep a few food depots open on the remote west coast. State-aided emigration from the poorest areas he believed was imprudent without further enquiry into the employment opportunities overseas. Lord John's conclusion was that the

[6] Irish Council meeting, 28 Sept., *Nation*, 2 Oct. 1847; *The Times*, 11 Oct. 1847; Irish Confed. meeting, 20 Oct., *Nation*, 23 Oct. 1847.

[7] Graham to Peel, 28 Aug. 1847, Peel papers, Add. MS 40452, ff. 230–1.

[8] Clarendon to Wood, 12 Aug. 1847, Clarendon papers, letterbook I.

[9] Clarendon to Wood, 21 July 1847, Clarendon papers, letterbook I.

[10] Sir C. Trevelyan to Clarendon, 18 Oct. 1847, Clarendon papers, Ir. box 60.

only legitimate means of helping the people was the poor rate which should have precedence over all other claims since, 'proprietors and their tenants have raised up, encouraged and grown rich, upon a potato-fed population. Now that the question is between rent and sustenance, I think rent must give way, and the whole rental if necessary given to support the people'.[11] The Prime Minister would have liked to put Irish famine relief on a strictly local basis. That had long been his inclination but the circumstances in Ireland, in 1847–8, were such as to make it just as difficult as in the preceding year. In pressing for a strict adherence to the Poor Law, Russell was strongly backed by Charles Wood, the Chancellor of the Exchequer, who remained a steadfast advocate of non-intervention by the state in economic affairs.[12]

In Ireland, the new Lord Lieutenant, Lord Clarendon, was able to see more clearly that 1847–8 could not be regarded as a normal year.[13] The potato crop had again failed and the poor had even fewer resources than in previous years. Again, the problem remained of what was to be done about the relief works which had been left in an unfinished state.[14] In the end, under pressure from Dublin, a compromise solution was devised. Funds were to be made available to complete unfinished public works in the summer of 1848, but the sum to be advanced was to be limited to the amounts repaid to the Treasury by the different localities in Ireland.[15] A few food depots were to be retained in some remote areas, and a close watch was to be kept on the operation of the Poor Law. To guard against exceptional hardship in impoverished Poor Law unions, it was conceded that some state aid might ultimately have to be

[11] Memorandum by Lord John Russell, Russell papers, P.R.O. 30/22/6.
[12] Wood to Clarendon, 15 Aug. 1847, Clarendon papers, Ir. box 9, bundle 42; Wood to Russell, 26 Aug. 1847, Russell papers, P.R.O. 30/22/6.
[13] George William Frederick Villiers, fourth Earl of Clarendon and fourth Baron Hyde (1800–70). Attaché at St Petersburg, 1820. Ambassador at Madrid, 1833–9. Lord Privy Seal, 1839–41. President of the Board of Trade 1846. Foreign Secretary, 1853–8, 1865–6, and 1868–70.
[14] Clarendon to Russell, 18 Aug. 1847, Clarendon papers, letterbook I; Clarendon to Russell, 28 Aug. 1847, Russell papers, P.R.O. 30/22/6.
[15] *Hansard*, c. 484–90; Wood to Russell, 1 Sept. 1847, Russell papers, P.R.O. 30/22/6; Sir G. Gray to Clarendon, 20 Mar. 1848, Clarendon papers, Ir. box 5, bundle 21.

given.[16] But the main burden of meeting the needs of the people was to have fallen on the Irish Poor Law system. It was expected, by the Government, to fulfil a task for which it was not intended: to support a famine stricken people in a very poor country. The inevitable happened and in 1848 money had to be voted by Parliament to relieve distress in twenty-two of the most impoverished Irish unions, and the Treasury had to accept the fact that Ireland was in no position to repay quickly the funds which had been advanced in 1846–7.[17] But these concessions were too limited to undo the harm caused by a rigid and shortsighted application of the Poor Law during a national emergency.[18]

Clarendon, the Lord Lieutenant, was quick to realise the political dangers of the social and economic crisis in Ireland. He urged the Government to take up once again the question of the relations between landlord and tenant in the belief that 'it is always better for a government to precede and to guide opinion where it is founded on justice'.[19] But, while the Government in the closing months of 1847 agreed on the need for a measure, the difficulty was to devise a formula which would please all interests. The cabinet was fearful of taking any step which could alienate the landed interest, or set a precedent which might lead to complications in the rural areas of England.[20] This helped to produce a rather curious situation in which Lord John found himself in an ineffective minority within his own cabinet. At first, the cabinet considered as being too daring Clarendon's moderate proposals to compensate evicted tenants for authorised improvements they had made in the lands during their tenancy.[21] In contrast to his colleagues, Russell, however, argued that the legal recognition of some form

[16] Clarendon to Russell, 8 Oct. 1847, Clarendon papers, letterbook I.
[17] *Hansard*, ci. 461–3; Wood to Clarendon, 1 June 1848, Clarendon papers, Ir. box 9, bundle 42.
[18] Clarendon to Sir. G. Grey, 15 Jan. 1848, Clarendon papers, letterbook II.
[19] Clarendon to Russell, 18 Oct. 1847, Russell papers, P.R.O. 30/22/6.
[20] Wood to Clarendon, 26 Oct. 1847, Clarendon papers, Ir. box 31, bundle 42; Clarendon to Wood, 28 Oct. 1847, Clarendon papers, letterbook I.
[21] Clarendon to Russell, 23 Oct. 1847, Russell papers, 30/22/6, and Clarendon papers, letterbook I.

of tenant-right rather than mere compensation for improvements was necessary. Occupancy of land over a period of years, he suggested, even without evidence of improvements should give a legal right to compensation for disturbance in the event of an eviction.[22] Russell would have liked, as well, to introduce a bill 'for giving some security and some provision to the miserable cottiers who are now treated as brute beasts'.[23] Against the combined opposition of the Lord Lieutenant, who viewed tenant-right with disfavour, and the rest of the cabinet, Russell's advocacy of a radical land reform made little progress, especially as Russell was not prepared to press his colleagues to accept his point of view.[24]

It was only after a tedious struggle, that the cabinet, in the end, agreed to a compensation measure which included Clarendon's principal recommendations. Indeed, at one stage the cabinet, in the Prime Minister's absence through illness, seemed on the point of virtually jettisoning the whole measure.[25] Yet the bill which provoked so much discussion and misgivings proved to be no more ambitious than the Conservatives' inadequate proposals in 1846. It offered a limited measure of compensation, not to exceed three years' rent, to dispossessed tenants who had held land at rents of £10 or less per annum. This compensation was to be paid only in respect to improvements made by the tenant with the landlord's approval or the approval of arbitrators where landlord and tenant failed to agree. After a period of twenty-one years, if the tenant had continued to hold at the same rent, the landlord would be released from paying compensation.

The bill, introduced in February 1848, received a cool welcome from Irish land reformers. Since no improvements could be made without prior notice to the landlord, the criticism was made that the bill contributed little towards the solution of the problem of insecurity of tenure. Again, the bill

---

[22] Russell to Clarendon, 10 Nov. 1847, Russell papers, P.R.O. 30/22/6.

[23] Russell to Clarendon, 15 Nov. 1847, Russell papers, P.R.O. 30/22/6.

[24] Clarendon to Palmerston, 21 Nov. 1847, Clarendon papers, letterbook I; Lansdowne to Russell, 14 Jan. 1848, Russell papers, P.R.O. 30/22/7; Clarendon to Russell, 5 Feb. 1848, Clarendon papers, letterbook I.

[25] Sir G. Grey to Clarendon, 21 Jan. 1848, Clarendon papers, Ir. box 5, bundle 21; Sir G. Grey to Russell, 21 Jan. 1848, Russell papers, P.R.O. 30/22/7.

was seen as a possible threat to the Ulster tenant custom because the Government now offered less than what the Ulster farmers had long claimed as of right. It was further argued that the machinery for arbitration included in the bill was too cumbersome.[26] The debate in Parliament on the bill never progressed very far. Early in April 1848, it was referred to a select committee, a step which the Earl of Lincoln rightly took as meaning that the Government had decided quietly to bury a measure for which it had never felt much enthusiasm.[27] Instead of facing the hazardous task of reform in Ireland, Government and Parliament were content to go on propping up the existing social structure with hastily devised expedients, such as the Crime and Outrage Bill.

Lord Clarendon, on the death of Lord Bessborough, in May 1847, had been appointed Lord Lieutenant. He undertook the commission to govern Ireland with some misgivings. 'The real difficulty', he explained to his friend Henry Reeve, of *The Times*, 'lies with the people themselves. They are always in the mud . . . their idleness and helplessness can hardly be believed.'[28] Clarendon was an able, somewhat cynical man and an experienced diplomat who, as foreign secretary, was to play an important part in the shaping of British foreign policy in the eighteen-fifties and sixties. His letters dealing with Irish affairs are vivid and outspoken, but he lacked that close knowledge of the country which Lord Bessborough, a resident Irish landlord, had possessed. Clarendon did not agree with Charles Wood that there was no salvation for Ireland except 'through a purgatory of misery and starvation', but quickly he came to the conclusion that no matter what the Government did to aid the people, 'we shall be equally blamed for keeping them alive or letting them die, and we have only to select between the censure of the economists or the philanthropists . . .'.[29] The

[26] *Hansard*, xcvi. 680–98; *Freeman's Journal*, 15 Feb. 1848; *Nation*, 19 Feb. 1848.

[27] *Hansard*, xcviii. 60–9.

[28] Clarendon to Henry Reeve, 18 Sept. 1847, Clarendon papers, letterbook II. See also H. E. Maxwell, *The Life and Letters of George William, fourth Earl of Clarendon*, i. 280.

[29] C. Wood to Clarendon, 23 July 1847, Clarendon papers, Ir. box 31, bundle 42; Clarendon to Russell, 10 Aug. 1847, Clarendon papers, letterbook I.

maintenance of public order became for Clarendon a major preoccupation in the difficult months of 1847–8. The growing unrest in the rural areas troubled him and he considered that the hostile attitude of a section of the Catholic clergy, especially the younger priests, made the task of government more difficult than it might otherwise have been.[30] To curb their activities, he worked hard to win the confidence of the Catholic bishops, but, as we shall see, these efforts to secure greater ecclesiastical goodwill soon provoked suspicion and uneasiness in nationalist circles.[31]

By November 1847, agrarian outrages in Ireland had become a serious problem. The evictions of tenant-farmers brought with them unrest particularly in the counties Limerick, Tipperary, Clare, Roscommon, King's County and Fermanagh. The unrest was, therefore, to some extent localised but Lord Clarendon feared that the disturbances might well spread to other counties. In the event of an emergency, the Lord Lieutenant argued that the simplest and most effective procedure would be for parliament to suspend, for a limited period, the Habeas Corpus Act. Nothing less, he made it clear, would be of real use to him.[32] Clarendon, however, indicated that until the position in Ireland grew more alarming, he would be satisfied with new legislation to regulate the licensing of arms and to permit the imposition of collective fines on disturbed districts.[33]

These demands put Lord John Russell in a difficult position, especially as Clarendon threatened to retire from office unless the additional powers were given to him.[34] Russell was conscious of the fact that he and his friends had helped to drive Peel from office, ostensibly over an Irish coercion bill. Now he was being asked to introduce a coercion bill of his own. Russell was doubtful about the possible reactions of Parliament to new repressive measures and Sir George Grey, the Home Secretary,

[30] Clarendon to Russell, 10 Aug. 1847, Clarendon papers, letterbook I.
[31] Clarendon to Russell, 1 Oct. 1847, Clarendon to Russell, 13 Oct. 1847, Clarendon papers, letterbook I; MacHale to Clarendon, 9 Dec. 1847, B. O'Reilly, op. cit., ii. 34–6.
[32] Clarendon to Russell, 12 Nov. 1847, Clarendon papers, letterbook I; Clarendon to Russell, 10 Nov. 1847, Clarendon papers, letterbook I.
[33] Clarendon to Russell, 12 Nov. 1847, Clarendon papers, letterbook I.
[34] Russell to Clarendon, 10 Nov. 1847, Clarendon to Russell, 18 Nov. 1847, Russell papers, P.R.O. 30/22/6.

agreed with him on the inadvisability of asking Parliament to accept a new coercion bill, but the pressure on Russell to take action was considerable.[35] Lord Palmerston advocated a vigorous measure and, despite Russell's misgivings, the response of Parliament to the Government's proposals was to prove the accuracy of Sir William Somerville's view that not merely did public opinion in Britain favour some coercion in Ireland, but that 'Parliament would grant any powers which the Government might think fit to demand'.[36] To meet the situation, the cabinet found a compromise solution in the Crime and Outrage (Ireland) Bill. It was a mild measure enabling the Lord Lieutenant to proclaim disturbed districts and to draft additional police into such areas. As a further precaution, the carrying of unlicensed arms was prohibited in the proclaimed areas on penalty of two years imprisonment and the constabulary were authorised to search for such arms.[37]

The Lord Lieutenant was not particularly satisfied with the bill, but he accepted it in the hope that 'it will answer not so much by its own provisions as by the evidence it will afford that Parliament and the Government are in earnest'.[38] When Parliament met, in November, the Crime and Outrage (Ireland) Bill was supported by the principal political groups in both Houses and such criticism as it did encounter was largely confined to the complaint that the bill was not strong enough.[39]

Russell had little to fear from Parliament, because apart from this police measure and the Tenant Compensation Bill, which was abandoned before the session ended, he had now no controversial Irish policy which could endanger his Government.[40] Parliament met, however, under the shadow of a major com-

[35] Russell to Clarendon, 15 Nov. 1847, Russell papers, P.R.O. 30/22/6.
[36] Palmerston to Russell, 20 Nov. 1847, Russell papers, P.R.O. 30/22/6; Sir W. Somerville (Chief Secretary) to Clarendon, 21 Nov. 1847, Clarendon papers, Ir. box 27, bundle 38. Sir William Meredith Somerville, Bart. (1802–73). Irish landowner. Succeeded to the baronetcy 1831. M.P. for Drogheda 1837. 1847 Chief Secretary for Ireland. Created Baron Athlumney 1863.
[37] *Hansard*, xiv. 270–312.
[38] *The Greville Memoirs* (2nd part), iii. 104–6.
[39] *Hansard*, xcv. 342–3, 347–55; *The Times*, 1 Dec. 1847; Clarendon to Russell, 30 Nov. 1847, Clarendon papers, letterbook I.
[40] *Hansard*, xcv. 11–14. See p. 197.

mercial crisis, which reached its climax in October. The general food shortage in Western Europe, in 1846–7, had resulted in sharp competition in the American and Russian grain markets, and had caused a rise not merely in grain prices, but in the prices of a wide range of other commodities as well. These developments put a heavy strain on Britain's financial reserves and the intensive efforts of the railway promoters to secure capital for their schemes helped to tie up considerable sums in dubious and speculative undertakings. Discount rates and grain prices were both high in the summer of 1847, but August brought a very sudden reversal in price trends. In May, London wheat prices were as high as 115/- per cwt. but by mid-September the average price had fallen to 49/6d. This rapid fall in prices helped to pull down the unsteady superstructure erected on grain speculation and over-investment in railway schemes. The crisis was financial rather than industrial in character, and the Bank of England succeeded in riding the storm with its credit intact. But though the crisis passed quickly enough, it left behind it a feeling of insecurity and a distaste for economic experiment which hardly encouraged courageous action in relation to the social ills of Ireland.[41] Britain's economic difficulties rather than Irish affairs held the centre of the stage, and the fumbling repeal opposition did little to force the urgent needs of Ireland on the attention of Parliament.

The repealers approach to the new Crime and Outrage Bill illustrates their weakness as a political pressure group. No sustained effort was made in Parliament by a united party to halt the progress of the bill or even to secure substantial reforms as the price for allowing the bill an easy passage. The burden of opposition was borne by John O'Connell, Smith O'Brien and three or four other members. John O'Connell, for his part, made it clear that he would abandon his opposition to the bill if the Government, having first introduced remedial legislation, could then show that the criminal law needed strengthening in Ireland.[42] Some of the other repeal members, however, did not

[41] Sir John Clapham, *The Bank of England; a History*, ii. 197–9; Redcliffe N. Salaman, *The History and Social Influence of the Potato*, pp. 298–9; Halévy, *The Age of Peel and Cobden*, pp. 170–82.

[42] *Hansard*, xcv. 312–17, 701–13, 328–34, 341–2, 976–9; Somerville to Clarendon, 10 Dec. 1847, Clarendon papers, Ir. box 27, bundle 38.

even wait for the remedial legislation to be brought forward. Both Henry Grattan, the repeal member for County Meath, and R. Dillon Browne, the member for County Mayo, spoke in favour of the bill, while Morgan John O'Connell, Daniel O'Connell's nephew, supported the Government on the third reading.[43]

After the general election, it was estimated that some 39 repealers had been elected, yet only 20 members in all could be found to vote against the first reading of the bill and of these two were Radicals representing English constituencies.[44] On the second reading only 19 votes were cast against the bill and 5 fewer still on the third reading.[45] With such slight opposition to contend with it was not surprising that the bill sped swiftly through Parliament. First introduced on November 29, it received the royal assent on December 20.[46]

The feeble efforts of the repeal members to induce Parliament to devote greater attention to Irish issues were in no way aided by the disagreements between Feargus O'Connor, the Chartist leader, and John O'Connell at this time. The relations between the Chartist movement and repeal had never been particularly cordial. Daniel O'Connell had long criticised the Chartists' tendency towards violence and the Young Irelanders had looked with suspicion on Chartism as a mere class movement rather than a political movement superior to sectional interests. On many practical questions, however, such as electoral reform, Irish repealers and British Chartists shared common aspirations. Again, the personal backgrounds of some of the principal Chartists, such as Feargus O'Connor and his critic James Bronterre O'Brien, strengthened the associations between Chartism and Ireland.

Feargus O'Connor had first sat in Parliament, in 1832, as a supporter of Daniel O'Connell. He soon found O'Connell's leadership both too firm and too moderate and turned to English Radicalism. O'Connor, however, did not lose interest in the Irish repeal campaign nor did he forget his grievances against the O'Connell family.[47] O'Connor's dislike of the Anti-

---

[43] *Hansard*, xcv. 720–6.

[44] Scholefield, the member for Birmingham, and Feargus O'Connor both opposed the bill. *Nation*, 11 Dec. 1847.

[45] *Hansard*, xcv. 355–6.   [46] Ibid., xcv. 976–9.

[47] Mark Hovell, *The Chartist Movement*, pp. 95, 163; *Labourer*, i. 206–11.

Corn Law League and his advocacy of the interests of the small holders helped him, with Tory assistance, to secure for the declining Chartist movement its sole success in the general election of 1847. Returned for Nottingham, he lost no time in putting himself forward as a champion of the repeal of the Union and as an outspoken critic of John O'Connell's leadership of the repeal party.[48] Both inside and outside the House of Commons, O'Connor propounded radical solutions for many Irish problems. In his journal the *Labourer*, which he edited with Ernest Jones, it was urged that the Irish tenant-farmers should be given perpetuity of tenure as a fair rent.[49] O'Connor argued, too, that there was only one cure for Ireland's plight and it was to give 'the Irish their own, restoring the soil to its children— but the physician must be a home government, established under the banner of repeal'.[50]

John O'Connell lacked the great qualities of command and decision possessed by his father and the obvious contrast in character between the two men may well have encouraged Feargus O'Connor to attempt to oust John O'Connell from the leadership of the rather dispirited repeal party by a show of daring and courage. Whatever O'Connor's motives may have been, he made no attempt to hide his strong hostility towards John O'Connell.[51] In the course of the debate on the Crime and Outrage Bill, he criticised O'Connell's opening speech as being nothing better than a 'humble adjuration'.[52] His attack on O'Connell was followed up by a resolution asking for a select committee of the House of Commons to report on the means by which the Act of Union was accomplished, the effects of the Union on both Britain and Ireland and the probable consequences of its maintenance.[53]

With the great majority of the members of Parliament opposed to the repeal of the Union, O'Connor's attempt to interest the House in repeal was destined to failure. In bringing forward the resolution, however, he no doubt hoped to demonstrate his qualities as the advocate of a more vigorous repeal policy in

---

[48] *Hansard*, xcv. 317–21.　　[49] *Labourer*, i. 19–23.
[50] Ibid., ii. 143.　　[51] Hovell, op. cit., p. 382.
[52] Somerville to Clarendon, 10 Dec. 1847, Clarendon papers, Ir. box 27, bundle 38; *Hansard*, xcv. 317–21, 728–38.
[53] Ibid., xcv. 752–65.

Parliament. Though he appears to have acted without any prior consultation with the repeal members, they did make a rather half-hearted attempt to support O'Connor, but the debate rapidly degenerated into a series of trivial exchanges, with the Home Secretary, Sir George Grey, protecting the closing repeal speakers from constant interruptions.[54] O'Connor's resolution met its expected fate when it was defeated by 255 votes to 23. Only one English member supported him in the division, Wakley, the member for Finsbury.[55] Though a Chartist versifier might write that 'Each true British spirit will join with Eirin for repeal of the Union—the land and the charter', the chances of such a combination emerging at the close of 1847 must have seemed remote indeed.[56]

The weakness and lack of unity which characterised the repeal party at Westminster helped to strengthen the resistance of the more radical elements in Ireland to any suggestion that the Irish Confederation should concentrate its activities largely on organising support throughout the country in preparation for any future parliamentary elections.[57] This growth of radical criticism, however, served to confirm Gavan Duffy and Smith O'Brien in their fear that the Confederation might become 'purely democratic' in character.[58] As we have seen, the task of formulating a programme for the Confederation soon caused a major clash within the organisation.[59] Men such as John Mitchel and Devin Reilly saw in the social and political developments of the weeks between August and December ample proof of the futility of relying on any policy which was not firmly based on a widespread agitation to encourage the farmers to enforce tenant-right and withhold all payments of the poor rate.[60] Such an approach neither Gavan Duffy nor Smith O'Brien could accept and the consequence of this sharp disagreement was that

[54] *Nation*, 11 Dec. 1847; *Hansard*, xcv. 769–74, 752–65, 766–8, 769–74; Sir G. Grey to Clarendon, 8 Dec. 1847, Clarendon papers, Ir. box 11, bundle 21.

[55] *Hansard*, xcv. 797–8.   [56] *Labourer*, i. 92–3.

[57] *Nation*, 8 Jan. 1848; Doheny, *The Felon's Track*, pp. 120–6; McGee to Smith O'Brien, 30 Dec. 1847, Smith O'Brien papers, vol. 439, no. 2040.

[58] Gavan Duffy to Smith O'Brien, [late 1847], Smith O'Brien papers, vol. 441, no. 2232.

[59] See p. 155.

[60] *Nation*, 4 Dec. 1847, 8 Jan. 1848.

Mitchel withdrew from the committee on Confederate policy and ceased to write for Gavan Duffy's newspaper, the *Nation*.[61]

The Confederation, in February 1848, adopted, on the recommendation of the Council of the organisation, and in the face of Mitchel's opposition, a series of resolutions designed to confine the activities of the movement to a policy based primarily on a parliamentary campaign.[62] Though Mitchel and his friends did not formally leave the Confederation, he, along with Devin Reilly and John Martin, of Newry, resigned from the Council. Mitchel henceforth was to devote much of his energy to his new and radical newspaper, the *United Irishman*, which appeared for the first time on 12 February 1848.

The rejection of Mitchel's approach to political action by the Confederation did not mean that all the leading Young Irelanders were in complete agreement with Gavan Duffy's and Smith O'Brien's advocacy of moderation. Some Young Irelanders, such as Richard O'Gorman and Thomas Francis Meagher, for example, considered that Gavan Duffy and Smith O'Brien were showing poor judgement when they discouraged any strong opposition to the Crime and Outrage Bill. Gavan Duffy feared that too outspoken an attack on the bill might imperil the Confederates' chances of winning the support of the gentry, but O'Gorman and Meagher argued that any undue consideration for the landlords at such a time could only result in the loss of whatever popular support the Confederation had been able to secure.[63] Again, despite the set-back he had suffered, Mitchel found many active supporters among the members of the Confederate clubs, especially in Dublin where six out of a total of seventeen clubs in Ireland had been established by the beginning of 1848.[64]

[61] R. O'Gorman to Smith O'Brien, 14 Dec. 1847, Smith O'Brien papers, vol. 439, no. 2033; Minute book of the Irish Confederation, R.I.A. MS 23 H. 44.

[62] *Nation*, 5 Feb. 1848. See also p. 155.

[63] R. O'Gorman to Smith O'Brien, 3 Dec. 1847, Smith O'Brien papers, vol. 439, no. 2030; Gavan Duffy to Smith O'Brien, [late 1847], Smith O'Brien papers, vol. 441, no. 2232; T. F. Meagher to Smith O'Brien, [late 1847], Smith O'Brien papers, vol. 441, no. 2298.

[64] McGee to Smith O'Brien, 30 Dec. 1847, Smith O'Brien papers, vol. 439, no. 2040; Mitchel to Fintan Lalor, 4 Jan. 1848, Fogarty, *James Fintan Lalor*, pp. 120–2; *Nation*, 15 Jan. 1848.

Though they could not accept Mitchel's drastic proposals, even the most conservative Young Irelanders viewed with concern the plight of the peasant population. Smith O'Brien perhaps best expressed the growing sense of apprehension in Ireland when he declared that the famine was not so much the outcome of an 'inevitable doom', as the result of the 'stolid incapacity of British misgovernment'.[65] The moderate Young Irelanders rejected the conclusions drawn by Mitchel and Fintan Lalor, but with troubled spirits they could only pursue a course of action which seemed destined to achieve little of practical worth. Such active popular political feeling as survived in the country remained loyal to the Repeal Association and the O'Connell name. The machinery of agitation was there, but there was little on which the agitators could work.

If political issues were primarily responsible for the initial secession within the repeal movement, there can be but little doubt that the hardship produced by the famine was the irritant that led to the fresh division within the ranks of the secessionists themselves. From the point of view of the development of Irish political thought and the discipline of political action, the second secession, if it may be so called, was in some ways more significant than the first. It was the expression of a new approach to Irish political problems. It took, perhaps, a narrower view of nationalism than its critics could accept, but it realised the latent possibilities of the economic grievances of the rural population. It was, however, something more than a mere technique of agitation, for this 'new departure' assumed a criminal neglect of duty rooted in antipathy towards the people of Ireland on the part of both government and landowners. Mitchel and Fintan Lalor may have disagreed, to some extent, as to the precise mode of procedure to be followed in enlisting the aid of the rural population, but both were convinced of the need for a radical change in the existing political and social structure, which they saw as a closely integrated whole opposed to the interests of the exploited and impoverished people.[66]

[65] Irish Confed. meeting, 12 Jan., *Nation*, 15 Jan. 1848.
[66] Gavan Duffy, *Four Years of Irish History*, p. 175; Irish Confed. meeting, 2 Feb., *Nation*, 5 Feb. 1848.

X

THE REPEAL MOVEMENT IN
/
1848

~~~~~~

(1)

FREEDOM OF WORSHIP was secure in mid-nineteenth century
Ireland, but the Catholic church, the greatest single organised
force in the country, had no legally-defined place in public
affairs. The question of the relations between the Catholic
church and the Government had long troubled Peel, and the
Whigs saw in the contrast between the status of the established
church in Ireland and the Catholic church an injustice which
should be redressed. It was not surprising, therefore, that
Russell, once in office, should have sought to improve the
position of his Government in Ireland through a settlement with
Rome.[1] It was a task which called for caution. The storm of
criticism over the Maynooth grant in 1845 had shown how
sensitive Protestant opinion in Britain could be to any further
recognition of Catholic claims. In Ireland, any contact between
the Government and Rome was regarded by Irish Catholics
with profound suspicion as a possible threat to their independence of action. It was, therefore, in the most discreet of
fashions that Russell sought the assistance of the Holy See, at
the beginning of 1847, using the British Ambassador at Vienna
and the Papal Nuncio there as intermediaries. Russell had the

[1] John F. Broderick. *The Holy See and the Irish Movement for the Repeal of
the Union with England. 1829–1847*, passim.

174

message conveyed to Rome that the Government would appreciate it highly if the Pope addressed the Irish bishops and urged them to continue in their efforts to preserve good order and to get the people to confide in the Government.[2] The response to this approach by the Government was most encouraging, particularly as the Holy See was anxious to maintain friendly relations with Britain. Early in April 1847 a private letter was sent by Pope Pius IX to the four Irish Archbishops counselling them to work for the preservation of peace and order in the country, and a copy of the letter was given to the British Ambassador at Vienna.[3] In the course of the secret but friendly discussions with the Ambassador, the Nuncio put forward the suggestion that for the future it would be wiser to consult directly with Rome over Irish ecclesiastical matters rather than to engage in negotiations with the rival Catholic factions in Ireland. The Court of Rome let it be known in Vienna, too, that the Pope would be satisfied with the recognition by the British Government of the Catholic church in Ireland as a legal entity, backed by a promise that the Government would not interfere with the priests in the discharge of their duties.[4]

This rather friendly attitude led the Ambassador to hope that, for the future, Rome would no longer be 'misled' by English and Irish Catholics.[5] His optimism was premature. Over the 'Godless' colleges, the Irish clerics in Rome scored a minor success with the promulgation of a papal rescript in October condemning the colleges' scheme because it did not make adequate provision to meet the religious needs of the students.[6] There were signs, too, that some of the Pope's advisers remained very suspicious of British motives.[7]

The decision to send Lord Minto, the Lord Privy Seal, on a mission to Italy was, therefore, taken at an opportune time. Palmerston's Italian policy was aimed at minimising ultra-conservative and especially French influence in Italy, in the

[2] Ponsonby to Russell, 29 Mar. 1847, Russell papers, P.R.O. 30/22/6.

[3] Ponsonby to Russell, 3 May 1847, Russell papers, P.R.O. 30/22/6.

[4] Ponsonby to Russell, 29 Mar., 3 May 1847, Russell papers, P.R.O. 30/22/6.

[5] Ponsonby to Russell, 3 May 1847, Russell papers, P.R.O. 30/22/6.

[6] *Freeman's Journal*, 25 Oct. 1847.

[7] Clarendon to Russell, 1 Oct. 1847, Clarendon papers, letterbook I.

hope that the Italian rulers would be prepared to make some constitutional concessions of a liberal kind to their subjects.[8] Lord Minto's task was to further this policy at the papal and other courts of Italy and he set out on his mission encouraged by the knowledge that the Holy See had indicated its willingness to welcome such a mission.[9] It was expected in London, however, that Minto would concern himself with more than Italian issues while in Rome, since Irish ecclesiastical affairs offered another urgent theme for discussion and negotiation. The outspoken comments of the Catholic hierarchy on the inadequacy of the Government's famine relief measures indicated the importance of the Church as a potentially formidable critic of state policy.[10] Again, the open association of many Catholic priests with the tenant-right agitation was a further source of concern for the administration, and, indeed, these quasi-political activities had already provoked some sharp attacks on the clergy, both inside and outside Parliament.[11]

Careful preparations were made to provide Minto with a detailed statement of the Government's attitude on Irish ecclesiastical affairs. He was advised by Clarendon, in a special memorandum, to inform the Pope that in Ireland religious issues had become so confused with political ones—due to past conditions in the country—that if the clergy showed any inclination to abandon a strongly nationalistic policy they became objects of attack. For the clergy to be 'the slaves of the people', Clarendon wrote, was a degrading situation, but only the Pope could provide a remedy. The remedy Clarendon would have liked was an instruction to the clergy directing them not to join political movements or attend political meetings. To prevent any misunderstandings, he was anxious that a

[8] Gilbert Elliot, 2nd Earl of Minto (1782–1859), 1832 British Ambassador in Berlin, he became First Lord of the Admiralty in Sept. 1835. He was appointed Lord Privy Seal in 1846 and held office until the fall of the Russell ministry in 1852. He was Lord John Russell's father-in-law. Halévy, *The Age of Peel and Cobden*, pp. 194–6.

[9] Palmerston to Russell, 21 Aug. 1847, H. M. Addington to Russell, 11 Sept. 1847, Russell papers, P.R.O. 30/22/6.

[10] Clarendon to Russell, 1 Oct. 1847, Clarendon papers, letterbook I.

[11] *The Times*, 9 Dec. 1847; *Hansard*, xcv. 675–96; Clarendon to Russell, 17 Nov. 1847, Russell papers, P.R.O. 30/22/6.

papal representative should be sent to Ireland to enforce the decrees.[12]

When Lord Minto met Pope Pius for the first time he was careful to explain that while his Government sought no advantages from Rome, they felt it only right to draw attention to the political activity of the Irish clergy and to the fact that the Pope had been misled into sanctioning the measures directed against the new colleges in Ireland. The Government, Minto assured the Pope, was in reality willing to make arrangements which would prove satisfactory to the Catholics.[13]

In the negotiations stress was laid on the colleges' question, and the need for decisive action to check clerical agitation. But though the Pope had received Minto in a most favourable manner and had shown his anxiety to establish diplomatic relations with Britain, the business in Rome proceeded slowly.[14] The influential Irish clerics in Rome, led by the rector of the Irish college there, Dr Paul Cullen, the later Archbishop of Dublin, were active in opposing Minto's representations.[15] In this they were supported by Archbishop MacHale in Ireland, who in open letters to Russell pointed out that the clergy took part in public affairs merely to protect their flock from starvation and death.[16] Minto, as a result, came to the conclusion that it might be more prudent not to ask the Pope to issue a prohibition against political activities, but merely to seek a strong intimation of his disapproval of such activities. Any other course he feared might lead to the papal directive being ignored 'by the turbulent portion of the clergy' in Ireland, which would only leave things in a more difficult situation than before.[17] Faced with the conflicting claims of the British Government and the more extreme party among the Irish Catholics, Rome endeavoured to meet both as far as possible without entering into any definite commitments. A papal

[12] Clarendon to Russell, 1 Oct. 1847, Clarendon papers, letterbook I (Memorandum enclosed).

[13] Minto to Russell, 15 Nov. 1847, Russell papers, P.R.O. 30/22/6.

[14] Minto to Russell, 2 Jan. 1848, Russell papers, P.R.O. 30/22/7.

[15] Minto to Palmerston, 30 Dec. 1847, F.O. papers, 44/2.

[16] *Freeman's Journal*, 2 Dec. 1847; MacHale to Russell, 17 Dec. 1847, O'Reilly, op. cit., ii. 21.

[17] Minto to Palmerston, 30 Dec. 1847, F.O. papers, 44/2.

rescript was issued at the beginning of January 1848 on the political activities of the Irish clergy.[18] It was, however, a mildly and cautiously worded document. The Congregation of Propaganda, it declared, could not believe that the Irish clergy condoned murder, but to prevent any false allegations it urged the clergy to attend to spiritual affairs alone and in no wise to involve themselves in secular matters. Before taking further action the Holy See requested the Archbishops of Armagh, Dublin and Tuam to provide information on the position in Ireland.[19]

This judicious enquiry was received with considerable satisfaction by the British Government, for its implications were obvious enough; that Rome disliked the Irish clergy interfering in political matters. The unofficial agent of the British Government in Rome was instructed to express the Government's thanks to the Pope for the letter to the Irish bishops.[20] But this papal rescript represented not the first but the only fruits of intense British pressure on Rome. The course of events, in 1848, soon left Pope Pius with little opportunity to concern himself with developments in Ireland.[21] For its part, the British Government did introduce, in February 1848, a measure to establish diplomatic relations with Rome. But though the bill was passed by Parliament it never achieved any practical importance because of an amendment, accepted by the Government, which required the papal envoy in Britain to be a layman.[22]

The rumours about Minto's activities in Rome and the publication of the papal rescript had, however, a disturbing effect on public life in Ireland. The repealers naturally feared for the independence of the Catholic church, since the Repeal Association was closely identified in the minds of the people not only with the vindication of their political liberty, but with the

[18] *Dublin Evening Post*, 5 Feb. 1848; Clarendon to Palmerston, 23 Jan. 1848, Clarendon papers, letterbook II.

[19] *Dublin Evening Post*, 5 Feb. 1848; Clarendon to Russell, 5 Feb. 1848. Clarendon papers, letterbook II.

[20] Minto to Petre, 26 Feb. 1848, F.O. papers, 43/42.

[21] Petre to Minto, 5 Mar. 1848, F.O. papers, 43/42.

[22] Clarendon to Russell, 21 Feb. 1848, Clarendon papers, letterbook II; *Hansard*, ci. 495–768.

defence of their religious position as well.[23] Repealers were, therefore, watchful and suspicious of the negotiations with Rome, and this feeling of uncertainty spread outside the ranks of the declared nationalists. Even so moderate a man as Archbishop Murray was for a time worried about the activities of Minto and Petre, the unofficial British agent in Rome.[24]

In the circumstances, it was hardly surprising that a new attempt should have been made to unite all sections of the nationalist movement. Other factors encouraged such a move too. The disputes between the rival groups and Young Irelanders had helped to strengthen the influence of the moderates within the Irish Confederation. This development was not lost on John O'Connell who was anxious to win new friends at a time when the Whig alliance was not faring well. One indication of this had been John O'Connell's personal opposition to the coercion bill and ever since Lord Bessborough's death, in May 1847, the relations between O'Connell and the Whigs had not been easy. Bessborough, an old acquaintance of Daniel O'Connell, had been on good terms socially with the O'Connells.[25] Clarendon from the outset, however, was doubtful of John O'Connell's motives and of the value of his influence in Ireland.[26] He pressed Russell to make no concessions to O'Connell, at the time of the coercion bill, because 'he is a thoroughly ill conditioned wilful man and the only honest thing about him is his bigotry'.[27] Even before that he had made it clear that in his opinion no patronage or favour should be shown to those who maligned the 'members or the measures of the Government'.[28] A certain irritation over the repeal successes in the general election added to the strain between the Whigs and the Repeal

[23] *Freeman's Journal*, 3 Jan. 1848; Clarendon to MacHale, 5 Dec. 1847, Clarendon papers, letterbook II; W. J. O'Neill Daunt to Smith O'Brien, 5 Jan. 1848, Smith O'Brien papers, vol. 441, no. 2348.
[24] Clarendon to Palmerston, 23 Jan. 1848, Clarendon papers, letterbook II.
[25] Bessborough to Russell, 16 Jan. 1847, Russell papers, P.R.O. 30/22/6.
[26] Clarendon to Russell, 12 July 1847, Clarendon papers, letterbook I; Clarendon to Sir George Grey, 24 Aug. 1847, Clarendon papers, letterbook I.
[27] Clarendon to Russell, 30 Nov. 1847, Clarendon papers, letterbook I.
[28] Clarendon to Russell, 23 Aug. 1847, Clarendon papers, letterbook I.

Association, though there was no formal breach between the two in 1847–8.[29]

A much milder tone than in the past was adopted towards the moderate Young Irelanders by speakers in the Repeal Association. On the occasion of a visit to his constituency, Limerick, at the end of 1847, John O'Connell was received warmly not merely by the O'Connellite party but by the local Young Irelanders as well. He made use of the occasion to stress the necessity of forgetting past differences and on his return to Dublin he told the Repeal Association that a reconciliation with the Young Irelanders was 'the most anxious wish' of his heart.[30] These friendly gestures were on the whole well, if cautiously, received by the Confederate leaders. Negotiations for reunion followed, but they quickly broke down on two issues. The Young Irelanders, especially Smith O'Brien, wanted both organisations to be dissolved and a new one established in its place. Smith O'Brien feared that a return to the Association might be generally interpreted as a humiliating surrender and he still apparently regarded with some suspicion the strength of Catholic clerical influence on the existing Association. John O'Connell was adamant in maintaining that the Repeal Association should be preserved as it was and that unity could best be achieved within its framework.[31] The second point of disagreement was closely related to the first one. The Confederate leaders felt that a pledge against place hunting should be incorporated in the rules of a united repeal movement so as to prevent any reliance in the future on Whig patronage. John O'Connell again replied that the Young Irelanders would have to return to the Association as it stood.[32]

The failure of these negotiations could not disguise the fact that there was a strong feeling in favour of reunion within the

[29] Palmerston to Russell, 19 Aug. 1847, Russell papers, P.R.O. 30/22/6; Clarendon to Henry Reeve, 21 Jan. 1848, J. K. Laughton, *Memoirs of the Life and Correspondence of Henry Reeve*, i. 192–5.

[30] Repeal Assoc. meeting, 17 Jan., *Freeman's Journal*, 18 Jan. 1848; *Nation*, 4 Jan. 1848.

[31] O'Neill Daunt to Smith O'Brien, 5, 14 Jan, 1848, Smith O'Brien papers, vol. 441, nos. 2348 and 2352; *Nation*, 22 Jan. 1848.

[32] John B. Dillon to Smith O'Brien, 3 Jan. 1848, Smith O'Brien papers, vol. 441, no. 2347; John O'Connell to the people of Ireland, 21 Jan. 1848, *Dublin Evening Post*, 27 Jan. 1848.

repeal movement. Few practical differences, it now seemed, divided John O'Connell and his party from the moderate wing of the Young Irelanders. John O'Connell, it is true, was elusive on the question of place-hunting, but he was at one with men like Gavan Duffy and Smith O'Brien in demanding some generous concessions to the tenant-farmers, better relief measures and the creation of a strong parliamentary party. How these aims could be realised was a difficult problem to resolve in a prostrate country and at a time when parliamentary agitation appeared to have little prospect of success.[33]

The difficulties facing the moderate section of the Young Irelanders in attempting to build up a strong parliamentary representation were well illustrated by the outcome of the Waterford city by-election of February 1848. The vacancy occurred when the Liberator's youngest son, Daniel, accepted a post from the Whig administration in the consular service.[34] Thomas Francis Meagher was invited by the local Confederates to contest the seat and he agreed to do so with the approval of the Confederate Council though Mitchel sharply criticised the decision in the *United Irishman* as a move which might raise false hopes of winning just measures from Parliament.[35] Meagher seemed to be a strong candidate. He was popular in Waterford, his native city, and his father, an O'Connellite repealer of independent views, was a sitting member for the constituency. John Dillon hoped that a decision in Waterford in favour of Meagher would decide the issue of repeal leadership between the Young Irelanders and John O'Connell, but the outcome of the election was something of an anti-climax.[36] The seat was not won by Meagher or the O'Connellite candidate put up in opposition to him but by Sir Henry Barron, a local landowner of liberal sympathies, who was inclined to favour a domestic legislature. Meagher was at the bottom of the poll, but, as elsewhere, the Confederates appear to have won a measure of support among the urban artisans who did not enjoy the franchise.[37]

[33] *Freeman's Journal*, 10 Jan. 1848; Repeal Assoc. meeting, 17 Jan., *Freeman's Journal*, 18 Jan. 1848.   [34] *Nation*, 26 Feb. 1848.
[35] *United Irishman*, 19 Feb. 1848; John B. Dillon to Smith O'Brien, 11 Feb. [1848], Smith O'Brien papers, vol. 438, no. 1788.
[36] Ibid.   [37] Gavan Duffy, *Four Years of Irish History*, pp. 187–8.

In the circumstances of the time, the sudden overthrow of the French monarchy, in February 1848, naturally excited a great deal of interest and political speculation in Ireland.Throughout Europe, the February revolution in Paris was seen as a dramatic proof that France was again to take the lead in the struggle between a militant liberalism and the forces of reaction. Nationalists and liberals asserted that the French revolution of February had an almost mystical significance because, in contrast to earlier revolutions, it had been almost bloodless and had, it seemed, been achieved by the disciplined action of men drawn from all sections of the community.[38] With France as a model, it appeared as if the armed yet peaceful peoples of Europe were to be led to victory not by soldiers and men of violence but by poets, social reformers and simple working men. The reputed harmony in France, in February and March, impressed the Irish repealers of all shades of opinion because it was such a union of interests they had long sought but failed to find.

In March, the opinion was widely held in repeal circles that the British Government, fearful of attack by a warlike and revolutionary France, would quickly capitulate to a really united Irish demand for repeal, in an attempt to avoid the two-fold task of having to suppress social unrest in Britain and a national revolution in Ireland.[39] Such an approach, however, overestimated the missionary ardour of revolutionary France and the actual strength of the Chartist agitation in Britain.[40] With sturdy republicans, like Ledru Rollin and Louis Blanc, in the ascendant for the moment in France, there seemed little reason to doubt the firmness of purpose of the new republic.

John O'Connell, who was in Paris in February 1848, wrote with enthusiasm to Ledru Rollin, the Minister of the Interior in the Provisional Government, describing the revolution as 'the really sublime spectacle presented to the world'.[41] With equal

[38] Pouthas, *Démocraties et capitalisme*, pp. 69–79; Seignobos, *La révolution de 1848, le second empire, 1848–1859*, pp. 285–6.

[39] *Nation*, 4 Mar. 1848; *Freeman's Journal*, 11 Mar. 1848.

[40] Seignobos, op. cit., p. 282; Lord Palmerston to Earl of Clarendon, 9 Mar. 1848, Ashley, *The Life and Correspondence of Henry John Temple, Viscount Palmerston*, ii. 74–5.

[41] J. O'Connell to Ledru Rollin, 29 Feb. 1848, *Freeman's Journal*, 7 Mar. 1848.

enthusiasm the Young Irelanders responded to the events in France. Smith O'Brien wrote to Lord Cloncurry, a member of the Repeal Association, suggesting that the time had come for all repealers to unite. If that were not possible, then Smith O'Brien proposed that the Association and the Confederation should, at least, adopt a joint address to the Queen asking for a repeal of the Union.[42]

An almost immediate consequence of the developments in France was that even the more conservative of the Young Ireland leaders began to speak in more vigorous terms. Gavan Duffy, for example, could say that the men, like himself, who had voted in the past against 'rash words and rash courses' were bound when the hoped for opportunity arose, 'to prove that wise caution, not slavish cowardice' had been their motive.[43] Other Young Irelanders urged the people to arm or even to form a national guard, while the *Nation*, in a leading article, asserted that 'the new government to a man desire to make France a deliverer of the oppressed nations . . . already the young republic is familiar to the heart and imagination of every man in Ireland . . .'.[44] The belief that Britain would bow before the forces the French revolution had released gave a new hope to a divided, unsuccessful and dispirited repeal movement in Ireland.

The proceedings at political meetings and the leading articles in the nationalist newspapers reveal, in March and April, a conscious cultivation of the arguments and even of the phrases made popular by the Paris revolution. The *Pilot*, an O'Connellite newspaper, advised the people to emulate the 'most glorious revolution recorded and consecrated in history' while the *Nation* considered that the members of the Repeal Association in Dublin were 'animated by the same noble spirit of fraternity and forgiveness' as the Young Irelanders.[45] At the same time the Repeal Association, in an address to the people of Ireland, asked for a revival of the spirit of the monster meeting campaign of 1843.[46] This enthusiasm for unity was not confined to Dublin.

[42] Smith O'Brien to Cloncurry, 29 Feb. 1848, *Nation*, 11 Mar. 1848.
[43] *Nation*, 4 Mar. 1848.
[44] Ibid., 4, 11 Mar. 1848.
[45] *Pilot*, 1 Mar. 1848; *Nation*, 4 Mar. 1848.
[46] *Freeman's Journal*, 4 Mar. 1848.

Throughout the provinces the news from France was received with satisfaction by repealers. In Kilkenny, a joint meeting of both sections was held and it was resolved that past differences should be forgotten. The repealers of Limerick came together to congratulate the French republic, while in towns such as Cashel, Roscrea, Drogheda and Clonmel demonstrations took place in honour of revolutionary France.[47]

Hopes of French encouragement were raised by the warm reply John O'Connell received from Ledru Rollin who assured him that 'soon without doubt, shall better days dawn for Ireland'.[48] Again, Lamartine's manifesto, of March 7, to the great powers denouncing the territorial settlement of 1815 was optimistically interpreted in Ireland as an additional proof that France was firm in her resolve to help the suppressed nationalities of Europe.[49] Encouraged by these developments, the view soon gained ground among Irish nationalists that they should send fraternal delegates to France to greet the representatives of the new republic. In Dublin, O'Connellites, moderate Young Irelanders and John Mitchel and his friends agreed to establish a committee which was to organise a public demonstration and send an Irish mission to Paris. Had the new committee retained its representative character, if might have served as a useful link between the repeal factions but, in practice, jealousies and old suspicions prevented the committee from winning any lasting significance.

The committee soon lost favour with John O'Connell who claimed that Mitchel's inflamatory comments, as a member of the committee, might well involve it in serious difficulties with the authorities.[50] Alarm at Mitchel's radicalism was not confined to John O'Connell. The moderates among the Young Irelanders were by no means anxious to be left isolated on the committee with only Mitchel for company.[51] Gavan Duffy urged John O'Connell to co-operate with the committee, but the hurried negotiations which took place made it clear that O'Connell would only lend his support on condition that the Repeal Association was allowed to control the committee.[52]

[47] Ibid., 9 Mar. 1848; *Nation*, 11 Mar. 1848.   [48] Ibid.
[49] Ibid., 18 Mar. 1848.   [50] *Freeman's Journal*, 8 Mar. 1848.
[51] Doheny, *The Felon's Track*, p. 127.
[52] *Nation*, 25 Mar. 1848.

The public demonstration, held on March 20, proved to be a considerable success despite threatening military preparations and the refusal of the Repeal Association to take part in it. Between ten and fifteen thousand people were estimated to have attended and the artisan class of Dublin appear to have been well represented. The gathering, however, did not mark, as some Conservatives feared, the beginning of a revolution.[53] Instead, those present contented themselves with voting a fraternal address to the people of France, which was to be brought to Paris by a special delegation, and another resolution called upon Queen Victoria to restore self-government to Ireland as the Union had resulted in starvation and misrule.[54]

Proceedings of this kind illustrate the very confused state of mind prevailing in Ireland at this time. While John O'Connell sought to combine great caution with timid praise of the French revolution, the Confederate leaders sought to appear as radical as possible without, however, committing themselves fully to Mitchel's republicanism or to the prospect of revolution. The Confederates were to discover that, in a year of revolutions and exciting political change, keeping to a middle path was a difficult and exacting task.

The drift towards radicalism could be seen in a variety of ways. At a Confederate meeting, on March 15, Smith O'Brien boldly urged the people to form a national guard. Meagher, on the same occasion, assured his audience that if the Queen did not receive an Irish delegation and grant repeal, then the next time they demanded 'an admission to the throne room of St. James it shall be through the accredited ambassador of the Irish Republic'.[55] In the past the Confederates had disassociated themselves from the Chartists, but at the demonstration in Dublin, on March 20, Meagher admitted that 'we have been guilty of sad injustice in our abuse of the English democracy'.[56] In the same spirit of new-found friendship, combined Chartist and Confederate meetings were held in the north of England. Meagher and other leading Confederates spoke from the same

[53] *Dublin Evening Mail*, 8 Mar. 1848; Clarendon to Sir. G. Grey, 20 Mar. 1848, Clarendon papers, letterbook II.
[54] *Nation*, 25 Mar. 1848.
[55] Ibid., 18 Mar. 1848.
[56] Ibid., 25 Mar. 1848.

platform as Feargus O'Connor, in Manchester, on March 17, when Meagher was particularly enthusiastic in renouncing what he described as his false sentiments. The revolution in Paris, he said, had made him a democrat.[57]

This unity of purpose was again emphasised at the Chartist demonstration at Kennington Common, on April 10, which was the prelude to the presentation of the third petition for the People's Charter to Parliament. Large numbers of Irish Confederates, drawn up 'in military array' and carrying an Irish flag took part in the confused and indecisive proceedings. They heard Feargus O'Connor tell the gathering that 'I look upon Ireland and the Irish cause as I view England and the English cause and I hold, after the demonstration of to-day, and the petition which is to be presented, that it will be impossible to withhold from Irishmen their just rights, justly demanded'. Some of the other speakers who followed him seemed equally enthusiastic about their new alliance with the Irish nationalists.[58] Irish representatives, too, were invited to attend the projected national assembly and in Dublin a short-lived Irish Universal Suffrage Association was founded with John Mitchel's support and the encouragement of a Chartist delegation from England.[59]

The new radicalism in Irish politics expressed itself in other ways too. When, for example, the Irish Confederation voted an address to the people of France, a Dublin workingman was included in the official party which was to bring the message to Paris.[60] The radical enthusiasm was infectious and yet, in their more cautious moments, the moderates among the Young Irelanders, such as Gavan Duffy and Smith O'Brien, feared that a repetition in Ireland of what had happened in Paris might well result in a democratic revolution and disaster for the middle class. John Mitchel's decision to resume his place on the Council of the Confederation only helped to confirm their apprehensions.[61]

On March 22, Smith O'Brien and Meagher were prosecuted

[57] *United Irishman*, 25 Mar. 1848; *Nation*, 25 Mar. 1848.
[58] *The Times*, 11 Apr. 1848.
[59] *Nation*, 22, 29 Apr., 6 May 1848; *The Times*, 12, 14 Apr. 1848.
[60] *Nation*, 11, 18 Mar. 1848.
[61] Gavan Duffy to Smith O'Brien, [Mar. 1848], Smith O'Brien papers, vol. 441, no. 2255.

for making seditious speeches at a Confederate meeting and John Mitchel for printing seditious articles in three issues of his newspaper, the *United Irishman*.[62] Though the Government viewed all three as potential disturbers of the peace, Smith O'Brien was quite resentful that his opinions should have been identified in any way with those of Mitchel.[63] The Government's apparent indifference to the distinctions between moderates and radicals was not, however, shared by John O'Connell and his brother Maurice, who at once offered their services as bailsmen to enable Smith O'Brien and Meagher to set out on their mission to Paris. Their gesture was one which touched Smith O'Brien.[64]

The decision taken by the Confederates and their allies in Dublin to send a mission to Paris soon made the question of Anglo-Irish relations a factor of some importance in the negotiations between the United Kingdom and the new French republic. The British Government may not have taken too serious a view of repeal activities in March 1848, but it could not afford to permit any official French encouragement of the repeal movement to go unchallenged.[65] On a diplomatic level, determined and successful efforts were made to forestall any French intervention in Irish affairs.

The task of neutralising French influences was simplified by the fact that Lamartine was both head of the Provisional Government and Foreign Minister. The February revolution had brought many elements together in an uneasy alliance, which was quickly to resolve itself into a struggle for leadership between the moderates led by Lamartine and the representatives of a more radical and republican tradition. Had Ledru Rollin and the Jacobins secured undisputed control, France might well have offered armed support to nationalists elsewhere in Europe, but Lamartine and the moderates insisted that it was wiser to concentrate on winning British goodwill rather than to embark on a series of dangerous revolutionary

[62] *Nation*, 25 Mar. 1848; *United Irishman*, 19 Feb., 4, 18 Mar. 1848.

[63] *Nation*, 25 Mar. 1848; Smith O'Brien to Gavan Duffy, 24 Mar. 1848, Gavan Duffy, *Four Years of Irish History*, p. 202.

[64] *Nation*, 25 Mar. 1848.

[65] Memorandum by Sir Charles Wood, 31 Mar. 1848, Russell papers, P.R.O. 30/22/7.

adventures.[66] Lamartine knew that Palmerston and the Whigs generally had received the news of the overthrow of Louis Philippe with little regret because they had come to regard the House of Orleans as a threat to British interests. The French Foreign Minister also recognised that Britain, the one great parliamentary power in Europe, would only accept the new order in France on condition that the French did not meddle in the affairs of other states, particularly in those of the United Kingdom.[67] The British Government, for its part, was uncertain about what course revolutionary France might pursue and so, at first, refused to give the republic more than informal recognition. Anxious to prove the respectability of the Second Republic and so win full diplomatic recognition, Lamartine set himself against any effective French assistance to the Irish repealers.

Lamartine's position was a difficult one in March 1848. The Provisional Government, lacking unity and without any effective means of enforcing its authority, was very much at the mercy of the armed revolutionaries of Paris. The advocates of a social republic were active in early March and the more radical ministers tended to forget discretion in their replies to the foreign delegations which crowded into Paris. Even Lamartine, in his attempts to appease the Radicals, often had to use brave words in public when receiving the revolutionary missions from abroad. In private, however, Lamartine was quick to assure the British Government, early in March, that he never could consider Irish nationality 'in any other sense except as identical with English nationality'.[68] It was not easy to dismiss the Irish with a reply in similar terms, especially as the popular and formidable Minister of the Interior, Ledru Rollin, was an outspoken friend of Irish nationalism.[69]

The first test of Lamartine's skill in dealing with the Irish

[66] Seignobos, op. cit., p. 282; Halévy, *The Age of Peel and Cobden*, pp. 182–98.

[67] Palmerston to Lord Normanby (British Ambassador, Paris), 26 Feb. 1848, Ashley, *The Life and Correspondence of Henry John Temple, Viscount Palmerston*, ii. 71; Normanby to Palmerston, 2 Mar. 1848, F.O. papers, 27/804.

[68] Normanby, *A Year of Revolution*, i. 226. 'Identified' instead of 'identical' in Normanby to Palmerston 15 Mar. 1848, F.O. papers, 27/804.

[69] See p. 54, n. 86.

came when he received a deputon from the Irish residents of
Paris, on March 17. The reception was a public one and it took
place at a time when the Socialists and Radicals were obviously
dissatisfied with his cautious foreign policy.[70] March 17 was a
tense and critical day of left-wing demonstrations and a trying one
for Lamartine. In an effort to justify himself before his critics he
may have been incautious in his warm words of praise of Irish
patriotism and of Daniel O'Connell, who 'has taught the world
the most energetic, although wisest means for the people to
regain their rights . . . peaceful agitation'.[71] What alarmed the
British Government even more than Lamartine's words of
encouragement was the report that the Irish deputation had
presented an Irish flag to Lamartine and that he had accepted
it as a symbol of French respect for Ireland's national aspirations.

The British authorities lost no time in making strong representations to the French Foreign Minister. Already on March
18, Lord Normanby, the British representative in Paris,
demanded a full explanation of the incident. Lamartine denied
ever receiving or even seeing an Irish flag when he met the
Irish deputation. This disclaimer, however, did not satisfy
Normanby who warned Lamartine that unless the reports were
publicly contradicted, the worst possible impression would be
created in Britain.[72] Lamartine at once met the British demand
and in a public message he declared that France recognised in
the case of the United Kingdom only one national flag. He
further explained that the remarks he had made relating to
Ireland were merely intended as an expression of French
sympathy with the Irish claims to true religious freedom and
liberal reforms.[73]

Lamartine's willing disclaimer did not altogether meet Lord
Palmerston's objections. The British Government's official
answer to Lamartine, therefore, took the form of a stern rebuke
to which was joined a demand that no French minister, for the
future, should make public observations about the political

[70] *Moniteur Universel*, 18 Mar. 1848.
[71] *The Times*, 20 Mar. 1848.
[72] Normanby to Palmerston, 18 Mar. 1848. F.O. papers, 27/805;
Normanby, op. cit., i. 243–6.
[73] *Moniteur Universel*, 19 Mar. 1848.

affairs of the United Kingdom.[74] In his diplomatic offensive Normanby also made effective use of the argument that only a violent faction in the repeal party was associated with the efforts to enlist French support and that O'Connell's Repeal Association remained loyal to the Crown. Even before the arrival in Paris, on March 26, of Smith O'Brien and the other members of the Irish mission, Lamartine had reached the decision that no encouragement should be given to the Irish nationalists.[75]

Lamartine, having had to explain away his observations to the deputation from the Irish of Paris, was not particularly anxious to get involved in difficulties with yet another group of Irish nationalists, at a time when his own political position was far from secure. He, therefore, suggested to Lord Normanby that, in the circumstances, it would be better to let his radical colleague, Ledru Rollin receive the Irish, provided the Jacobin minister could be induced to 'answer them without saying anything that could give offence'.[76] Normanby's obvious lack of enthusiasm for this suggestion and possibly Ledru Rollin's unwillingness to identify himself with Lamartine's moderating zeal appear to have led Lamartine to abandon this plan. He decided that the safest course would be for himself to undertake the task of receiving Smith O'Brien and his companions. Before meeting the Irish in public on April 3, Lamartine carefully outlined to Normanby what he proposed to say to them and it would also appear that he told Smith O'Brien in private that the Irish nationalists could expect neither support nor encouragement from the French Government.[77]

The Irish addresses presented to Lamartine were of a moderate character. They did not ask for armed assistance, but merely sought a declaration of French sympathy with Irish national claims. Instead of making any such declaration, Lamartine, true to his undertaking to Lord Normanby, said it was the wish of France to remain at peace with the whole of the United Kingdom and that he could not encourage any

[74] Palmerston to Normanby, 20 Mar. 1848, F.O. papers, 27/805; Palmerston to Normanby, 21 Mar. 1848, Correspondence, Archives des Affairs Étrangèrs (Paris), vol. 669, no. 116.

[75] Normanby, op. cit., i. 254–8.

[76] Normanby, op. cit., i. 250–4, 272–4; Normanby to Palmerston, 23 Mar. 1848, F.O. papers, 27/805.

[77] Normanby to Palmerston, 31 Mar. 1848, F.O. papers, 27/805.

action which might result in civil war between citizens of the one country.[78] Lamartine's public assertion of friendship towards Great Britain and his polite but definite refusal to make any significant comment on Irish affairs won the approval of the British Government. Palmerston at once requested Normanby to thank him for so loyally fulfilling the promise he had made.[79]

Though Lamartine 'courageously and effectually kept his promise', as Lord Normanby put it, the Irish were given a much more friendly reception in the revolutionary clubs of Paris.[80] Ledru Rollin, too, appears to have told Smith O'Brien of his personal sympathy with Irish nationalist claims, though even he seems to have stressed the need for proceeding with caution.[81] Bold words in the clubs and Ledru Rollin's goodwill were no compensation for the public refusal of the Foreign Minister to commit the French republic to open support for the cause of Irish nationalism.[82]

Efforts were made, however, for a time to minimise the effect of Lamartine's words and Smith O'Brien was at pains to explain, before he left Paris, that Lamartine had been compelled 'to repress the utterances of sentiments which his heart and his intellect suggested'.[83] There is, indeed, no reason to doubt that Lamartine was well inclined towards the Irish claims, but the necessity of maintaining and improving Anglo-French relations remained the primary consideration in the shaping of the decisions which he took in March and April.

The Irish mission had to return to Dublin without those public assurances of French goodwill which they had hoped would give a new strength to the claims of Irish nationalism.[84] It is, perhaps, significant that in speeches and discussions from this time onwards much less attention is devoted to France than in the months of February and March. Mitchel may well have expressed more than his own personal view when he wrote: 'we

[78] *Moniteur Universel*, 4 Apr. 1848.
[79] Palmerston to Normanby, 6 Apr. 1848, F.O. papers, 27/806.
[80] Normanby to Palmerston, 5 Apr. 1848, F.O. papers, 27/806; Gavan Duffy, *Young Ireland*, i. 148–54.
[81] Ledru Rollin to Smith O'Brien, 30 Mar. 1848, Smith O'Brien papers, vol. 442, no. 2406; Normanby, op. cit., i. 286.
[82] *Freeman's Journal*, 8 Apr. 1848.   [83] *Nation*, 15 Apr. 1848.
[84] Irish Confed. meeting, 5 Apr., *Nation*, 8 Apr. 1848.

are well pleased that M. Lamartine has let us know distinctly we must rely on ourselves'.[85]

The obvious failure of the mission to France did not produce any real change in the general pattern of developments in Ireland. The exciting events on the continent, the apparent strength of the Chartists in Britain and the Government's determination to bring Smith O'Brien, Meagher and Mitchel to trial on the sedition charges, all helped to strengthen the new radical tendencies in the repeal movement. Speeches in both the Repeal Association and the Confederation became more militant and among the Confederates a great deal of emphasis was put on the importance of raising an armed national guard. They urged, too, that a representative national council should be convened to compel the British Government to grant repeal.[86]

The growing popularity of advanced views in repeal circles put John O'Connell and his brothers in a difficult position. As early as April 10, Maurice O'Connell had to warn the members of the Repeal Association against attending the meetings of the Confederate clubs, but such admonitions did not prevent a number of prominent members of the Association from joining in the celebrations, on April 15, to mark the return of the Confederate deputation from France and from making defiant speeches on the same occasion.[87]

Gavan Duffy's 'Creed of the *Nation*', published in the *Nation* newspaper shortly after the passing of the new Treason-Felony Act, probably best sums up the position of the majority of the Young Irelanders at this time. Though the famine had become for Gavan Duffy 'a fearful murder committed on the mass of the people', he still firmly rejected any suggestion that the struggle for national independence should be conducted on a class basis and said that any doctrine which led the labouring classes to regard their own interest 'as the only honest one' was in fact 'as selfish and fraudulent as the worst dogmas of despotism'. He wanted all sections of society to turn to nationalism, because 'nationality is broad, comprehensive and universal'. Politically he remained conservative. An independent Irish Parliament

[85] *United Irishman*, 8 Apr. 1848.
[86] Irish Confed. meeting, 5 Apr., *Nation*, 8 Apr. 1848.
[87] Repeal Assoc. meeting, 10 Apr., *Freeman's Journal*, 11 Apr. 1848; *Nation*, 22 Apr. 1848.

under the Crown, a responsible Irish ministry and an Irish-born Viceroy, he argued 'will content the country'. Such a Parliament would give the farmers tenant-right, support the clergy of all denominations and 'endeavour to settle the claims of labour'. Gavan Duffy favoured a monarchy rather than a republic, a negotiated settlement rather than a violent revolution and yet he was prepared to say that 'if independence must come by force, a republic is inevitable and welcome'.[88] Gavan Duffy did not hestitate, then, to advise an ultimate recourse to arms though he, like so many of his fellow Confederates still clung to the hope that a negotiated settlement could somehow still be brought about. In practice it was to prove extremely difficult to work for such a settlement while making preparations, however inadequate and tentative they might be, for a revolution.

The increasingly warlike tone of the Young Irelanders' speeches and articles was hardly likely to lessen the suspicion of the repeal movement among the more conservative elements in the country. Nevertheless, a new attempt was now made to draw the Conservatives and the Protestants generally into the repeal movement. Because the majority of repealers, Confederates and followers of John O'Connell alike, continued to view with considerable suspicion John Mitchel's republicanism and social radicalism, they naturally saw in any indication of interest in nationalism among the conservative elements a welcome sign.[89] A short-lived Protestant Repeal Association was founded by a small group of Protestants which included Samuel Ferguson the poet. But the new association achieved nothing of importance. The prevailing temper among Irish Protestants was hardly conducive to the success of such an experiment, especially as the Government was beginning to show signs that in an emergency it would not abandon the Irish landed ascendancy.[90]

(II)

Despite the symptoms of political unrest, the Whig ministry, in the spring of 1848, showed no particular readiness to take

[88] Ibid., 29 Apr. 1848.
[89] John Mitchel to Smith O'Brien, 5 May 1848, Smith O'Brien papers, vol. 442, no. 2445.
[90] Gavan Duffy, *Four Years of Irish History*, pp. 208–9.

repressive action in Ireland. It was only under strong pressure from the administration in Dublin that new coercive legislation was eventually introduced. The Lord Lieutenant, Lord Clarendon, at the beginning of the year, had shown himself reasonably well satisfied with the steps already taken to preserve public order and even went so far as to predict that the Repeal Association might soon cease to exist through having 'little money in their till and that vapouring fellow, J. O'Connell, for their champion'.[91] Clarendon, however, was sensitive to possible dangers in Ireland and his reactions to the demonstrations of sympathy with France, which were organised in March, were sharp enough. He was quick to report on the enthusiasm with which the Paris revolution had been greeted in Ireland, but though Clarendon was, by this time, obviously uneasy, he still could say: 'The worst enemy we have to deal with, however, is destitution—if the people were employed we should have little fear of agitation . . .'.[92] On balance, the authorities in London and Dublin felt, in early March, that a policy of watchful inactivity was for the moment the wisest. Sir George Grey, the Home Secretary, considered that it would be better not to prosecute at once the editors of the advanced nationalist newspapers 'without very good grounds for expecting success', while Lord John Russell vacillated between indifference to the threat of agitation and alarm at the tone of the *Nation* and of John Mitchel's newly founded newspaper, the *United Irishman*.[93]

For both the administration and the repealers the first really significant development was the decision to stage in Dublin, on March 20, a great public demonstration in favour of Franco-Irish friendship.[94] The much publicised preparations made Lord Clarendon rather more apprehensive than he had been because he feared that the Dublin demonstration might only be the prelude to a great deal of turbulent agitation throughout the country. To halt any such drift into radicalism, he resolved that once the Dublin demonstration was safely over, Thomas Francis

[91] Clarendon to Russell, 9 Jan. 1848, Clarendon papers, letterbook II; Clarendon to Henry Reeve, 21 Jan. 1848, Laughton, *Memoirs of the Life and Correspondence of Henry Reeve*, i. 192–5.

[92] Clarendon to Russell, 2 Mar. 1848, Clarendon papers, letterbook II.

[93] Grey to Clarendon, 8 Mar. 1848, Clarendon papers, Ir. box 12, bundle 21.

[94] See p. 185.

Meagher, John Mitchel and, after some initial doubts, Smith
O'Brien should be prosecuted for sedition.[95] Clarendon was
busy in other ways too. In an effort to reach a popular audience,
he had placards posted on walls throughout Dublin 'paradying'.
as he put it, 'one issued by the Confederates'. Surprisingly, the
actual author of this curious excusion into journalism of a very
humble kind was the Lord Lieutenant himself. With obvious
pride in his achievement, he let Sir George Grey know that the
placard was a really good means of reaching the 'plebs'.[96]
Again, to meet any possible emergency, Clarendon worked out a
careful plan. If the demonstration resulted in riot and bloodshed, then he intended having Mitchel and Gavan Duffy immediately arrested 'as accessories before the fact'. But if the day
passed off quietly, he would simply proceed with the prosecutions for sedition against Mitchel, Meagher and Smith O'Brien.[97]

In Government circles opinion was divided on the issue of
prosecuting the Young Irelanders. Wood, the Chancellor of
the Exchequer, believed that prosecutions were what the Young

[95] Grey to Clarendon, 15 Mar. 1848, Clarendon papers, Ir. box 12,
bundle 21; Clarendon to Grey, 18 Mar. 1848, Clarendon papers, letterbook II.

[96] Clarendon to Grey, 16 Mar. 1848, Clarendon papers, letterbook II.
Lord Clarendon, in March 1848, showed his interest in popular journalism
with more embarrassing and costly consequences when he engaged the
services of an adventurer and, as it proved, an attempted blackmailer,
James Birch, the proprietor of a small Dublin newspaper, the *World*. In
return for financial aid, met in part out of secret service funds, Birch agreed
to write in defence of the established order and to oppose the designs of
the nationalists (Clarendon to Sir G. Grey, 28 Mar. 1848, Clarendon
papers, letterbook II). In the course of two years Birch received more than
£1,100. Dissatisfied with these payments, Birch, in 1850, threatened to
bring an action against Lord Clarendon. Anxious to avoid the public dis-
closure of the fact that Birch had received secret service money, Clarendon
agreed, in Nov. 1850, to pay Birch £2,000 on condition that he discontinued
the action (Clarendon to Sir Charles Wood, 29 Nov., 10 Dec. 1850,
Maxwell, *The Life and Letters of George William, fourth Earl of Clarendon*, i.
317–18). Though he received the £2,000 from the Lord Lieutenant, Birch
commenced a new action against Sir William Somerville, the Chief Secretary, to recover £7,500 expenses claimed to have been incurred by him in
the public service. Somerville fought the case successfully, but Clarendon
had to give evidence of the payments he had made to Birch (Maxwell, op.
cit., i. 318–19). See also James Birch, *Narrative of a connexion between the Lord
Lieutenant of Ireland, the British Government and James Birch, esq.*

[97] Clarendon to Grey, 12, 18 Mar. 1848, Clarendon papers, letterbook II.

Irelanders wished to bring about. 'John Russell, etc.', he wrote, 'think it alright, Graham thinks it right but augurs ill of it, Peel has very serious doubts . . . my private advice to you is to be forbearing to excess . . . .'[98] The Dublin demonstration proved, as we have seen, something of an anti-climax, but the prosecutions of Smith O'Brien, Meagher and Mitchel in no way served to strengthen the Government's position as Clarendon had hoped.[99] Instead, as Wood had rightly predicted, the sedition trials, which were not held until May, only served to arouse sympathy for the three accused.

The fear of serious unrest in the coming months troubled Lord Clarendon a great deal from the end of March onwards, especially in view of the economic plight of the people. 'I should care little', he wrote, as on previous occasions 'for the most reckless agitators, but it is this distress which affects all classes and which must during the next four months become immeasurably greater that alarms me.'[100] His uneasiness was in no way lessened when he discovered that his law officers could find no provision in the existing law under which a projected national guard could be declared to be illegal.[101]

Clarendon's persistent demand for additional legal powers to check possible revolutionary preparations put the cabinet in a difficult position.[102] With mixed feelings the Government had gone some distance with repressive measures. They had approved of the prosecutions of Smith O'Brien and the other two Young Irelanders, but could they, without provoking much political controversy, ask Parliament to accept new repressive legislation? In coming to any decision the Government had to take into account the widespread Chartist agitation in Britain and especially the much discussed preparations for a Chartist convention, which was to be held in London early in April.[103]

[98] Wood to Clarendon, 27 Mar. 1848, Clarendon papers, Ir. box 31, bundle 42.

[99] Grey to Clarendon, 18 Mar. 1848, Clarendon papers, Ir. box 12, bundle 21; Clarendon to Grey, 20 Mar. 1848, Clarendon papers, letterbook II.

[100] Clarendon to Wood, 30 Mar. 1848, Clarendon papers, letterbook II.

[101] Clarendon to Russell, 25 Mar. 1848, Clarendon papers, letterbook II.

[102] Clarendon to Russell, 30 Mar. 1848, Russell papers, P.R.O. 30/22/7.

[103] Clarendon to Russell, 31 Mar. 1848, Clarendon papers, letterbook II; Hovell, *The Chartist Movement*, pp. 288–92.

The Government, therefore, conscious of the difficulty of putting down disturbances in Britain and Ireland, was anxious to avoid taking any action which might provoke rebellion in Ireland or even lead to protracted obstructionist debates in Parliament.[104] It was hoped that the sending of more troops to Ireland might suffice to keep the peace there, but a show of force of this kind was not sufficient to influence seriously the course of political development in Ireland. To strengthen his hand, Clarendon would have favoured a suspension of Habeas Corpus, but he was very conscious of the difficulties the Government might well encounter in trying to carry any such suspension unless the position became far more critical in Ireland. 'If you could carry a bill for suspending the Habeas Corpus act', he wrote to the Prime Minister, 'it might save this country but have you any chance of doing so? I fear every Irish member would oppose it and obstruct all other business . . . because he would expect to be assassinated on his return here.'[105] Despite the melodramatic touch in Clarendon's comments at this time, Sir George Grey, the Home Secretary, held firmly to the view that it would be 'very impolitic' to propose the suspension of Habeas Corpus. They could, he considered, only carry public opinion with them in any drastic action against the Young Irelanders 'by letting these gentlemen put themselves completely in the wrong'.[106] In contrast, Lord John Russell, argued that the Government could even ask Parliament to suspend Habeas Corpus for a year provided useful measures of social reform were also introduced. With characteristic indecision, however, the Whig ministry failed to reach agreement either on the issue of an immediate suspension or on any worthwhile proposals for reform in Ireland.[107]

In the cabinet memoir circulated at the end of March, in which he recommended the temporary suspension of Habeas Corpus, Russell again returned to the Irish land question. He

[104] Grey to Clarendon, 3 Apr. 1848, Clarendon papers, Ir. box 12, bundle 21; Clarendon to Russell, 31 Mar. 1848, Clarendon papers, letterbook II.

[105] Clarendon to Russell, 31 Mar. 1848, Clarendon papers, letterbook II.

[106] Grey to Clarendon, 3 Apr. 1848, Clarendon papers, Ir. box 12, bundle 21.

[107] Memorandum by Lord John Russell, 30 Mar. 1848, Russell papers, P.R.O. 30/22/7; Walpole, *Life of Lord John Russell*, ii. 64–5.

suggested that restrictions should be placed on the landlords' power of eviction, and in contrast to his earlier qualms on the question of advancing public moneys, proposed that £1,000,000 in exchequer bills be made available for necessary works in Ireland. As a further gesture of goodwill, Russell considered that a land tax of £400,000 should be raised in Ireland and be employed there either to purchase glebe houses and land for the Catholic parish clergy or to provide them with salaries. If some such measures were introduced, he argued, the Government could safely ask Parliament to suspend Habeas Corpus for one year as a temporary security measure.[108]

These proposals were given a rather unenthusiastic reception by Russell's colleagues. Earl Grey doubted whether the Catholic endowment plan was immediately practicable and suggested that negotiations with Rome and the bishops should take place first.[109] Charles Wood was not in favour of using a land tax to raise the necessary funds and both he and Earl Grey felt that the situation in Ireland did not yet justify a suspension of Habeas Corpus.[110] On the issue of limiting the powers of the landlords to evict, Russell encountered the massive opposition of Lansdowne and Palmerston, both of them Irish landlords. Lansdowne warned of the danger of further alienating the Irish gentry, while Palmerston urged that '. . . it is useless to disguise the truth that any great improvement in the social system of Ireland must be founded upon an extensive change in the present state of agrarian occupation, and that this change necessarily implies a long continued and systematic ejectment of small holders and of squatting cottiers'.[111]

The British Government was in the unhappy position of being unable to decide what should be done in Ireland, at a time when Chartism threatened to become a serious menace in Britain. A possible way of meeting the immediate problem of

[108] Memorandum, 30 Mar. 1848, Russell papers, P.R.O. 30/22/7; Walpole, *Life of Lord John Russell*, ii. 64–5.
[109] Memorandum by Earl Grey, 30 Mar. 1848, Russell papers, P.R.O. 30/22/7.
[110] Memorandum by Sir Charles Wood, 31 Mar. 1848, Russell papers, P.R.O. 30/22/7.
[111] Memorandum by Lord Palmerston, 31 Mar. 1848, Russell papers, P.R.O. 30/22/7; Memorandum by Lord Lansdowne, 30 Mar. 1848, Russell papers, P.R.O. 30/22/7.

maintaining order was, however, suggested by Lord Campbell, a former Irish Chancellor and the future Lord Chancellor of England. Lord Campbell considered it was quite impracticable to take action against the Young Irelanders under an antiquated and harsh treason law, especially as the French had abolished capital punishment for political offences. He, therfore, suggested that a new statutory offence of treason-felony should be instituted, a move which he believed would also be welcomed by the reformers. 'Thus,' as he put it, 'while you had the glory of mitigating the severity of the penal code, you would be armed with the effectual means of sending Messrs. Mitchel, Meagher and Smith O'Brien to Botany Bay.'[112] The Government adopted Lord Campbell's suggestion and embodied it in the Crown and Government Protection Bill. This measure, which applied to Great Britain as well as Ireland, provided that the capital offence of compassing and designing to levy war against the sovereign could be dealt with as an ordinary felony and be punished by transportation instead of death. In an important provision the offence was, however, extended to include all persons who should promote treasonable designs 'by open and advised speaking'.[113]

The Government, as we have already seen, was slow to bring forward any new coercive measures. Troubled about the attitude of Parliament, the ministry even rejected Clarendon's suggestion that the Crown and Government Protection Bill should include provisions to authorise the suppression of the rifle clubs and make it illegal to manufacture or possess pikes without a licence.[114] It was believed that in the absence of fuller evidence of an armed conspiracy, the Government could hardly ask Parliament to meet the Lord Lieutenant's request. The actual debates on the Crown and Government Protection Bill soon made it quite clear that the administration had seriously over-estimated the strength of its critics in the House of Commons. John O'Connell, aided by a small number of Irish mem-

[112] *Hansard*, xcvii. 1205–7; Lord John Campbell to Russell, [Apr. 1848], Russell papers, P.R.O. 30/22/7.

[113] *Hansard*, xcviii. 20–34.

[114] Clarendon to Sir G. Grey, [12] Apr. 1848, Clarendon papers, letter-book II; Grey to Clarendon, 17 Apr. 1848, Clarendon papers, Ir. box 12, bundle 21.

bers and a mixed group of Radicals, including Sharman Crawford, O'Connor, Muntz, Wakley and Hume, did oppose the bill. The Irish members, however, with the exception of Smith O'Brien remained content with formal protests.[115] John O'Connell made it clear that he was opposing the bill with some regret and would vote against it simply because there appeared to be no immediate necessity for it. Smith O'Brien, back from Paris, alone made a defiant and angry speech before a very hostile House. His defiance was made all the more lonely by the fact that the one other Confederate in Parliament, Chisholm Anstey, not merely voted for the bill but spoke in its favour.[116] Fearful of Chartists in Britain and of revolution and republicanism in Ireland, Parliament willingly accepted the new measure. On the third reading in the Commons, the Opposition could only muster 40 votes while 295 supported the bill.[117] Introduced on April 7, it received the royal assent fifteen days later.[118]

Alarmed at the violence of the language used even at meetings of the Repeal Association, John O'Connell, early in April, gladly accepted a suggestion that he should co-operate with the Government in helping to preserve order in Ireland.[119] Two days before the debate on the Treason-Felony Bill, he sought and was granted an interview by Russell.[120] At this interview, O'Connell stressed the importance of new measures to relieve distress and he urged Russell to bring forward a landlord and tenant bill and to amend the Charitable Bequests Act so as to meet Catholic criticism of it. He felt, too, that more attention should be paid to Catholic opinion on such issues as education and diplomatic relations with Rome. On the immediate political level, O'Connell told Russell that some good might be done were the Government to permit some discussion of a repeal bill in Parliament and abandon the prosecutions of Smith O'Brien, Meagher and Mitchel.[121] Russell was careful not to

---

[115] *Hansard*, xcviii. 34–7, 119, 92–6, 383–5, 463–70.

[116] Ibid., xcviii. 103–4.   [117] Ibid., xcviii. 480.   [118] Ibid., xcviii. 537.

[119] Clarendon to Grey, 28 Mar. 1848, Clarendon papers, letterbook II; Repeal Assoc. meeting, 10 Apr., *Freeman's Journal*, 11 Apr. 1848; *Nation*, 22 Apr. 1848.

[120] John O'Connell to Russell, 4 Apr. 1848, Russell papers, P.R.O. 30/22/7.

[121] Sir William Somerville to Clarendon, 5 Apr. 1848, Clarendon papers, Ir. box 27, bundle 38; *Nation*, 15 Apr. 1848.

commit himself to O'Connell. The Prime Minister's suggestion, however, that provision might be made for the purchase of glebes for the Catholic clergy seems to have pleased O'Connell even though he considered that a great deal more needed to be done.[122] O'Connell followed up this exchange of views with Russell by subscribing to a loyal declaration denouncing agitation which had been drafted by the Irish Conservative members of parliament. Later, in a more contrite mood, he was to admit that this declaration was of a slavish character, but for the moment it was not surprising that Lord Clarendon should have claimed that, 'the steam goes down here every day'.[123] As on previous occasions his optimism was short lived.

From the nationalist point of view the position, therefore, was by no means easy in April. John O'Connell made his long promised attempt to interest the Commons in repeal but it was a failure. The House showed itself well content with the answer given by the Chief Secretary, Sir William Somerville, that the repeal of the Act of Union would leave Ireland no better off, particularly in view of the fact that Ireland could not maintain herself in time of famine.[124] The spiritless debate on O'Connell's motion did nothing to strengthen the position of the advocates of peaceful methods. But the Confederates, too, suffered a grave set-back at this time. The dispute between the radical wing, led by John Mitchel, and the majority of the Confederate Council flared up again in early May, when John Mitchel and his friend Devin Reilly finally withdrew from the Irish Confederation.

The nominal cause of the trouble was an unhappy incident involving both Smith O'Brien and Mitchel. Smith O'Brien had indicated that he would not take part in the same meetings as John Mitchel so as to prevent their political views being confused in the public mind. Mitchel accepted this arrangement. However, through a misunderstanding both men were present at a meeting held in Limerick, on April 29, in honour of the 'prosecuted patriots'. Smith O'Brien was popular and respected in Limerick but the local repealers, angered by some comments on Daniel O'Connell in the *United Irishman*, were determined to

[122] Ibid.

[123] *Freeman's Journal*, 13 Apr. 1848; *Nation*, 29 Apr. 1848; Clarendon to Grey, 28 Apr. 1848, Clarendon papers, letterbook II.

[124] *Hansard*, xcviii. 178–210.

treat Mitchel as nothing better than a vilifier of the good name of the dead Liberator. It was of little avail for Mitchel to assert that he was indeed a republican but no Jacobin or Communist. The mob, with a show of violence, broke up the meeting and Smith O'Brien, who was slightly injured in the disturbance, withdrew in mortification, disgusted both with the mob and what he considered was a breach of faith on Mitchel's part.[125]

The affair took a still more serious turn when Smith O'Brien indicated plainly to both John Mitchel and Devin Reilly that either he or they would have to resign from the Confederation. In similar terms both Devin Reilly and Mitchel, on May 3, resigned from the Confederation and its Council, Devin Reilly stating that he believed that the majority of the Council supported Smith O'Brien's moderate views. In his letter of resignation, John Mitchel made it quite clear that more fundamental matters were involved than the Limerick riot. The primary causes of his resignation were really differences on policy with Smith O'Brien and the latter's decision to force the issue. Unlike Smith O'Brien, he believed that 'the time for conciliation of the landlord class is past' and, in consequence, the national movement '. . . *must* become a class movement also—or it will stand still'.[126]

The news of the Limerick incident was received with considerable satisfaction by the Lord Lieutenant, who described it as a great blow to the Young Irelanders. Rather than give them any chance to recover the influence he felt they had lost, Clarendon urged that prompt action should now be taken against them. The repeal movement was divided but, he argued, the agitation was potentially dangerous as 'in another month will begin the great pressure of distress and as no assistance in any shape is to be given, we must expect some disturbance'.[127] In the months of shortage ahead the Lord Lieutenant feared that the agitators might gain supporters from among the poor of the countryside as well as in the towns.[128] As a result, even before

---

[125] *United Irishman*, 6 May 1848; Gavan Duffy, *Four Years of Irish History*, p. 211; Mitchel to Smith O'Brien, [Apr.–May 1848], Smith O'Brien papers, vol. 440, no. 2202.

[126] *United Irishman*, 6 May 1848; *Nation*, 6 May 1848.

[127] Clarendon to Russell, 2 May 1848, Clarendon papers, letterbook II.

[128] Clarendon to Henry Reeve, 10 May 1848, Laughton, *Memoirs of the Life and Correspondence of Henry Reeve*, i. 200–1.

the much delayed sedition trials took place, Clarendon had decided, as an 'experiment', to prosecute John Mitchel under the new Treason-Felony Act and to drop in his case the lesser charge of seditious libel.[129] This decision was an important one because, on May 15, Smith O'Brien came up for trial on the sedition counts and won a minor victory over the authorities. Despite efforts by the prosecution to exclude possible repealers from the jury, the Crown failed to secure a conviction, as the jurors were unable to agree on a verdict, and Smith O'Brien was discharged. Next day the case against Meagher ended in a similar way. The arrest and prosecution of Mitchel for treason-felony now became the principal weapon in the Government's attempt to frighten the agitators into silence and inactivity.[130]

The outcome of Mitchel's trial, which began on May 26, could hardly ever have been in doubt. Remembering what had happened in the sedition proceedings against Smith O'Brien and Meagher, the sheriff made careful arrangements to exclude possible repeal sympathisers from the jury by replacing the original panel of jurymen with another one containing few Catholics. Though the defence protested, the trial judge refused to interfere with what the sheriff had done.[131] Again, the prosecution's task was made easier by the fact that neither Mitchel nor his counsel attempted to deny the accusation that he advocated warlike action as a national necessity in the pages of the *United Irishman*.[132] The packing of the jury and the severity of the sentence, fourteen years transportation, immediately won for Mitchel the sympathy of men drawn from all sections of the divided repeal movement. Repealers were angry but despite the threats and demonstrations Mitchel was removed from the country without the peace being disturbed. He had apparently expected that some attempt would be made to rescue him, but the Council of the Confederation decided against any such action because of their followers' utter inexperience in military

129 Clarendon to Grey, [10–11] May 1848, Clarendon papers, letter-book II.
130 Grey to Clarendon, 16 May 1848, Clarendon papers, Ir. box 12, bundle 21; Clarendon to Russell, 23 May 1848, Clarendon papers, letter-book II.
131 *Hansard*, xcviii. 1325–7; *Nation*, 27 May 1848.
132 *United Irishman*, 29 Apr., 6 May 1848.

matters.[133] Many meetings of protest were held, however, which at least provided an opportunity for speakers from both the Confederation and the Repeal Association to join in vigorous attacks on the Government's Irish policy.[134]

Mitchel's trial and sentence had repercussions in Britain too. Already in March and April Confederates and Chartists had held joint meetings in many parts of the provinces, while in London the Irish Confederate clubs appear to have had close associations with the radical wing of the Chartists led by men such as Ernest Jones, P. M. MacDouall and William Cuffey.[135] Though the Kennington Common demonstration of April 10 had failed completely to intimidate the Government and Parliament, the Chartist leaders made yet another attempt to rally their supporters in early June. In this new and short-lived agitation the Irish living in Britian played an important part and, as proof of their unity of purpose, Chartists and Irish nationalists joined in vigorous condemnation of the Treason-Felony Act and Mitchel's trial and sentence. At Oldham, at the end of May, banners inscribed with the words 'Mitchel and Liberty' were carried. At Nottingham the cry was 'Mitchel should be free'.[136] The critical point in this combined action was reached when June 12 was selected by the Chartist executive in London as the date on which a number of meetings of Chartists and Irish nationalists were to be held in the London area. Like the Kennington Common demonstration in April, this plan came to nothing because of the resolute stand taken by the authorities.[137] The 'physical force Chartists', like the Confederates in Ireland, were ill-prepared for a serious defiance of the Government despite fiery speeches and threatening attitudes.

The severity of the sentence imposed on Mitchel did, however, help to bring all sections of the Irish repeal movement closer together. Already on the eve of the trial, John O'Connell had spoken at a protest meeting and he went so far as to say that if Mitchel were convicted of treason-felony, he would be a martyr for Ireland.[138] Afterwards, the conviction of Mitchel was con-

[133] Gavan Duffy, *Four Years of Irish History*, pp. 212–13; John Mitchel, *Jail Journal; or Five years in British Prisons*, passim.

[134] *Nation*, 27 May 1848.

[135] *United Irishman*, 25 Mar. 1848; *The Times*, 12 June 1848.

[136] *Nation*, 12 June 1848; *The Times*, 1 June 1848.

[137] Ibid., 12 June 1848.   [138] *Freeman's Journal*, 26 May 1848.

demned by both the Repeal Association and the Confederation, a development which helped to open the way for new attempts to bring all nationalists into one organisation.[139] Whatever passing optimism the outcome of the trial may have produced in official circles, it was soon to be replaced by a realisation that more would be needed to end the activities of the Confederate clubs than the transportation of John Mitchel to Tasmania.[140]

In bringing Mitchel to trial, the Government gave, as John O'Connell had predicted, a martyr to the nationalist cause. In Ireland, Mitchel had been something of an embarrassment to his more moderate colleagues. In banishment he became a symbol which helped to bring nationalists a little closer together, and long after his death Mitchel's teachings on republican nationalism continued to have their effect on the shaping of revolutionary movements in Ireland.[141] The events in France convinced him of the validity of republicanism, and he thereby brought back into Irish nationalism a belief which had languished in the early nineteenth century following the failure of the 1798 rebellion and Emmet's rising in 1803.[142]

Mitchel's conversion to the belief that an agrarian conflict

---

[139] Repeal Assoc. meeting, 29 May, *Freeman's Journal*, 30 May 1848.

[140] Grey to Clarendon, 29 May 1848, Clarendon papers, Ir. box 12, bundle 21. John Mitchel was first transported to Bermuda. He finally reached Tasmania in April 1850. In 1853 he surrendered his convict's ticket of leave and escaped from Australia to the United States. In America he quickly won the reputation of being a vigorous, controversial journalist strongly sympathetic to the claims of the southern states. He boldly defended negro slavery as it existed in those states. In 1865, after the Civil War had ended, he was arrested for continuing to write pro-southern articles and was imprisoned under harsh conditions for some months. Despite his interest in American politics, Mitchel remained associated with advanced Irish nationalism. Though he doubted the value of the methods employed by the Fenians, he supported the movement for a time. He refused however, to accept the leadership of the Fenians in America. In 1874 he visited Ireland. In Feb. 1875 he was returned unopposed as an M.P. for Co. Tipperary, having indicated to the electorate that he was no supporter of moderate Home Rule and that he would not attend Parliament. Unseated as a convicted felon, he was again returned for Tipperary, in March 1875. Long in bad health, John Mitchel died at his old home near Newry on 20 March 1875 shortly after his re-election. Two of his sons fell while serving with the confederate forces during the American Civil War.

[141] James Connolly, *Labour in Irish History*, pp. 174–90.

[142] *United Irishman*, 15 Apr. 1848.

was necessary had been a gradual one and he undoubtedly drew heavily on Fintan Lalor's teachings.[143] But though Mitchel openly embraced republicanism without qualifications for the first time in 1848, his own special contribution to the development of Irish nationalism lay in his efforts to link the agrarian struggle with a militant republicanism. In his uncompromising way, Mitchel, in 1848, wanted the repealers 'to strike for a republic' and to raise 'the Irish tricolour, orange white and green, over a forest of Irish pikes'.[144] Through a bold, armed rebellion, he believed the nationalists could best hope to win practical aid from abroad. Mitchel rejected secret conspiracy in favour of open defiance, but in doing so he overestimated both the warlike spirit of the countryside and the natural discipline of a famine-weakened people. Angered by the famine, John Mitchel saw in armed revolt a worthier way for men to die than from starvation.[145]

Before the end of May, on the suggestion of the Repeal Association an informal joint committee was set up to devise some means of bringing the two sections of the repeal movement together on a permanent basis. On May 29, John O'Connell, having expressed sympathy with John Mitchel, announced that he had met Smith O'Brien that day and while no plan for reunion had yet been decided upon 'there may be courses upon which we can agree with those with whom we have been hitherto at dissensions . . .'.[146] Negotiations followed between the two organisations and by June 3 or 4 it had been agreed, subject to the ratification of the proposal by both bodies, that the Repeal Association and the Irish Confederation should be dissolved and be replaced by a new association, the short-lived Irish League. It was further agreed that the Confederate clubs were not to be disbanded but were to remain, as independent bodies, the nucleus of a national guard. At the same time, however, the clubs were to be 'connected with the association by machinery . . . to be arranged and if they chose to arm themselves the association is not to interfere'.[147] For the moment it

[143] See p. 148.   [144] *United Irishman*, 15 Apr. 1848.
[145] Ibid., 11 March, 8 Apr. 1848.
[146] Repeal Assoc. meeting, 29 May, *Freeman's Journal*, 30 May 1848.
[147] Sir Colman O'Loghlen to Smith O'Brien, 4 June 1848, Smith O'Brien papers, vol. 442, no. 2465.

seemed that the way was, at last, open for a successful reunion of the repeal forces, especially as the principle had apparently been accepted that members were free, in their private capacity and outside of the League, to advocate the use of arms. The repeal movement, however, remained true to its history. Unexpected difficulties arose for which John O'Connell was not altogether to blame, difficulties that both delayed the formation of the League and deprived it of the prestige value of the O'Connell name.

Gavan Duffy's handling of the situation was hardly the most tactful. Proposing, on June 6, that the Confederation should adjourn indefinitely, once the preliminary agreement had been finally adopted, he described that agreement as a victory for the Confederation, since he believed the League would provide a convenient means of introducing armed clubs into the rural areas where the Confederation had made little progress.[148] Though Gavan Duffy was careful to say that by joining the new movement the O'Connellites were not abandoning their principles, the general suggestion of a Confederate victory proved distasteful to John O'Connell. O'Connell, it would appear, had hoped that the clubs would quietly be allowed to fall into the background once the new movement got under way. To avoid the possibility of the League being used in the way suggested by Gavan Duffy, he soon resorted to a variety of expedients to prevent the final dissolution of the Repeal Association.[149]

O'Connell's position was by no means an easy one. The finances of the Association were now so weak that he had to admit, late in June, that even were the Association not disbanded, it could hardly survive much longer.[150] Within the Association, too, John O'Connell had to face a new threat in the form of a growing body of critics who resented his efforts to hinder the establishment of the League.[151] Though working under difficulties, O'Connell was at least partially successful

[148] Irish Confed. meeting, 6 June, *Nation*, 10 June 1848.

[149] *Freeman's Journal*, 12 June 1848.

[150] John O'Connell to the people of Ireland, 23 June 1848, *Nation*, 24 June 1848.

[151] Sir Colman O'Loghlen to Smith O'Brien, 11 June 1848, Smith O'Brien papers, vol. 442, no. 2472.

in opposing the dissolution of the Repeal Association. On the plea that his father's old organisation should not be swept away until the provincial repealers had been consulted, the final decision to wind up the Association was postponed for two weeks.[152] This move made the task of concluding a speedy and satisfactory settlement more difficult since it gave John O'Connell an opportunity to rally his supporters especially among the Catholic clergy, and to raise the old cry that the organised repeal movement should be kept free of illegal activities.[153]

John O'Connell proved unable to sustain any prolonged opposition to the formation of the League. The letters received from the country were inconclusive. Some of the Catholic bishops, for example, welcomed the League, while others regretted any action which could lead to the dissolution of the old Association. Outvoted on a resolution, which he had brought forward, that the new organisation should only employ peaceful methods, and convinced that the Repeal Association's days were numbered, John O'Connell finally declared that he would no longer resist the foundation of the League though he could never join it. Instead of taking part in the new movement, he said he would rather confine himself to his duties as a member of Parliament.[154]

This clash with John O'Connell, however, taught the Confederate leaders to be somewhat more circumspect in their comments and actions. At the final public meeting of Confederation, on June 21, the spokesmen were careful to stress that the Young Irelanders had no intention of using the Irish League to further their own particular views. The Confederation was then adjourned indefinitely but the clubs continued to exist and the Confederation, at its final meeting, approved of the formation of a small council to act as a caretaker body for the Confederation until the League was constituted.[155] The way was now open for the establishment of the Irish League. The Repeal Association had for all practical purposes ceased to exist, the

[152] *Freeman's Journal*, 13 June 1848.

[153] Clarendon to Grey, 12 June 1848, Clarendon papers, letterbook II.

[154] John O'Connell to the people of Ireland, 23 June 1848, *Nation*, 24 June 1848.

[155] Irish Confed. meeting, 21 June, *Nation*, 24 June 1848. Some meetings of this council may have been held even after the establishment of the Irish League (Gavan Duffy, *Four Years of Irish History*, p. 228).

Confederation had been adjourned *sine die* and the League, which met for the first time on July 11, became the only repeal organisation apart from the clubs.[156] It came much too late to achieve anything of importance and the elimination of the older organisations did not resolve the problem of how the Young Irelanders could make effective preparations for a possible rebellion and yet pursue a moderate policy based on parliamentary agitation and requiring middle and upper class support.[157]

In addition to the activities in the clubs, more confidential discussions took place between some of the leading Young Irelanders for the purpose of planning an armed rising which, they hoped, would take place later in the year. The widespread resentment over Mitchel's trial and sentence had helped to bring his friends and the other Young Irelanders closer together. Not surprisingly, it was one of Mitchel's most vigorous supporters, Rev. John Kenyon, a Catholic priest, who apparently suggested that these discussions should take place. The Young Irelanders involved in the conspiracy included Gavan Duffy and John Dillon as well as more radical figures such as Devin Reilly. Smith O'Brien, because of his known moderation and anxiety to avoid bloodshed, was not invited to join the conspirators though he knew of their activities.[158]

In addition to these discussions the Council of the Confederation, before that organisation finally adjourned, appointed 'a cabinet of organisation', as the secretary of the Confederation called it, to help establish new clubs throughout the country.[159] It was further planned by the Council to send representatives to America, and despite the rebuff the Young Irelanders had experienced in Paris, consideration was again given to the possibility of winning French support.[160] These activities, how-

[156] John O'Connell revived the Repeal Association in October 1849. The meetings were poorly attended and attracted little attention. The receipts, too, were meagre. In July 1850 the Association finally ceased to meet (*Freeman's Journal*, 9 Oct. 1849, 10 July, 1850).

[157] *Irish Felon*, 24 June 1848; *Nation*, 8, 15 July 1848.

[158] Gavan Duffy, *Four Years of Irish History*, pp. 217–18.

[159] Thomas Halpin to Smith O'Brien, 13 June 1848, Smith O'Brien papers, vol. 442, no. 2475.

[160] Thomas Halpin to Smith O'Brien, 29 June 1848, Smith O'Brien papers, vol. 442, no. 2484; Gavan Duffy, *Four Years of Irish History*, pp. 217–18.

ever, appear to have exhausted the Young Irelanders enthusiasm for secret or semi-secret conspiracy. The proceedings in the clubs were open and well known to the police and, from April 1848 onwards, John Donnellan Balfe, an active member of the Confederation, was able to supply the Dublin Castle authorities with reasonably accurate information about the Confederates plans, the differences on policy, and the personal rivalries within the movement.[161]

The nationalists' problem of reconciling the claims of constitutional and revolutionary methods did not remain for long a practical one, as the British Government, rather reluctantly, decided to make yet another attempt to end agitation in Ireland. By June, the Lord Lieutenant's easy optimism of a few weeks previously had given way to a nervous anxiety. The transportation of Mitchel had only helped to close the ranks of the nationalists and the activity in the clubs especially caused him a great deal of worry. The police and military reports, in June and July, showed that the members of the clubs were engaging quite openly in military exercises and buying arms, and yet legally it was difficult to take any effective action against them.[162] In the circumstances, Grey, the Home Secretary, believed that the only way to suppress the clubs was to suspend Habeas Corpus and imprison the leaders, but neither Grey nor Clarendon felt, in early June, that the Government could yet

---

[161] S.P.O. Ir. Outrage papers, cartons 1514, 6/828, 6/866. John Donnellan Balfe was, it would seem, a native of County Meath. He worked as a journalist in England where he was active in Radical and Irish repeal circles. Financial difficulties may have led him to seek employment as a government agent. Balfe returned to Ireland early in 1848, but he soon admitted to his employers that he was already suspected by the repealers of being an informer (J. D. Balfe to George E. Turner, 6 Apr. 1848, Clarendon papers, Ir. box 53). Gavan Duffy, however, in mid-April asked Balfe to help organise the new national guard and throughout 1848 he was in receipt of useful information (see enclosure with Balfe's report, 25 Apr. 1848, Clarendon papers, Ir. box. 53). He was present at Thurles railway station when Smith O'Brien was arrested after the 1848 rising. Subsequently Balfe appears to have obtained a post in the prison service in Tasmania. Though critical of the Young Irelanders and especially of Gavan Duffy, Balfe was careful to stress that the Confederate leaders were 'chivalrous, bold, courageous, eloquent and incorruptible' (Balfe's report, 2 June 1848, Clarendon papers, Ir. box 53). See also John Mitchel, *Jail Journal*, pp. 264-5.

[162] S.P.O. Ir. Outrage papers, cartons 1514, 6/947, 6/961.

approach Parliament with so drastic a proposal.[163] Again, they miscalculated the temper of Parliament.

The authorities, at first, contented themselves with taking action against the more radical of the newspapers and against some of the principal Young Irelanders. On July 8, Gavan Duffy, the proprietor of the *Nation*, was arrested and committed to prison on a charge of publishing articles of a treasonable nature. The owners of two other nationalist newspapers, the *Irish Felon* and the *Tribune* were also arrested and Meagher, Doheny and McGee were charged with making seditious speeches. But though both Meagher and Doheny were released on bail and the Wicklow grand jury refused to return a bill against McGee, the arrests provoked a great deal of anger in nationalist circles.[164]

Busy in the provinces organising their scattered supporters, the Young Ireland leaders now began to use more openly the language of revolution. Meagher, at a large, semi-military demonstration in County Tipperary, urged the people to hold the harvest and not to surrender it to the landlords, while Doheny told his listeners that 'we intend to realise the true gospel which was preached by John Mitchel'.[165] The temper among the clubbists was such that Smith O'Brien concluded that any attempt to transport Gavan Duffy and the others, if convicted of treason-felony, would result in an insurrection.[166]

The activities of the armed clubs, which had been established by the Confederates, and the revolutionary tone of the leaders' speeches soon convinced Clarendon that the time had come to end the threat of revolution by taking really vigorous action against the organisers of political unrest.[167] By the middle of July, as his tense, anxious letters testify, he had abandoned his earlier doubts about the wisdom of suspending Habeas Corpus and the Government under strong pressure from Dublin finally

---

[163] Grey to Clarendon, 1 June 1848, Clarendon papers, Ir. box 12, bundle 21; Clarendon to Russell, 4 June 1848, Clarendon papers, letterbook II; Clarendon to Russell, 15 June 1848, Clarendon papers, letterbook III.

[164] *Nation*, 15 July 1848.

[165] Ibid., 22 July 1848.

[166] Smith O'Brien to Lucy C. O'Brien, 20 July 1848, Smith O'Brien papers, vol. 442, no. 2491.

[167] Clarendon to Grey, 18 July 1848, Clarendon papers, letterbook III.

gave way and agreed to a suspension bill.[168] Clarendon may have exaggerated the dangers, but the possibility of an autumn rising in Ireland, when the harvest had been saved, was something even so irresolute a ministry as Russell's could hardly afford to ignore. The cabinet, on July 21, decided that Habeas Corpus should be suspended at once in Ireland. It was agreed, too, that more troops and naval vessels should be sent to the Irish stations as a precautionary measure.[169] The next day, Lord John Russell obtained leave to introduce the suspending bill which was to be effective until 1 March 1849.[170]

The ease with which this drastic measure passed almost undebated through Parliament in one day revealed the weakness, indeed, the utter ineffectiveness of the repeal party as a parliamentary force. Only eight members could be found, in the Commons, to oppose the Government's motion. Without sustained leadership or a strong organisation in Ireland to support them, the repeal members in the summer of 1848, had ceased to matter politically. Three days after it had been introduced, the bill received the royal assent.[171] The suspension of the constitutional guarantees made a humiliating surrender or a premature rising inevitable in Ireland. In late June and early July, the Young Irelanders had endeavoured to make some assessment of the actual numerical strength of the clubs. The result was not altogether encouraging. In the urban areas, especially Dublin, Cork and Waterford, the clubbists appear to have been relatively numerous and enthusiastic, but in the countryside the formidable task of winning significant support among a famine-exhausted population had yet to be accomplished.[172] The authorities, however, left the Young Irelanders little time to resolve their many problems. On July 21, the City and County of Dublin were proclaimed under the 1847 Coercion Act and all unlicensed holders of arms were directed to surrender their weapons to the police.

[168] Clarendon to Grey, 19 July 1848, Clarendon papers, letterbook III; Grey to Clarendon, 21 July 1848, Clarendon papers, Ir. box 12, bundle 21.
[169] J. D. Balfe's report, 15 July 1848, Clarendon papers, Ir. box 53; Russell to Clarendon, 30 July 1848, Clarendon papers, Ir. box 43, bundle 54; Grey to Clarendon, 21 July 1848, Clarendon papers, Ir. box 12, bundle 21.
[170] *Hansard*, c. 693–713. [171] Ibid., c. 743.
[172] Thomas Halpin to Smith O'Brien, 29 June 1848, Smith O'Brien papers, vol. 442, no. 2484.

A still more serious blow fell on July 26, when another proclamation was issued declaring that membership of a political club would be regarded as sufficient grounds for making arrests following the suspension of Habeas Corpus.[173] In a hurried effort to provide the clubs with a central directory to meet this emergency, the representatives of the Dublin clubs elected a council of five. These last-minute preparations, proved of no significance, since the directory apparently never met.[174]

The Suspension Act forced the Young Ireland leaders to scatter throughout the country. Many made their way to the south-eastern counties where they believed they could count on much support, and Smith O'Brien, who had hitherto hesitated to commit himself fully to an armed revolt, now accepted a rising as a practical necessity.[175] The confused and short-lived attempt at rebellion in the south-eastern counties, however, not only marked the end of Young Ireland but proved to be the effective extinction of the whole movement founded by Daniel O'Connell to secure the repeal of the Act of Union.

In deciding to stage a rebellion, the Young Irelanders were no doubt influenced by the fact that the clubs, in June and July, had won additional supporters.[176] They were aware, too, that in the Counties Tipperary, Wexford, Kilkenny and Waterford, the spirit of unrest was strong even in the rural districts. The Government shared this knowledge and, in the closing days of July 1848, an element of serious alarm entered into the communications between Dublin and London.[177] Clarendon believed that the insurgents would operate within a triangle formed by Kilkenny, Cashel and Waterford. He feared that, 'when they once commence it is impossible to say how far they may extend', and his forebodings were confirmed, it seemed, when he was able to report, on July 28, that Smith O'Brien was marching at

[173] *Nation*, 29 July 1848.

[174] The members of the directory were, John Dillon, Meagher, Richard O'Gorman, McGee and Devin Reilly (Gavan Duffy, *Four Years of Irish History*, pp. 229–30).

[175] Ibid., pp. 230–1.

[176] See p. 211.

[177] Gavan Duffy, op. cit., pp. 226–7; Grey to Clarendon, 27 July 1848, Clarendon papers, Ir. box 12, bundle 21.

the head of 2,000 armed men in south Tipperary.[178] The
authorities also knew that money and emissaries were reaching
Ireland from America and it was even thought that sympathisers
with the insurgents might cause disturbances in Liverpool.[179] In
the circumstances, Wellington thought it well to advise the
Prime Minister to send 10,000 troops to the south-east of
Ireland.[180]

The Government, for a time, even considered the possibility of
accepting the offer of some Orange elements to raise armed
units, but Russell feared that any such display of Protestant zeal
might only drive many Catholics into the ranks of the rebels.[181]
In practice, the need for such assistance never arose. The rebellion suddenly collapsed at Ballingarry, County Tipperary, on
July 29, when Smith O'Brien and his band of supporters had to
give way before a body of armed police.[182] The rising or rather
the armed demonstrations had not lasted a week.

Elsewhere in the country there were a few minor incidents.
Thomas Clarke Luby and some other Dublin clubbists planned
to march in force from Blanchardstown, near Dublin, to County
Meath where the agrarian secret societies were said to be
sympathetic. Only a small number of the Dublin club members
assembled and the plan was abandoned. Richard O'Gorman
succeeded in gathering some supporters at Abbeyfeale, County
Limerick, but they dispersed once the bad news from Tipperary
became known.[183] In early September, John O'Mahony, the
future Fenian leader, sought to organise a fresh rising in
Counties Tipperary and Waterford, and Clarendon claimed
that 'arms and plunder and non-payment of rent' were the
motives behind these new outbreaks. They were of short duration. On September 28, the Lord Lieutenant was able to write:

178 Clarendon to Grey, 26 July 1848, Clarendon papers, letterbook III;
Clarendon to J. T. Delane, 27 July 1848, Dasent, *John Thadeus Delane*, i.
77–9; Clarendon to Russell, 28 July 1848, Clarendon papers, letterbook III.
179 Clarendon to Grey, 26 July 1848, Clarendon papers, letterbook III;
Clarendon to Russell, 30 July 1848, Clarendon papers, letterbook III.
180 Russell to Clarendon, 27 July 1848, Clarendon papers, Ir. box 43,
bundle 54.
181 Russell to Clarendon, 24 July 1848, Clarendon papers, Ir. box 43,
bundle 54.
182 *Freeman's Journal*, 31 July 1848.
183 Gavan Duffy, *Four Years of Irish History*, pp. 241–4.

'things are quiet here—a good many of the minor figures engaged in the last insurrection (if it can be so called) have been arrested. O'Mahony . . . is trying to affect his escape and the other, Doheny, has arrived in Paris. O'Gorman is said to be again at Abbeyfeale trying to get up a rising but we have force enough there'.[184]

In official circles the sense of alarm quickly passed. Even as early as August 3, Clarendon could say, with confidence, that 'the news from the different parts of the country this morning may be summed up in these words *the rebellion is over.* The people are returning to their work, the farmers and middle classes are recovering from the *very wholesome* alarm they have undergone and the priests are still rebuking their flocks for their folly'.[185] Sir Robert Peel, a little later, expressed this same sense of relief in another way: 'Smith O'Brien has rendered more service than I thought he was capable of rendering by making rebellion ridiculous'.[186]

The rising of 1848 failed because of the lack of preparations, of effective military leadership and of any clear plan of action. Enthusiastic meetings and even local goodwill in the south-eastern counties were no substitute for careful planning and disciplined mass support. Other factors seriously hampered the leaders of the short-lived rising as well. The Catholic clergy generally advised the country people against taking part in a hopeless demonstration. Again, in some areas the O'Connellites proved hostile or indifferent to the insurgents and Smith O'Brien, who had assumed leadership, was a reluctant rebel.[187] His personal qualities of bravery and integrity were high but he was no guerrilla soldier.

As we have seen, the action of the Government in suspending Habeas Corpus had the effect of forcing the Young Irelanders to take premature action.[188] Had they waited until the harvest had been gathered, their chances of success might well have

[184] Clarendon to Russell, 14 Sept., 28 Sept. 1848, Clarendon papers, letterbook III.

[185] Clarendon to Russell, 3 Aug. 1848, Clarendon papers, letterbook III.

[186] Peel to Graham, 24 Aug. 1848, Graham papers.

[187] *Freeman's Journal,* 2 Aug. 1848; Clarendon to Russell, 3 Aug. 1848, Clarendon papers, letterbook III.

[188] 'It is perfectly true that the insurrection was forced on before the preparations were complete and that accounts for its being of the paltry

been greater, though even then the question remains an open one whether conservatives, like Smith O'Brien and Gavan Duffy, would have accepted a policy based on the seizure of the crops and possibly of the estates of the landlords by agrarian revolutionaries. The aims and methods of Fintan Lalor and John Mitchel were not really tested in 1848.

A number of those involved in the rising, including Smith O'Brien and Meagher, were captured eventually and put on trial, at Clonmel, County Tipperary, on charges of high treason.[189] Others, like Gavan Duffy and John Martin, were already in custody before the rebellion on treason-felony charges, and some 118 persons were arrested, in 1848–9, on suspicion of treasonable practices, following the suspension of Habeas Corpus.[190] Among those imprisoned without trial was Fintan Lalor, who had contributed many of the most violent of the articles published in the *Irish Felon* before the rising.

The high treason trials proved, perhaps, more of an embarrassment than an advantage to the British Government. There was little likelihood that the terrible sentence of hanging, drawing and quartering would ever be executed. When Smith O'Brien and his three companions were found guilty, Conservatives joined with Liberals and nationalists in seeking to have the sentences commuted and Lord Clarendon felt that the executions would only provide the nationalists with martyrs.[191] The Government was in fact quite willing to commute the sentences to transportation for life but the prisoners showed no enthusiasm for such a solution. They argued that, under the

---

[189] *Freeman's Journal*, 22, 23 Sept. 1848.

[190] *Return of all Persons who have been committed to or retained in Prison in Ireland since the Passing of the Act 11 and 12 Vict. c. 35 . . .*, H.C. 1849 (13), xlix. 381–4.

[191] *Morning Post*, 21 Oct. 1848; *Freeman's Journal*, 12, 14 Oct. 1848, 6 June 1849; Clarendon to Grey, 8 Oct. 1848, Clarendon papers, letterbook III. 'In any case we must not be too severe now that political excitement is over and public opinion will be against more punishment than is necessary . . .' (Clarendon to Grey, 9 May, 1849, Clarendon papers, letterbook IV).

---

character described by Dillon (in a letter to the *Freeman's Journal*), but that was no fault of the leaders. They meant to wait till the harvest was got in and the club organisation was completed throughout the country . . .' (Clarendon to Grey, 4 Feb. 1849, Clarendon papers, letterbook III).

law as it stood, the Crown had no legal power, in the case of treason, to exercise the prerogative of mercy by substituting transportation for the capital sentence.[192] In the end, the Government escaped from this strange legal impasse by having the Transportation for Treason (Ireland) Bill hurried through Parliament in June 1849.[193] The sentences were then commuted and early in July the four state prisoners, Smith O'Brien, Meagher, Bellew MacManus and Patrick O'Donoghue, began their long journey into exile in Tasmania.[194]

The sentences imposed on the state prisoners evoked no such sharp popular reaction as did the transportation of John Mitchel, because repeal in 1849 was no longer a living force. With no success, John O'Connell, in October 1849, sought to revive the Repeal Association. His efforts went virtually unnoticed and by the summer of 1850 Conciliation Hall had to close its doors once more.[195] Fintan Lalor, on his release from prison, due to ill-health, in November 1848, became the centre of a group of revolutionaries which included Thomas Clarke Luby and Joseph Brennan, but though they thought and planned in terms of secret conspiracy and armed rebellion, their impact on the Ireland of 1849–50 was slight. In September 1849, they organised an unsuccessful attack on a police station at Cappoquin, County Waterford.[196] The attack irritated the authorities but it was not the prelude to a general rising in the south-east as the conspirators had hoped.[197] Though the 1849 conspiracy was a complete failure, many of those involved in it did not lose faith in secret revolutionary methods as the history of the Fenian movement in the eighteen-sixties and later was to show.

[192] *Freeman's Journal*, 10 June 1849.
[193] *Hansard*, cvi. 158–63, 389–449, 830.
[194] Clarendon to Grey, 9 July 1849, Clarendon papers, letterbook IV; *Freeman's Journal*, 10 July, 1849.
[195] Ibid., 9 Oct. 1849, 10 July 1850.
[196] L. Fogarty, *James Fintan Lalor*, pp. xxxvii–xlii; Tomás Ó Néill, *Fiontán Ó Leathlobhair*, pp. 111–23; *Freeman's Journal*, 19, 21, 22 Sept. 1849.
[197] Clarendon to Grey, 22 Sept. 1849, Clarendon papers, letterbook IV.

XI

THE END OF REPEAL

~~~~~~~~~~~~~~~~~~~~~~~~~~~~~~

SOCIAL ISSUES, especially the relations between landlord and tenant, rather than the old demand for repeal were to determine much of the character of Irish politics from the autumn of 1848 onwards until late in the eighteen-fifties.[1] As early as September 1848, Lord Clarendon could account for some fresh outbreaks in south Tipperary by saying that 'arms and plunder and non-payment of rents appear to be the inciting causes . . .'.[2] Throughout 1848-9, there were many reports of hunger and distress in rural areas, of resistance by farmers to the payment of poor rates and rent and of evictions by landlords.[3] The poverty of the people and the discord between the classes remains a constant theme in contemporary reports and correspondence. Already at the beginning of December 1848, some 495,719 people were in receipt of poor relief and a few months later the Lord Lieutenant, appalled by the problems confronting him, complained to Russell that 'the accounts from the west are indeed dreadful, but it is disgraceful to the legislature of a civilised country to have gone on puzzling for three months about the means of relieving the misery which they knew was daily increasing'.[4]

[1] J. W. Whyte, *The Independent Irish Party 1850-9*, pp. 1-11.
[2] Clarendon to Russell, 14 Sept. 1848, Clarendon papers, letterbook III.
[3] *Abstract of Return of all Notices served upon Relieving Officers of Poor Law Districts in Ireland by Landowners and Others . . .*, H.C. 1849 (517), xlix. 279-314; *Freeman's Journal*, 22 Sept. 1849.
[4] Clarendon to Russell, 25 Dec. 1848, Clarendon papers, letterbook III; Clarendon to Russell, 26 Apr. 1849, ibid., letterbook IV.

That misery had deep-rooted causes in the social system of the Irish countryside, but the distress was heightened by the fact that the potato crop, in 1848 and 1849, failed yet again. The food shortage was accompanied, too, by the cholera.[5] The breakdown of the old pattern of society, in the circumstances, affected all classes. The landlords answered the tenants' unwillingness or inability to pay rents by evictions, often on a scale which warrants the description of 'clearances'. In 1849 alone, some 90,000 people were known to have been put off their family holdings. In 1850 the total was even higher.[6] The high rents they endeavoured to collect and the poverty of their tenants naturally made the evicting landlords the object of severe criticism.[7] The members of the landed class, however, faced difficulties of their own as a falling income from rents and rising tax demands for poor relief drove many heavily encumbered estates still further into insolvency. The proceedings of the Incumbered Estates Commission, set up under the 1849 Incumbered Estates Act, show that, between October 1849 and July 1850 alone, properties with a total estimated revenue of £665,470 were sold by order of the commissioners. The burden of mortgages and other charges on these lands was enormous, amounting to £12,400,348.[8]

Had the Government been able to meet the social problems of Ireland with a series of vigorous measures based on a coherent policy, a great deal of human suffering might have been avoided or at least mitigated. Unfortunately, though some members of the administration were to recognise the need for positive measures, weakness and indecision continued to characterise the approach of the Whig government to all the major issues in Ireland.

[5] *Freeman's Journal*, 10 Aug. 1848; Sir William P. MacArthur, 'Medical History of the Famine', in *The Great Famine*, pp. 306–7.
[6] *Return . . . of Cases of Evictions which have come to the knowledge of the Constabulary in each of the Years from 1849 to 1880*, H.C. 1881 (185), lxxvii.
[7] 'Hence the tears and groans of the Irish landlords—their own recklessness, cruelty and extravagance are made the scourges to flog their backs—and they make an outcry against the Government and English legislation' (Russell to Clarendon, 20 Dec. 1848, Clarendon papers, Ir. box 43, bundle 54). *Freeman's Journal*, 1 Sept. 1849; *Hansard*, cv. 1286, 1287–8.
[8] *Report of the Commissioners for the Sale of Encumbered Estates*, H.C. 1850 (1268), xxv. 55–8.

For a short time it seemed as though the Government might devise a constructive Irish policy. In September 1848, Lord John Russell paid a brief visit to Ireland to consult with the members of the Irish administration.[9] He returned to London with the outlines of a fairly comprehensive programme which he believed would provide a sound basis for his Government's Irish proposals in the coming session of Parliament.[10] Some of the measures were familiar ones. A landlord and tenant bill was to contain tenant compensation clauses which should be 'as certain and as extensive as possible'. A uniform franchise was to be created in Ireland based on an £8 poor law valuation. The land law was to be altered so as to make the sale of land easier. The key factor, however, in the whole scheme of reform was to be a new Irish land and house tax. On the credit of this tax, funds would be raised to support the Catholic parish clergy, assist emigration from Ireland to the British colonies, and finance poor relief, land drainage and railway projects. Russell's proposals had little chance of survival.[11] Divisions within the cabinet, the powerful influence of pressure groups and the fear that Parliament would be unwilling to make any further funds available for Irish purposes, led to the rapid abandonment of the Prime Minister's schemes.

Russell did not abandon his programme willingly. When the cabinet decided that there should be no special emigration tax, he threatened to resign but his colleagues were not over-awed by this gesture and Russell dropped his emigration plan. This dispute was only a prelude to more serious divisions within the ministry on Irish issues.[12] The rapid advance of the potato blight, in 1848–9, had once again made famine relief an urgent necessity and a matter for cabinet decision. There were those ministers, such as Charles Wood, the Chancellor of the Exchequer and Sir George Grey, who were inclined to question any fresh expenditure on relief as being contrary to sound economic teaching, the advocates of 'the operation of natural

[9] Clarendon to Russell, 16 Aug. 1848, Clarendon papers, letterbook III; *Morning Herald*, 4, 12 Sept. 1848.

[10] Memorandum by Lord John Russell, 8 Sept. 1848. Clarendon papers, Ir. box 43, bundle 54.

[11] Ibid.; *Freeman's Journal*, 5 July 1849.

[12] Russell to Clarendon, 29 Jan. 1849, Clarendon papers, Ir. box 26, bundle 34.

causes' as Clarendon called them.[13] In Parliament, too, this attitude had its supporters though, on the reluctant recommendation of Wood, the Commons, in February 1849, agreed to an advance of £50,000 to aid the more distressed Poor Law unions in Ireland.[14] It was obvious that £50,000 would not suffice, especially as many of the Poor Law unions in the most impoverished parts of the country were virtually bankrupt.[15]

Russell and his colleagues came to the conclusion that Parliament was in no mood to go on making advances indefinitely to Ireland, especially as the Government could give no firm indication of its future policy towards Ireland.[16] Russell, therefore, considered that the only possible ways of meeting British criticism would be to impose either an income tax on Ireland or a general rate-in-aid, whereby the more solvent Irish unions would come to the assistance of the poorer ones.[17]

Both propositions encountered massive and sustained opposition inside and outside the cabinet. Lansdowne at first threatened to withdraw from the ministry if the rate-in-aid were enforced, and in this stand he had the support of many other influential Irish landowners who saw in the rate-in-aid a further threat to their incomes from their Irish estates.[18] Some Irish members of Parliament did favour an income tax, since it would reach sections of the community little affected by the burden of the existing poor rate, but there were those, too, who argued that it was wrong to tax Ireland as a unit to meet a famine emergency which should be considered as affecting the United Kingdom as a whole.[19] In the end, the Government's

[13] *Hansard*, cii. 1–5; G. Trevelyan to Russell, 21 Aug. 1848, Russell papers, P.R.O. 30/22/7; Grey to Clarendon, 5 Dec. 1848, Clarendon papers, Ir. box 12, bundle 21; Clarendon to Russell, 27 Jan. 1849, ibid., letterbook III.

[14] *Hansard*, cii. 374–86, 433–6.   [15] Ibid., civ., 470–1.

[16] Somerville to Clarendon, 7 Feb. 1849, Clarendon papers, Ir. box 27, bundle 38.

[17] Russell to Clarendon, 25 Jan. 1849, Clarendon papers, Ir. box 26, bundle 34.

[18] Lansdowne to Russell, [Feb. 1849], Russell papers, P.R.O. 30/22/7, and see also Gooch, op. cit., i. 233–4; Landsowne to Russell, 15 Feb. 1849, Russell papers, P.R.O. 30/22/7, and partially quoted in Gooch, op. cit., i. 234–5; *Hansard*, cv. 637–62; *Greville memoirs* (2nd pt.), vi. 293–4.

[19] *Hansard*, civ. 249–52.

compromise of a low rate-in-aid of sixpence to be imposed on the better off Irish unions was accepted for a two-year period. A maximum of 7/- was fixed as the ordinary poor rate which could be levied in any Irish Poor Law union.[20]

The debate on these Poor Law issues dragged on into July 1849, accompanied not merely by prolonged discussions in Parliament and in the cabinet but by confused and unsatisfactory consultations between Russell and the Irish members drawn from all parties.[21] The Government had come forward ill-prepared and disunited on Irish social questions. Ruefully, Lord John Russell had to admit as early as February: 'Things are in a very bad way here. The consequences of coming forward without a plan are beginning to be felt very seriously'.[22]

Little effort was made to bring forward the other measures Russell had hoped his Government would sponsor in 1849. No tenant compensation bill was introduced and no measure to assist financially the Catholic clergy.[23] Even the long promised reform of the Irish franchise made only hesitant progress. A franchise bill was brought in but not proceeded with and it was not until August 1850 that the Parliamentary Voters (Ireland) Bill was finally passed. Even then the bill fell short of Lord John Russell's expectations. As first introduced, in February 1850, the bill would have established the Irish franchise on the basis of a uniform £8 poor law valuation and so would have increased the dwindling county electorate from a mere 30,000 voters to some 200,000.[24] Including the urban voters, the bill offered the prospect of a total electorate of under 300,000, sufficient, however, to establish a more balanced relationship between the total population of Ireland and the parliamentary franchise. The bill encountered strong Conservative opposition in the Lords, especially on the grounds that a

[20] Ibid., civ. 860–6.

[21] Ibid., civ. 999, cvi. 89; *Freeman's Journal*, 20, 21 Apr. 1849.

[22] Russell to Clarendon, 8 Feb. 1849, Clarendon papers, Ir. box 26, bundle 34. 'The error of meeting Parliament without any plan for Ireland becomes every day but too apparent, and I have for months past not disguised from you my fears that the doctrinaire policy of Trevelyan, reflected through C. Wood and supported by Grey would prevail' (Clarendon to Russell, 12 Feb. 1849, Clarendon papers, letterbook III).

[23] *Hansard*, cii. 669–70.

[24] Ibid., cviii. 699–700, 1363–5.

popular franchise would simply help to deliver political power into the hands of the agitators or make the popular vote, as Lord Stanley put it, an object of contention between the Catholic and Presbyterian clergy on the one hand and the landlords on the other.[25] In the end the ministry agreed to a compromise which established a £12 franchise and this met with a reluctant acceptance in the Lords.[26] Even in its altered form the 1850 bill was of some importance because it provided that increased electorate of 135,245 voters in the counties, which helped to return, in the general election of 1852, an apparently united body of some 48 Irish members pledged to independent opposition and the winning of tenant-right for the Irish farmers.[27] It was a result which may have given some gloomy satisfaction to Lord Derby, since the Irish Catholic clergy did play an important role in influencing the outcome of the election.[28]

The much amended franchise bill was the only significant measure for which the Whig administration could claim credit. For the rest it seemed that, already by the end of 1849, the Government had lost whatever enthusiasm it might once have had for comprehensive reform in Ireland. Even the final remission of the debts incurred by the Irish Poor Law unions to meet the famine did not come until 1853, when the income tax was extended to Ireland.[29]

At no time did the Russell administration take any effective steps to deal with the complex problem of landlord and tenant relations, but then it was a problem which was to challenge men's minds even at a later time when the laws of economic science had lost something of their immutability. Sir Robert Peel, it is true, did excite much attention, in March 1849, by certain proposals he made during the course of the Poor Law debates. He suggested that something like a new Ulster plantation was needed, shorn of that plantation's religious implications, if Irish rural society were to be saved. 'Almost the only measure', he said, 'from which I derive a hope of safety is the

[25] Ibid., cxi. 802–17.   [26] Ibid., cxiii. 863–5.

[27] J. H. Whyte, *The Independent Irish Party, 1850–9*, pp. 63, 90–1.

[28] Ibid., pp. 63–81. Lord Stanley succeeded to the Earldom of Derby in 1851.

[29] T. P. O'Neill, 'The organisation and administration of relief, 1845–52', in R. D. Edwards and T. D. Williams (eds.), op. cit., p. 256.

introduction of new proprietors who shall take possession of land in Ireland . . . .'[30] He would have liked the state to buy out the existing landlords in the more distressed areas and he urged, too, the necessity of remedial legislation so that the evils generally of the land system could be cured. Peel's bold and sympathetic words were well received in Ireland though Russell considered his suggestions 'hollow and unsound altogether'.[31]

Not surprisingly the year 1849 ended with few Irish measures of any significance having been passed. The Habeas Corpus suspension was extended for a further six months until the beginning of September 1849, the 1848 Incumbered Estates Act was amended, since the original measure had proved unworkable because of the slowness of the proceedings in chancery, and some additional funds were made available for drainage schemes.[32] Apart from these measures and the hurried changes in the Poor Law, there was little to show. Equally unpromising had been the Government's experience in the field of education and religion.

The Diplomatic Relations with the Court of Rome Act had, in September 1848, opened the way for the exchange of diplomatic missions between London and Rome but the measure remained a dead letter, not least because of an amendment added in the Lords which provided that the representative of the Holy See at the Court of St James would have to be a layman.[33] Apart from bettering the relations between the United Kingdom and the Holy See, the Government hoped to strengthen the link between the state and the Catholic church in Ireland. As we have already seen, this had proved a complicated task in the past, made difficult by political considerations and by a legacy of supicion of the motives of Government among many of the Irish bishops and lower clergy.[34] Undismayed by previous experiences, Lord John Russell, in the autumn of 1848,

[30] *Hansard*, ciii. 179–93.

[31] Ibid., civ. 87–117, 229–35, 471–83; *Freeman's Journal*, 7 Mar. 1849; Russell to Clarendon, 13 Mar. 1849, Clarendon papers, Ir. box 26, bundle 34.

[32] *Hansard*, civ. 892–900; *Freeman's Journal*, 5 July 1849.

[33] *Hansard*, cvii. 89; Palmerston to Russell, 20 July 1848, Russell papers, P.R.O. 30/22/7.

[34] See p. 174.

raised the matter of payments by the state to the Catholic clergy.

His scheme envisaged, in its original form, the payment of the clergy, the upkeep of the parish churches and the provision of glebes. The cost of the scheme was, as we have seen, to be met from an Irish land and house tax. He was also willing to make additional provision for the Presbyterian church in order to achieve an approximate equality between the three principal churches in Ireland.[35] Thomas Redington, the Under-Secretary and a Catholic, advised that the cost should be met out of the consolidated fund as a charge on the revenue of the whole United Kingdom. He was opposed to an exclusively Irish tax since the people had already to support the Anglican establishment in Ireland and he argued, too, that the time had come to curtail the revenues of that establishment.[36] Russell was not anxious to interfere with the Anglican church or its revenues for fear of an outcry, but the question of endowing the Catholic church was, for the time being at least, deprived of all practical significance by the attitude of the Catholic hierarchy.[37]

Russell had hoped to secure the approval of Pope Piux IX for the endowment scheme and the necessary preliminary diplomatic approaches were apparently made.[38] No formal intimation of the Government's plan was given to the Catholic bishops as Dr Daniel Murray, Archbishop of Dublin, had advised against doing so, since the majority of bishops would probably oppose a state endowment, though Lord Clarendon added in a letter to Russell, 'Dr Murray says that if the vote of the clergy could be taken by ballot the question would be carried by an immense majority though they will not dare express themselves favourably to it in the dioceses of opposing bishops'.[39] There was, in fact, little doubt about the attitude of the majority of the bishops on this question. At their meeting, held in Dublin in October 1848, the bishops pronounced against state aid, saying that, 'having shared in the prosperity

[35] Russell to Redington, 6 Sept. 1848, Russell papers, P.R.O. 30/22/7, and quoted in part in Gooch, op. cit., i. 230–1; Russell to Redington, 9 Sept. 1848, Russell papers, P.R.O. 30/22/7.

[36] Redington to Russell, 7 Sept. 1848, Russell papers, P.R.O. 30/22/7.

[37] Russell to Redington, 9 Sept. 1848, Russell papers, P.R.O. 30/22/7.

[38] Palmerston to Russell, 27 Oct. 1848, Russell papers, P.R.O. 30/22/7.

[39] Clarendon to Russell, 4 Oct. 1848, Clarendon papers, letterbook III.

of their faithful flocks the clergy of Ireland are willing to
share in their privations . . .'.[40] Resignedly Russell concluded, 'I begin to fear that the endowment may have to be
postponed'.[41]

The time was an inopportune one for raising the question of
state aid to the Catholic church. Russell had been critical of
many aspects of the much disputed scheme for Irish provincial
colleges, but he had inherited the project from his predecessors
and by the end of 1848 the preparations for the opening
of the 'Godless colleges' in Belfast, Cork and Galway were
well advanced.[42] The Whig Government had hoped to satisfy
the misgivings of the Catholic bishops about them and
in this task Russell and Clarendon had succeeded in securing
the goodwill and help of Dr Daniel Murray, the Archbishop of
Dublin.[43] Strong efforts were made, at Rome, to induce the
Congregation of the Propaganda to come to a decision which,
at least, would not be wholly adverse to the colleges.[44] In
October 1848, however, a papal rescript was issued which
proved a severe setback to the Government and to its friends
among the Irish bishops.[45]

The new rescript declared that the revised statutes of the
colleges, dealing with religious matters, in no wise satisfied
Propaganda. In effect, the rescript confirmed an equally hostile
one issued in October of the previous year and it went on to
advise the Irish hierarchy to set up an independent Catholic
university similar to the one which had been established at
Louvain in Belgium. Though Archbishop Murray continued
to advise Rome that the statutes of the colleges as revised by the
Russell administration would safeguard the religious interests
of Catholic students and protect them from anti-Catholic or

[40] *Freeman's Journal*, 13 Oct. 1848.
[41] Russell to Clarendon, 1 Nov. 1848, Clarendon papers, Ir. box 43, bundle 54.
[42] T. W. Moody and J. C. Beckett, *Queen's, Belfast 1845–1949*, i. 10, 47–62.
[43] Redington to Clarendon, 24 Oct. 1848, Clarendon papers, Ir. box 24, bundle 32.
[44] Clarendon to Dr Francis J. Nicholson (Coadjutor Ab. of Corfu), 4 Oct. 1848, Clarendon papers, letterbook III; T. W. Moody and J. C. Beckett, op. cit., i. 47–8.
[45] *Freeman's Journal*, 26 Oct. 1848.

irreligious influences, his intervention proved fruitless.[46] The condemnation of the colleges was a victory for Archbishop MacHale of Tuam and his temporary ally in Rome, Dr Paul Cullen, the future Archbishop of Armagh and later of Dublin. The final blow to the Government's hope of a compromise was struck when, in August 1850, the Synod of Thurles decreed that not merely should the Irish bishops and clergy abstain from taking any part in the work of the colleges but that the laity too should avoid the new institutions as being dangerous to faith and morals. When the colleges opened their doors for the first time in November 1849, they did so with little prospect of Catholic support.[47]

Russell again raised the question of an endowment for the Catholic church late in 1849, but in November of that year he had to write to Clarendon: 'I consulted Tufnell yesterday as to the probable fate of any proposal to pay the Catholic priests. His opinion is that it would upset the Government and that the measure would fail, so we must put it off for another year.'[48] The eighteen-fifties were a time of sharp religious conflict in both Britain and Ireland. Catholic missionary activity in Britain and the influx of Irish labourers into the industrial areas helped to strengthen Protestant suspicions of Catholicism and Roman influence. The Ecclesiastical Titles Bill dispute was only one aspect of a complex problem. Already in 1848 and 1849, partisan feelings were being roused in a variety of ways. In July 1849, Sir G. Grey, the Home Secretary, admitted in Parliament that there would be widespread opposition in Britain to any endowment to the Catholic church, while in contrast to this mood in Britain, 29 Irish Liberal members of Parliament joined in a declaration which described the Protestant established church in Ireland as 'a symbol of conquest' and a source of social depression which should be dispensed with.[49] The press, especially the more conservative sections in Britain, maintained a hostile or critical attitude towards the Catholic

[46] Dr D. Murray to Redington, 20 Nov. 1848, Clarendon papers, Ir. box 24, bundle 32; Dr D. Murray to Dr Paul Cullen, 30 Dec. 1848 (copy), Clarendon papers, Ir. box 28.

[47] T. W. Moody and J. C. Beckett, op. cit., i. 77–8.

[48] Russell to Clarendon, 22 Nov. 1849, Clarendon papers, Ir. box 26, bundle 34. Henry Tufnell was the Whig chief whip.

[49] *Hansard*, cvii. 137–45; *Freeman's Journal*, 28 July 1849.

clergy who were blamed for the unrest in the Irish countryside, while in Ireland religious friction in 1849 at times assumed a rather threatening form particularly in the border areas of Ulster where Catholics and Protestants were both numerically strong.[50] Catholic and Orange factions came into conflict, the most serious clash taking place at Dolly's Brae, near Castle-wellan, County Down, in July, when a number of Catholics were killed and some houses burned down.[51] The Castlewellan incident caused considerable alarm, especially as the Earl of Roden, one of the most influential of the Conservative Protes-tant landlords in Ulster, was associated with the Orange demonstrations which were held before the conflict occurred.[52]

Though the tension in the rural areas of the north of Ireland was of a religious character, it seems to have had social and agrarian implications too in 1849. There is considerable evi-dence of the formation of secret and semi-secret societies among the Catholic country people in the early eighteen-fifties. Frequently these agrarian bands are described as ribbonmen, with the suggestion that they had behind them an elaborate oath-bound organisation throughout Ireland. The proofs for such a widespread organised conspiracy are slight and it seems that ribbonism as such with its decidedly sectarian character was confined to those areas of Ulster where Catholic and Protestant had often been in competition for farms.[53] Elsewhere in Ireland, the agrarian conspiracies, and they appear to have been numerous in the late eighteen-forties and early eighteen-fifties, were less obviously sectarian in character. They were directed primarily against high rents and evictions though some

[50] '*Murder, perjury* and pecuniary *fraud* are practices, then, to which the peasantry of the south of Ireland are well accustomed. Do they teach the priests, or do the priests teach *them*, these awful lessons? Can there be a doubt as to the fact? But what madness will it be then, if we first discover that we have to thank the priesthood for nearly all the crimes of Ireland; and then take the extraordinary course of placing the whole of the three provinces south of Ulster under the care and guidance of those very priests of Rome . . .' (*Morning Herald*, 5 Sept. 1848). See comments in *Morning Chronicle*, 1 Aug. 1848, *Morning Post*, 9 Nov. 1849. Clarendon to Grey. 18 Mar. 1849, Clarendon papers, letterbook IV.
[51] *Freeman's Journal*, 16 July 1849.
[52] Clarendon to Grey, 21 July 1849, Clarendon papers, letterbook IV.
[53] *Report from the Select Committee on Outrages (Ireland)*, H.C. 1852 (438), xiv.

had political implications particularly in Tipperary and the south-east of the country.[54]

Taking these factors into account, it is not surprising that the lull in political activity in 1849 should have come to an end rather quickly.[55] At the beginning of September 1849, the Habeas Corpus suspension act lapsed and the following months saw the beginnings of a modest political revival in Ireland. Gavan Duffy, against whom the Government had failed to secure a conviction for treason-felony, recommenced the publication of the *Nation* in September. In the same month, as we have already seen, a group of ex-clubbists, who had organised a secret revolutionary movement, staged an unsuccessful attack on a police station at Cappoquin, County Waterford. In October, John O'Connell sought to re-establish the Repeal Association.[56]

To emphasise the firmness of the Union and the authority of the Government, it was decided to arrange a royal visit to Ireland, the first in Queen Victoria's reign. There were, to begin with, some misgivings in court circles, but the visit finally took place early in August 1849. The Queen was received with no great enthusiasm by the Irish public, but both she and the Lord Lieutenant appear to have been well satisfied with the response to the tour.[57] This royal occasion had, however, no serious political consequences. In late September, Clarendon was again complaining to London that secret conspiracies were becoming a serious problem especially as 'the secrecy with which the whole is conducted exceeds anything on record in the annals of Irish conspiracies which in general are betrayed'.[58] A further

[54] Clarendon to Grey, 29 May 1849, Clarendon papers, letterbook IV; Clarendon to Grey, 31 May 1849, ibid; *Freeman's Journal*, 22, 24 Sept. 1849.

[55] Clarendon to Russell, 7 Sept. 1849, Clarendon papers, letterbook IV.

[56] *Nation*, 1 Sept. 1849. The *Nation* had ceased publication on 29 July 1848 after the last issue had been seized by the police. *Freeman's Journal*, 9 Oct. 1849; Clarendon to Russell, 11 Sept. 1849, Clarendon papers, letterbook IV; see p. 217.

[57] Clarendon to Russell, 6 Aug. 1849, Clarendon papers, letterbook IV; *Freeman's Journal*, 7 Aug. 1849; *Hansard*, cviii. 1–6. There is some evidence to suggest that the Dublin revolutionary conspirators for a time contemplated kidnapping Queen Victoria as a hostage in order to secure the release of the state prisoners (Gavan Duffy, *Four Years of Irish History*, pp. 275–6).

[58] Clarendon to Grey, 22 Sept. 1849, Clarendon papers, letterbook IV.

recurrence of the potato blight made the prospect no more cheerful.[59]

Though for a short time, he may have been too optimistic about the future course of agitation in Ireland, the Lord Lieutenant had rightly predicted that there would be no serious attempt to revive the repeal movement. Instead of attempting that, he thought the popular leaders would 'probably take up and work skilfully particular grievances such as landlord cruelties, the tenure and distribution of land and the church question'.[60] Almost re-echoing these words of the Lord Lieutenant, Gavan Duffy wrote in the first number of the *Nation*, after its re-establishment, that 'independence is no longer the first achievement . . . but the end and result of many previous victories . . . Our first practical effort ought to be to bring back Ireland to health and strength by stopping the system of extermination . . .'.[61] Gavan Duffy had learned one lesson from Fintan Lalor's teachings and it was the importance of the agrarian agitation. He announced that he had now lost all faith in the landlords and the existing land system. 'I esteem it', he wrote, 'the first duty of a national association to assault this system . . .'. This was a task which was to be accomplished with the aid of an independent party in Parliament.[62]

Gavan Duffy, of course, was not alone in pointing to the possibilities of a political movement based on agrarian grievances and the demand for the legal recognition throughout the whole of Ireland of the tenant-right custom. In a country confronted with so many social ills as Ireland was in 1849–50, men's minds naturally turned to the evils of the land system. The Catholic hierarchy had drawn attention to the urgent need for reform, moderate nationalist newspapers like the *Freeman's Journal*, stressed its importance and in Ulster, too, there was a growing concern about the encroachments by landlords on the traditional rights of the Ulster tenant-farmers.[63] In a country divided by religious suspicions, the common grievances associated with

[59] *Freeman's Journal*, 1 Oct. 1849.

[60] Clarendon to Russell, 27 Aug. 1849, Clarendon papers, letterbook IV.

[61] *Nation*, 1 Sept. 1849.

[62] Ibid., 8 Sept. 1849.

[63] *Freeman's Journal*, 13 Oct. 1848, 26 Sept., 9 Oct. 1849; Clarendon to Russell, 20 Nov. 1849, Clarendon papers, letterbook IV; J. H. Whyte, op. cit., pp. 5–8.

the landlord system offered a new basis for political unity of action.

Gavan Duffy's National Conference, which met in November, and the various tenant-right associations, which came into existence or were revived in 1849 and 1850, helped to prepare the way for that remarkable experiment in Irish politics, the great tenant-right agitation of the early eighteen-fifties. It was a movement which seemed to promise much success, but, as we now know, it failed because of deep-rooted suspicions between Catholic and Ulster Presbyterian in an age of passionate religious controversy, and because the Irish parliamentary party of the eighteen-fifties no more than its repeal predecessor was possessed of that discipline and unity necessary in a sustained political action.[64]

The Government of Lord John Russell, already showing strong symptoms of indecision, was to cling weakly to office until its final fall in 1852, but by 1850 it was abundantly clear that it had no Irish policy on any of the vital social and political issues. The failure of the Russell administration must, however, be judged within the limitations of the age. Russell himself saw perhaps more clearly than his colleagues the need for reform, but he lacked the strength to overcome social prejudices and the powerful political influence of the landed interest. Good men with good intentions were to be found in high office in the eighteen-forties but it was to remain a tragic period of lost opportunities in Anglo-Irish relations.

The famine, the large-scale emigration to North America and the stubborn survival of the land problem were to influence profoundly popular political thinking and action in Ireland in the second half of the nineteenth century. In many ways the emergence of the revolutionary and republican movement, Fenianism, was perhaps the most striking measure of the failure of the Irish policies of both the Tories and the Whigs between 1840 and 1851. But in those years might be seen, too, the tentative beginnings of that reformist approach to Irish problems which was to make of Gladstone a pioneer in Irish land legislation and the first Prime Minister of the United Kingdom to champion Home Rule for Ireland.

[64] *Nation*, 3 Nov., 10 Nov. 1849; Clarendon to Russell, 20 Nov. 1849, Clarendon papers, letterbook IV; J. H. Whyte, op. cit., pp. 93–157.

BIBLIOGRAPHY

~~~~~~

A. NOTE ON THE SOURCES

B. ORIGINAL SOURCES

I. Manuscript material
II. Printed material
  1. Newspapers and other periodicals
  2. Parliamentary papers
  3. Parliamentary proceedings
  4. Collections of letters and papers
  5. Other works by contemporaries

C. SECONDARY SOURCES

A. NOTE ON THE SOURCES

In combination the Peel and Graham papers provide an extensive range of manuscript material for a study of the relations between the Government in London and the administration in Dublin. As far as possible reference has been made in this book to the original documents, since the selections from these papers edited by C. S. Parker are frequently defective (*Sir Robert Peel from his Private Correspondence* (vol. i), *Sir Robert Peel from his Private Papers* (vols. ii–iii); *Life and Letters of Sir James Graham, second Baronet of Netherby* (vols. i–ii)). Numerous and often important paragraphs and sentences are omitted by Parker, without any indication being given in the printed text. Letters of different dates are run together and there are frequent errors in transcription.

For the period after 1846, the extensive collections of papers of the fourth Earl of Clarendon, now in the Bodleian Library, Oxford, and of Lord John Russell, in the Public Record Office, London, are of considerable importance. The Clarendon papers, except for those printed in the small selection made by Maxwell or incidentally included in Laughton's *Memoirs of the Life and Correspondence of Henry Reeve*, were until recently not easy of access. As a source they are necessary for any full examination of the attitude of the Irish administration in the critical months of 1847–8, when Clarendon

232

Bibliography

was Lord Lieutenant. They are also helpful in throwing some light on the relations between the Whigs and the repealers in the period after O'Connell's death.

The great collections of semi-official papers proved, for the purpose of this study, more useful than the official records of the Home Office and the Foreign Office. This latter type of material, though extensive, too often tends to record the formal decisions rather than the reasons for them. In relation, however, to the negotiations with Rome and later with France, the Foreign Office papers must be employed to supplement the Aberdeen papers and the published Palmerston material. The same may be said of the records of the French Foreign Ministry, in Paris, though they contain relatively little on Irish affairs.

The papers in the Public Record Office, Dublin, and the State Paper Office, Dublin Castle, add little on policy questions to what is contained in other sources, though again, the Irish Government correspondence books and the abstracts of correspondence from the Chief Secretary's office are convenient sources of information on the detailed mechanism of government. For the famine period, the Relief Commission papers throw a great deal of light on the working of the emergency administration. On military matters, the Kilmainham papers, in the National Library of Ireland, being the records of the military commanders in Ireland, contain much routine information on troop movements.

Apart from the carefully arranged Smith O'Brien papers, in the National Library of Ireland, the Fintan Lalor papers and some of Gavan Duffy's correspondence in the same library, the surviving manuscript material of value from repeal sources is regrettably slight. The Smith O'Brien papers contain not merely correspondence with the Young Irelanders, but a number of letters from O'Connell. These are particularly welcome since little of O'Connell's political correspondence, for this period, has apparently survived. The O'Connell papers, in the National Library of Ireland, are not of great political value, while the dearth of O'Connell material is not made good by Fitzpatrick's two inadequate volumes. The Monteagle papers, also in the National Library, are useful in throwing some light on the Irish Whig connection, particularly as Lord Monteagle conducted an extensive correspondence with the Whig and to some extent the Tory leaders in England.

In examining the developments within the repeal movement greater use has had to be made of newspaper material than in the case of the successive Governments. The quality of the reporting of meetings appears to have been high, though naturally the repeal journals tended to give the most space to nationalist activities. For reports of repeal meetings, the accounts in the *Freeman's Journal* and the *Nation* were found to be the fullest. In policy, the *Pilot* and *Warden* represented, of the repeal papers, those most fully committed to O'Connell's attitude. The *Freeman's Journal*, especially after 1846, generally sought to steer a moderate course as between the *Nation* and the Repeal Association, though remaining loyal to the O'Connell connection. The *Dublin Evening Post* and the *Northern Whig* are useful in illustrating Irish Whig reactions, while the *Dublin Evening Mail*, as the principal Irish

Bibliography

Tory journal, became increasingly critical of Peel's Irish policy, especially from 1844–5 onwards.

As a source of information, published memoirs of the repeal leaders take on a special importance in the absence of other material. Apart from John O'Connell's sketchy *Recollections of a Parliamentary Career*, and O'Neill Daunt's *A Life spent for Ireland*, memoir material from orthodox repeal sources is slight. The Young Irelanders, however, more than make up for the deficiency. The writings of Sir Charles Gavan Duffy provide a valuable introduction to the history of the mid-nineteenth century in Ireland, though their merits should not be allowed to disguise their weaknesses. Possibly the greatest weakness in all Gavan Duffy's writings is that while he reveals the defects in the Repeal Association, he does not with equal clarity delineate the tensions and difficulties within the Irish Confederation.

John Mitchel's vigorous writings are of value in helping to show how social conditions influenced the shaping of political opinions. His contention that the great famine could have been averted were it not for British and landlord self-interest, proved the politically most significant interpretation of the events of the famine years. In the pages of his newspaper, the *United Irishman* and subsequently in his comments in the *Jail Journal* and in *An Apology for the British Government in Ireland*, he further elaborated his views. The suggestion of ill-will though less emphatically stated is also to be found in the works of Gavan Duffy (e.g. *My Life in Two Hemispheres*, i. 198–9).

The secondary material on the period is considerable, but much of it follows rather closely Gavan Duffy's interpretation of the events. In recent times, however, some valuable independent work has been done in the history of the first half of the nineteenth century. R. B. McDowell's *Public Opinion and Government Policy in Ireland, 1801–1846*, is an attempt to re-assess, in general terms, the post-Union period. Unfortunately, the study ends in 1846 and so the account has to break off at a rather inconclusive point. Denis Gwynn in his *Young Ireland and 1848* and his *O'Connell, Davis and the Colleges Bill* makes considerable use of the Smith O'Brien papers but in endeavouring to establish the importance of Smith O'Brien's contribution to the repeal movement, he underestimates the role of Daniel O'Connell in the later phases of the history of the Repeal Association.

Among the shorter studies R. Dudley Edwards' article, 'The Contribution of Young Ireland to the Development of the Irish National Idea' in *Féilscríbhin Tórna*, is an attempt to put Young Ireland in an historical perspective, as part of the slow emergence of a concept of an organic Irish nation. T. W. Moody in *Thomas Davis, 1814–45*, examines the part played by Davis and the men of the *Nation* in the development of an all-embracing doctrine of nationality.

For the question of relations with Rome, Rev. John Broderick's *The Holy See and the Irish Movement for the Repeal of the Union with England 1829–1847*, contains some valuable Roman material not otherwise readily available. *The Great Famine: Studies in Irish History 1845–52*, edited by R. Dudley Edwards and T. Desmond Williams, is an important collection of detailed studies by specialists on various aspects of the famine years, while *Queen's, Belfast, 1845–1949*, by T. W. Moody and J. C. Beckett, examines at some length public policy in relation to higher education during the eighteen-forties. Norman Gash's *Politics in the Age of Peel* includes some useful information on the Irish electoral system.

B. ORIGINAL SOURCES

I. MANUSCRIPT MATERIAL

Bodleian Library, Oxford
Clarendon papers.

British Museum, London
Aberdeen papers (Add. MS 43151).
Gladstone papers (Add. MS 44162).
Peel papers (Add. MS 40442–40540).

Ministry of Foreign Affairs, Paris
Correspondence, 1847–8.

National Library of Ireland, Dublin
Gavan Duffy papers (MS 2642).
Fintan Lalor papers (MS 340).
Kilmainham papers.
Monteagle papers.
Smith O'Brien papers.
O'Connell papers.
Repeal Association papers.

Netherby, Longtown, Cumberland
Graham papers.

Public Record Office, London
Foreign Office papers (F.O. 27/804–6, 43/38–42, 44/1–2).
Home Office papers.

Public Record Office, Dublin
Relief Commission papers.

State Paper Office, Dublin
Government correspondence books (iv. 6).
Chief Secretary's Office, civil office, abstract of correspondence (1A. 18J).
Outrage papers, 1848–9.

Royal Irish Academy, Dublin
Correspondence book of the Irish Confederation (MS 23 H 41).
Minute book of the Council of the Irish Confederation (MS 23 H 44).
Gavan Duffy papers (MS 12 P 15).

II. PRINTED MATERIAL

1. Newspapers and other periodicals

Dublin Evening Mail.

Bibliography

Dublin Evening Post.
Economist.
Edinburgh Review.
Freeman's Journal.
Globe.
Labourer.
Moniteur Universel.
Morning Chronicle.
Morning Herald.
Morning Post.
Nation.
Nonconformist.
Northern Whig.
Pilot.
Quarterly Review.
The Times.
Tribune.
United Irishman.
Westminster Review.

2. Parliamentary papers

Report of the Poor Law Commissioners on Medical Charities, Ireland, pursuant to the 4th section of the Act 1 and 2 Vict. c. 56, H.C. 1841 (324), xi. 1–96.
Seventh Report of the Commissioners of National Education in Ireland for the Year 1840, H.C. 1842 (353), xxiii. 217–21.
Return of the number of cases of Ejectment entered for Trial, and of the number actually tried at Quarter Sessions before the Assistant Barristers of the several counties of Ireland, during each of the last five years, H.C. 1843 (320), i. 227–34.
Returns of all National Schools which have been erected adjoining to, or within the precincts of Roman Catholic Chapels, etc. in Ireland, H.C. 1843 (520), li. 69–72.
Ninth Report of the Commissioners of National Education in Ireland for the Year 1842, H.C. 1843 (471), xxviii. 93–352.
Report from Her Majesty's Commissioners of Inquiry into the State of the Law and Practice in respect to the Occupation of Land in Ireland, H.C. 1845 (605), xix. 1–56.
Evidence taken before Her Majesty's Commissioners of Inquiry into the State of the Law and Practice in respect to the Occupation of Land in Ireland; together with Appendix and Plans, pts. i–iii, H.C. 1845 (606, 616, 657), xix, xx, xxi.
Copy of the Report of Dr Playfair and Mr Lindley on the present state of the Irish Potato Crop, and on the prospect of approaching Scarcity, H.C. 1846 (28), xxvii. 1.
Correspondence explanatory of the measures adopted by Her Majesty's Government for the relief of Distress arising from the Failure of the Potato Crop in Ireland, H.C. 1846 (735), xxxvii.
Correspondence from July 1846 to January 1847, relating to the measures adopted for the Relief of Distress in Ireland, H.C. 1847 (761), li. 511.
An Account of the Sums which have been advanced on Loans since the Commencement

of the last Session of Parliament for the Relief of Distress and other Purposes in Ireland, H.C. 1847 (444), liv. 3.

A Return showing the Average Daily number of Persons employed on Relief Works in Ireland, during the week ending the 6 March 1847 etc., H.C. 1847 (185), liv. 23–4.

Account of the Quantities of Wheat, Barley, Oats, etc. imported into Great Britain from Ireland, from 1842 to 1845; also Account of the Quantities of Wheat, Barley, Oats, etc. imported into Great Britain from Ireland between 5 July 1845 and 5 January 1846, H.C. 1846 (16), xliv. 547–8.

Returns of the number and descriptions of Outrages specially reported by the Constabulary throughout Ireland, in each of the years, 1845 and 1846, H.C. 1847 (64), lvi. 231–4.

Returns of all Sums of Money granted or advanced on account of the Distress and Famine, or in aid of the Administration of the Poor Law in Ireland, during the years 1846, 1847, 1848 and 1849 with amount of repayments, H.C. 1849 (352), xlviii. 5–6.

Fifth, Sixth and Seventh Reports of the Relief Commissioners constituted under the act 10 Vict. c. 7 and Correspondence connected therewith: with Appendix, H.C. 1847–8 (876), xxix. 27–206.

Abstract of Returns of the number of Persons committed for Trial in the Year 1847, H.C. 1847–8 (146), lvii. 131–72.

3. Parliamentary proceedings

Hansard's Parliamentary Debates, 3rd series, London 1830.

4. Collections of letters and papers

Ashley, Evelyn. *The Life and Correspondence of Henry John Temple, Viscount Palmerston*. 2 vols. London 1879.

Cusack, M. F. *The Speeches and Public Letters of the Liberator*. 2 vols. Dublin 1875.

Daunt, William J. O'Neill. *A Life spent for Ireland; being Selections from the Journals of the late W. J. O'Neill Daunt, edited by his Daughter*. London 1896.

Davis, Thomas. *Essays, Literary and Historical* (ed. D. J. O'Donoghue). Dundalk, 1914.

Dasent, Arthur Irwin. *John Thadeus Delane, Editor of 'The Times': his Life and Correspondence*. 2 vols. London 1908.

Fitzpatrick, W. J. (ed.). *Correspondence of Daniel O'Connell, the Liberator*. 2 vols. London 1888.

Fogarty, L. (ed.). *James Fintan Lalor, Patriot and Political Essayist*. Dublin 1947.

Foster, Thomas Campbell. *Letters on the Condition of the People of Ireland*. London 1847.

Gooch, G. P. (ed.). *The Later Correspondence of Lord John Russell, 1840–1878*. 2 vols. London 1925.

Greville, Charles Cavendish Fulke. *The Greville Memoirs (second part). A Journal of the Reign of Queen Victoria from 1837 to 1852*. 3 vols. London 1885.

Lalor, James Fintan. *The Writings of James Fintan Lalor*. Dublin 1895.

Laughton, John Knox. *Memoirs of the Life and Correspondence of Henry Reeve, C.B., D.C.L.* 2 vols. London 1898.

Marlowe, Nathanial (ed.). *James Fintan Lalor: Collected Writings.* Dublin 1918.

Maxwell, Sir Robert E. *The Life and Letters of George William, fourth Earl of Clarendon.* 2 vols. London 1913.

Meagher, Thomas Francis. *Meagher of the Sword: Speeches of T. F. Meagher in Ireland, 1846–8.* (ed. Arthur Griffith). Dublin 1916.

Normanby, Constantine Henry, marquis of. *A Year of Revolution; from a Journal kept in Paris in 1848.* 2 vols. London 1857.

O'Brien, William Smith. *Reproductive Employment: a Series of Letters to the Landed Proprietors of Ireland.* Dublin 1847.

O'Reilly, Bernard. *John MacHale, Archbishop of Tuam: his Life, Times and Correspondence.* 2 vols. New York 1890.

Parker, Charles Stuart. *Life and Letters of Sir James Graham, second Baronet of Netherby.* 2 vols. London 1907.

Parker, Charles Stuart. *Sir Robert Peel from his Private Correspondence.* (vol. i), *From his Private Papers* (vols. ii–iii). London i. (1891): ii–iii (1899).

Peel, George. *The Private Letters of Sir Robert Peel.* London 1920.

Peel, Sir Robert. *Memoirs of the Right Honourable Sir Robert Peel; published by the trustees of his papers.* 2 vols. London 1857.

Rolleston, T. W. (ed.). *Prose Writings of Thomas Davis.*

Sillard, P. A. *The Life and Letters of John Martin.* Dublin 1893.

5. Other works by contemporaries

Butt, Isaac. *A Voice for Ireland: the Famine in the Land.* Dublin 1847.

Cavour, Camille Benso. *Thoughts on Ireland: Its Present and its Future.* London 1868.

Dodd, Charles R. *The Parliamentary Companion for 1843.* London 1843.

Doheny, Michael. *The Felon's Track: or History of the Attempted Outbreaks in Ireland embracing the Leading Events in the Irish Struggle from the year 1843 to the close of 1848.* Dublin 1914.

Duffy, Sir Charles Gavan. *The League of North and South: an Episode in Irish History, 1850–1854.* London 1886.

Duffy, Sir Charles Gavan. *My Life in Two Hemispheres.* 2 vols. London 1898.

Duffy, Sir Charles Gavan. *Young Ireland: a Fragment of Irish History 1840–1845.* Dublin 1884 (Irish people's edition).

Duffy, Sir Charles Gavan. *Young Ireland: Part 2 or Four Years of Irish History, 1845–1849.* Dublin 1887 (Irish people's edition).

Duffy, Sir Charles Gavan. *Thomas Davis, the Memoirs of an Irish Patriot 1840–1846.* London 1890.

Kennedy, J. P. *Digest of Evidence taken before Her Majesty's Commissioners of Inquiry into the State of the Law and Practice in respect of Land in Ireland.* pts. i & ii. Dublin 1848.

Mitchel, John. *An Apology for the British Government in Ireland.* Dublin 1905.

Mitchel, John. *The History of Ireland from the Treaty of Limerick to the Present Time.* 2 vols. Dublin 1869.

Bibliography

Mitchel, John. *Jail Journal, or Five Years in British Prisons* (ed. by Arthur Griffith). Dublin 1913.

Mitchel, John. *The Last Conquest of Ireland (perhaps)*. London.

O'Connell, John. *Recollections and Experiences during a Parliamentary Career from 1833 to 1848*. 2 vols. London 1849.

Pim, Jonathan. *The Condition and Prospects of Ireland and the Evils arising from the present distribution of Landed Property*. Dublin 1848.

Wyse, Francis. *Federalism*. Dublin 1844.

C. SECONDARY SOURCES

Allen, Rev. Robert. 'Henry Montgomery, 1788–1865', in *Essays in British and Irish History in Honour of James Eadie Todd* (ed. H. A. Cronne, T. W. Moody and D. B. Quinn). London 1949.

Aspinall, Arthur. *Lord Brougham and the Whig Party*. Manchester 1939.

Aspinall, Arthur. *Politics and the Press. c. 1780–1850*. London 1949.

Auchmuty, James J. *Sir Thomas Wyse 1791–1862*. London 1939.

Balfour, Lady Frances. *The Life of George fourth Earl of Aberdeen*, 2 vols. London 1922.

Bell, Herbert C. F. *Lord Palmerston*. 2 vols. London 1936.

Black, R. D. Collison. *Economic Thought and the Irish Question, 1817–1870*. Cambridge 1960.

Broderick, John F. *The Holy See and the Irish Movement for the Repeal of the Union with England 1829–1847*. Rome 1951.

Clapham, Sir John. *The Bank of England, a History*. 2 vols. Cambridge 1944.

Clark, George Kitson. *Peel and the Conservative Party 1832–41*. London 1929.

Clark, George Kitson. *The Making of Victorian England*. London 1962.

Clark, George Kitson. 'The repeal of the Corn Laws and the politics of the forties', in *Economic History Review*, second series, iv, no. i.

Clarke, Randall. 'The relations between O'Connell and the Young Irelanders', in *Irish Historical Studies*, iii (1942–3). 18–30.

Connell, K. H. *The Population of Ireland 1750–1845*. Oxford 1950.

Davidson, W. D. 'The history of the potato and its progress in Ireland', in *Department of Agriculture Journal*, xxxiv. 286–307.

Dictionary of National Biography. 22 vols. London 1908–9.

Dillon, William. *Life of John Mitchel*. 2 vols. London 1888.

Dolleans, Edouard. *Le Chartisme*. 2 vols. Paris 1912–13.

Edwards, R. Dudley. 'The contribution of Young Ireland to the development of the Irish national idea', in *Féilscribhin Tórna*, pp. 115–33. Cork 1947.

Edwards, R. Dudley, and Williams, T. Desmond (ed.). *The Great Famine: Studies in Irish History 1845–52*. Dublin 1956. New York 1957.

Erickson, Arvel B. *The Public Career of Sir James Graham*. Oxford 1952.

Eversley (George J. Shaw-Lefevre, first Baron). *Peel and O'Connell: a Review of Irish Policy of Parliament from the Act of Union to the Death of Sir R. Peel*. London 1887.

Fay, Charles R. *The Corn Laws and Social England*. Cambridge 1932.

Gash, Norman. *Politics in the Age of Peel*. London 1953.

Bibliography

Gash, Norman. *Mr. Secretary Peel: the Life of Sir Robert Peel to 1830*. London 1961.

Gash, Norman. 'F. R. Bonham: Conservative "Political Secretary", 1832–47', in *English Historical Review*, lxiii (1948), 502–22.

Gwynn, Denis. *Daniel O'Connell, the Irish liberator*. London 1929.

Gwynn, Denis. *Young Ireland and 1848*. Cork 1949.

Gwynn, Denis. *O'Connell, Davis and the Colleges Bill*. Cork 1948.

Halévy, Elie. *The Age of Peel and Cobden*. London 1947.

Hart, Jenifer. 'Sir Charles Trevelyan at the Treasury', in *English Historical Review*, lxxv no. 294 (Jan. 1960), 92–110.

Hovell, Mark. *The Chartist Movement*. Manchester 1950.

Kennedy, B. A. 'Sharman Crawford's federal scheme for Ireland', in *Essays in British and Irish History in honour of James Eadie Todd*, pp. 235–54.

Lampson, Godfrey Locker. *A Consideration of the State of Ireland in the Nineteenth Century*. London 1907.

Lecky, William E. H. *Leaders of Public Opinion in Ireland*. Vol. ii (Daniel O'Connell).

McGrath, Fergal. *Newman's University: Idea and Reality*. London 1951.

Mansergh, Nicholas. *Ireland in the Age of Reform and Revolution*. London 1940.

Monypenny, William F., and Buckle, George E. *The Life of Benjamin Disraeli*. 2 vols. London 1929.

Moody, T. W. *Thomas Davis, 1814–45*. Dublin 1945.

Moody, T. W. and Beckett, J. C. *Queen's, Belfast, 1845–1949: the History of a University*. 2 vols. London 1959.

Morley, John. *Life of Richard Cobden*. 2 vols. London 1881.

Namier, L. B. '1848; the Revolution of the Intellectuals', in *Proceedings of the British Academy*, xxx. 1–124. London 1945.

Nowlan, Kevin B. 'Writings in connection with the Thomas Davis and Young Ireland centenary, 1945', in *Irish Historical Studies*, v (1946–7), 265–72.

Nowlan, Kevin B. 'The meaning of Repeal in Irish History', in *Historical Studies IV* (ed. G. A. Hayes McCoy). London 1963.

O'Brien, George. *The Economic History of Ireland from the Union to the Famine*. London 1921.

O'Brien R. Barry. *Fifty years of Concessions to Ireland, 1831–1881*. 2 vols. London 1883–5.

Ó Néill, Tomás. *Fiontán Ó Leathlobhair*. Dublin 1962.

Ó Raifeartaigh T. 'Mixed education and the Synod of Ulster', in *Irish Historical Studies*, ix (1955), 281–99.

O'Rourke, Rev. J. *The History of the Great Irish Famine of 1847*. Dublin 1875.

O'Sullivan, T. F. *The Young Irelanders*. Tralee 1945.

Pouthas, Charles H. *Démocraties et capitalisme, 1848–1860*. Paris 1941.

Salaman, Redcliffe N. *The History and Social Influence of the Potato*. Cambridge 1949.

Seignobos, Charles. *La révolution de 1848, le second empire, 1848–1859*. Paris 1921.

Sillard, P. A. *The Life of John Mitchel*. Dublin 1901.

Strauss, E. *Irish Nationalism and British Democracy*. London 1951.

Bibliography

Tierney, Michael (ed.). *Daniel O'Connell, Nine Centenary Essays*. Dublin 1949.

Vale, Mary. 'The origins of the Catholic University of Ireland, 1845–1854', in *Irish Ecclesiastical Record*, lxxxii (1954).

Walsh, William J. *O'Connell, Archbishop Murray and the Board of Charitable Bequests*. Dublin 1916.

Whyte, J. H. *The Independent Irish Party 1850–9*. Oxford 1958.

Whyte, J. H. 'The influence of the Catholic clergy on elections in nineteenth century Ireland', in *English Historical Review*, lxxv, no. 295 (April 1960).

Woodham-Smith, Cecil. *The Great Hunger, Ireland 1845–9*. London 1962.

Young, G. M. *Early Victorian England, 1830–1865*. 2 vols. London 1934.

INDEX

Index

Index

Index

Index

Powell, Caleb, *M.P.*, 57
Presbyterian Church, 34–5, 225
Propaganda, Congregation of,
  178, 226
Protection of Life (Ireland) Bill
  (1846), 100–4
Protestant Repeal Association, 193
Public Works (Ireland) Bill
  (1846), 104

Queen's County, 151

Rebecca riots, 49
Redington, Thomas, *M.P.*, 121, 225
Reeve, Henry, 165
Reilly, Thomas Devin, 13, 149,
  156–7, 171–2, 201–2, 209
Remonstrants (repeal 1846),
  112–14
Repeal Association, 2, 6, 9, 11, 22–3,
  25, 38–40, 41–2, 45–6, 53, 56–8,
  67, 72–3, 76–8, 87–9, 90, 98–9,
  101–2, 108–9, 111–14, 125, 127,
  138–43, 151–2, 157, 173, 178–80,
  183–5, 190, 192, 194, 200, 204–5,
  206–8, 229
Reproductive Works Committee,
  126–7
Ribbonism, 228–9
Roden, Robert Jocelyn, third
  Earl of, 52, 90, 228
Roebuck, John Arthur, *M.P.*, 137
Rollin, Ledru, 54n.86, 182, 184,
  187–8, 190–1
Rome, 69, 174–9, 198, 224, 226
Roscommon, county of, 101, 166
Roscrea, Co. Tipperary, 184
Ross, David, 70, 74–5
Russell, Lord John, *M.P.*, and
  Daniel O'Connell, 16–17, 24, 50–
  1, 58, 61, 70–2, 102–4, 139, 141;
  and Irish land reform, 50, 92,
  106, 115–16, 132, 163–5, 198,
  220, 222–4, 231; attempted formation of govt. by (1845), 95;
  and Protection of Life (Ireland)
  Bill, 102, 104; and famine relief,
  111, 116–24, 129–32, 137, 161–2,
  218, 220–2; return to office of
  (1846), 115; and the Irish landlords, 127; and land improvement schemes (1847), 131, 137–8;
  and the Irish franchise, 132; and

Lord George Bentinck's Irish
  railway scheme, 133–4; and the
  Young Irelanders, 138, 194; and
  parliament (1847), 141–2; and
  Irish agrarian unrest, 166–7; and
  the Catholic Church, 174–8, 226;
  and John O'Connell, 179, 200–1;
  and unrest in Ireland (1848),
  197–8, 212, 214; and endowment of
  Catholic Church in Ireland, 220,
  224–7; and the Irish franchise,
  222–3

St. Germans, Earl, *see* Eliot, Lord
Scrope, George Julius Poulett,
  M.P., 137
Shaw, Frederick, *M.P.*, 126,
  126n.4
Sheil, Richard Lalor, *M.P.*, 24,
  34, 61, 70–1, 109, 143
Smith, Thomas Barry Cusack,
  M.P., 34
Somers, John Patrick, *M.P.*, 24
Somerville, Sir William Meredith,
  M.P., 167, 167n.36, 201
Soup-Kitchen Act, *see* Destitute
  Poor (Ireland) Act
Special Relief Commission, 105
Stanley, Lord Edward George
  Geoffrey, 21, 28, 30, 55, 59, 63,
  82–3, 84, 91–2, 95, 223
Sturge, Joseph, 57
Sugden, Edward Burtenshaw, 46–7

Tasmania, 217
Tenant-right, 90–1, 116, 139–40,
  143, 146–8, 151, 153–4, 164–5,
  223, 230–1
The Times, 91, 110, 165
Thurles, Synod of (1850), 227
Tipperary, county of, 101, 151,
  166, 211, 213–14, 218, 229
Tory protectionists, 132–3
Transportation for Treason
  (Ireland) Act (1849), 216–17
Treason-Felony Act, *see* Crown and
  Government Protection Act
Trevelyan, Charles Edward, 119–
  20, 120n.45
Tribune, 211
Trinity College, Dublin, 42, 84,
  88, *see also* Dublin University
Tufnell, Henry, *M.P.*, 227